UP above the clouds to die

*A tragic error. An epic battle.
An oral history*

The Kassel Mission of 27 Sept. 1944

Published by

Chi Chi Press

"A good little publishing company"*

1-888-KASSELM (5277-356)

ISBN: 978-0-9727330-8-3

Copyright © 2022, Aaron Elson

In memory of George Collar, Bill Dewey

and Walter Hassenpflug

*"Chi chi" was my mother's term of endearment for my father. One day, when they got a used Mercedes sedan from a relative, my dad called it "a good little car." My parents ran a small school transportation company. The illustration was by one of their drivers. – Aaron Elson

Contents

"Another fighter came up under the tail of Isom's ship but couldn't get him so he swung around hard to his left and came in at us at 2 o'clock, with all his guns blazing . . ." --**Paul Pouliot, co-pilot, Mercer's crew**

"There were planes blowing up. I saw engines go flying out of their holes. I saw parachutes. Parts of planes. It was just one hell of a mess. And we had our .50-caliber guns, we had eight of them shooting like hell. This is above 20,000 feet." -- **George Noorigian, bombardier, Mercer's crew**

"I flew alongside my victim and stared at the meter-high flames which were pouring out of this Liberator all the way back beyond the elevator. Then this great machine clumsily laid itself over on its back and went down." -- **Ernst Schroeder, fighter pilot, Jagdeschweder 4**

Chapter 1: Bandits at 6 O'Clock

On the morning of September 27, 1944, thirty-nine B-24 Liberators of the 445th Bomb Group were scheduled for a mission from their base at Tibenham, England. Their target: Kassel, Germany; specifically, the Henschel factory where the dreaded Tiger tank was assembled. Four planes aborted, leaving 35 bombers to join up with some 280 other bombers from the Second Air Division.

The target was obscured by a thick layer of clouds, causing the group to rely on a radar machine that enabled through-the-clouds bombing. Although there are several theories about what caused the group's lead plane to fly off course, the most widely accepted explanation is that the radar machine malfunctioned.

At the initial point, where the planes were to begin the bomb run, the lead plane made too wide a turn. Thirty-four planes had little choice but to follow, and the group became separated from the bomber stream.

Major Don McCoy, the command pilot, now had to make a decision: Should he lead the group to a secondary target, or turn around and pick up the tail end of the bomber stream. He opted for the former. It was a decision that would cost him his life, along with the lives of 116 other flyers.

Jack Mercer, a pilot; and Paul Pouliot, his co-pilot, wrote their accounts of the battle soon after it took place. I interviewed bombardier George Noorigian in 1999. Ernst Schroeder, a German fighter pilot, wrote his account for a 1989 issue of the 8th Air Force News.

Jack Mercer

And there we were – 26,000 feet, 10:06 a.m., Sept. 27, 1944, somewhere south of Kassel, Germany, flying above a nine-tenths overcast – and then "BOOM!"

We had just completed our group turn away from the target and were beginning to get the formation tightened up. On this day we were flying the No. 3 position on the wing of squadron leader Cecil Isom. The officers in Isom's crew shared the same Quonset hut with us and were good friends.

Just then tail gunner Harry Lied broke in on the intercom with "Bandits at 6 o'clock level, ten or twelve across." And thus began the most hectic eight to ten minutes imaginable, followed by two hours of "walking on eggshells" flying an aircraft that was a virtual time bomb.

I immediately began an intercom check to assure all crew members were alerted, but before completing the "check-in," Lied interrupted – "They're firing – looks like their wings are on fire, they're closing fast ..." but the intercom went dead before he completed his message. Without the intercom I had no idea of the degree of destruction going on around us but I did see that the sky was filled with gun bursts like flak. My concentration immediately centered on those things necessary to keep us flying.

We had taken a number of hits I knew. The controls went slack, the No. 2 engine began to run very rough and I could see the oxygen pressure had dropped considerably. As I struggled to find our problems I quickly realized formation flying was out of the question, and we had separated from Isom – about 200 feet below and to his left rear. I engaged the autopilot and to ensure adequate flying speed increased RPM and boost. By then we had FW-190s swarming around us and our whole plane was shaking from the firing of our .50s.

While we were alerting the crew, co-pilot Paul Pouliot, who had been standing by on the fighter channels throughout the mission, began to contact fighter groups. The German fighters' first pass knocked out all of our radios just as he made first contact, but Paul did not realize this immediately. He was trying so hard to reach someone he got red in the face as if he were trying to yell at them in frustration. So neither Paul nor radio operator Bob Bennett could let anyone know our position and situation.

Basically the German fighters attacked en masse from the rear, lobbing their 20-millimeter shells into our formation until they came in range of our .50s, then they peeled off and came up under our formation – hanging on their props as they pumped shells into our bellies uncontested. This confirmed that they knew our ball turrets had been removed (to improve handling characteristics at high altitudes – and it sure did make the 24s easier to fly in formation). But the ball turrets wouldn't have helped much this day – there were just too many German fighters.

By then I could begin to sense the unbelievable catastrophe taking place in the sky to our right and high. Our position in the formation on the extreme low left gave us a near complete view of the entire group that was left – but all I could see was Isom. Planes on fire, planes blowing up, parachutes cascading from damaged planes, 20-mm shell bursts like heavy flak, smoke – but the most eerie – the sight of two groups of four props corkscrewing forward from their ships but maintaining formation, and then slowly turning over to a horizontal plane as they lost forward momentum and began floating downward like loose windmill blades. No doubt these aircraft were lost because pilots did not follow proper procedures for increasing power rapidly. They sheared their props by ramming thrust to the wall before increasing RPMs sufficiently.

In the ensuing air battle we encountered two special situations which we will always remember. Apparently one of the FW-190s misjudged his vertical attack from below on Isom's ship which was about 200 feet ahead of the position we were able to maintain. He nearly stalled out, then rolled out directly towards us at 12 o'clock level firing wildly when he saw he could not complete his attack on Isom. Both Paul and I were trying frantically to get some gunner's attention, but what can you really do to contact a gunner some 20 feet away when you have no means of communicating? Here was this guy looking right down our throat firing away like mad and we

7

could do nothing. We both knew we had been had! But suddenly both the nose gunner (Ted Hoiten) and top turret (flight engineer Kenneth Kribs) picked this guy up. They both fired in a continuous burst for such a long time I wondered why their guns didn't burn up or jam. Finally after what seemed like an eternity this guy blew up – and we flew safely through his debris.

Near the middle of the attack I found an FW-190 camped very close under our left wing – far enough forward that I could look very clearly into his cockpit (nearly could read his instruments). We knew previously that the Germans were wanting a PFF (or radar) ship, and this guy was apparently looking us over. He was able to get in a position where neither the left waist gunner, the top turret nor the nose turret could touch him because the Jerries knew our ball turrets had been removed.

He looked quite comfortable sitting so close under our wing knowing our guns could not touch him. Boy, I'll remember that portrait – the piercing eyes looking out over his oxygen mask, his goggles on top of the black helmet – and again so clear that I could have read his instruments if I had the time to look more closely. Oh, how I wished for the .45 they took away from us before D-Day. I would have even used the "Very" pistol or maybe thrown a rock or something if I had it. Just to do something.

I used the autopilot aileron control to lower the left wing towards the 190 as quickly as possible. Apparently the pilot flinched and drifted from his safe position so that Harry Wheaton (left waist gunner) got a good shot at him. Suddenly, without any sign of damage to the FW-190, the canopy came off and the pilot ejected into space – no more than 100 feet from us. Apparently Harry's shots hit his ejection control. The last I saw of the German pilot his chute had opened and the 190 was headed straight down, still with no outward appearance of damage.

As soon as we could be sure the attack was over I asked Paul and Kribs to check on each crew member and for damages. I wasn't about to leave the cockpit so long as we didn't know what was wrong. I tried to stay close to Isom (the only remaining ship in our squadron) but could only keep him in sight – formation was out of the question.

George Noorigian

Mercer was up in the front. I was in the back, in the waist. Normally I would be in the nose with the navigator, but the B-24s are different. The 17 had room up there, but the 24s were terrible for the bombardier. They had a nose turret, so you couldn't see anything. You had to look down underneath. But when you flew on a mission, you didn't have to worry about bombing yourself. The lead bombardier, just like the lead navigator, the lead pilot, you just followed them. So instead of being up there in that hole, they said I could go into the turret in the front. But there wasn't much room, and if I had to get out of it, forget about it. So I said, "Give me a waist position." So I went into the right waist. And I wanted a gun, a .50-caliber gun. In case something comes up, I wanted a gun.

That's where I flew most of my missions. And according to Mercer, we were credited with seven planes, and I was credited with one Focke-Wulf 190. And the co-pilot verified it. See, the co-pilot was on the right side, and this fellow was coming in. They were coming in so close, they were coming in between us. Not this long-distance, they were right on top of you. In fact, I looked up, out the window, and I saw this FW-190 with the big swastika on it, and I could see the pilot, real clear. He was hunched over.

And that day, the squadron was in the low position. There's low and medium high and high. Usually you wanted to go into the high position because of anti-aircraft, but this day we were in the low position, which was a good idea because the German fighters came from up above [actually they originally came from below] and they swooped down on the squadron, on the whole group.

Within less than ten minutes, 25 of us were shot down. There were planes blowing up. I saw engines go flying out of their holes. I saw parachutes. Parts of planes. It was just one hell of a mess. And we had our .50-caliber guns, we had eight of them, shooting like hell. This is above 20,000 feet. It was one hell of a mess.

We got one shot from a Messerschmitt that came in. He was on the left side. It wasn't on my side. He came in low, and the Messerschmitt had four 20-millimeter cannons. Four of them! Along the wing. And he gave us a shot there, the one hit the tail, you know the double tails they have? The one hit the tail, and it made a mess out of the tail.

9

The second one came in – I was sitting when I was firing. There's no seats in the back, and we had boxes of what they call chaff. The chaff you distributed in certain positions, and what that did was knock out the radar. They would throw out bunches of it, and from the ground, especially when you had cloud cover, it would look like there's a squadron of planes there. So we had boxes of chaff and I sat on a box with my .50-caliber gun. Another one came in on the side of the plane, blew a hole I could put my head in it, and it went into the box. It went into the box and blew up. But the box of chaff, what it did, it blew in such a way that it blew the other way. It's a lucky thing I'm still here. And when it blew up, one section of the plane in the back was all full of oxygen tanks because we had to be on oxygen over 15,000 feet. And it blew out five or six tanks. Blew them out! Everything is white smoke. And the radio went out.

You didn't know what the hell was going on in the front. Everything was white smoke. And I had a flak jacket on. We all had parachutes, but we could not put the parachute on because the parachute was attached to the flak jacket in the front, so when you put your flak jacket on, there was nothing you could do unless you took the parachute off. So I said to the other gunner, "Take the damn jacket off! This goddamn plane's gonna blow up!"

He took it off so I could put the chute on. I didn't want to be up in the air with a flak jacket with no chute. You didn't know whether you were gonna get out alive or not. But it blew out the tanks over there, and it made a hole in the side of the plane. And another one came through the bomb bays, where the gasoline tanks are, it made a hole in one of the bomb bays and went into one of the tanks. It knocked out part of the hydraulic system. But it went into the tank, and since there was no fire, it made a big hole in the tanks. Those are self-sealing tanks, but this hole that went in, the 100 octane gas was just going all over the plane. Hundred octane. Eight .50-caliber guns going.

I was ready to jump out of the goddamn thing. The plane was gonna blow up. And another one came in and it went into one of the engines, like Mercer said, it hit the prop. And when we landed, you should have seen the mark that was on that prop. But that's what happened. So I'm here by the grace of God.

Paul Pouliot

Early in the morning on September 27, about 3:30, the "Gremlin" (as we call the boy from operations) came into our Nissen hut. The door creaked lightly and I heard his shuffling footstep in the dark going around the edge of George's bed to turn on the lights. Someone was going on a mission. The lights went on and he came toward our end of the barracks, shook Jack, our pilot, and said to be ready for briefing at 4:30.

Instead of getting up immediately, I covered up my head with the blankets for a last luxurious minute in the sack, all the time shivering at the thought of getting up in the cold. Finally we could put it off no longer. Jack was the first out, as usual; myself next, then George (the bombardier) and finally the boy who really loves his sack time, Milton (a good navigator even so).

I went to the washroom to scoop a couple handfuls of water on my face, then stubbed my way down the long path to the mess hall, where the boys were already waiting in line. I pushed a plateful of messy looking powdered eggs aside, and ate a peanut butter sandwich between gulps of G.I. coffee. We hurried so as not to miss the briefing.

Cigarettes were tossed at the briefing room door, no smoking allowed. The lights blinded us temporarily as we entered. It was crowded as usual, but not very noisy. Everyone is tense and anxious just then, to know where we are going. At 4:30 sharp, the door was closed and the briefing officer stood up. A hush came over everyone, as he raised the curtain and disclosed our route on the large map covering the front wall. The target was Kassel, Germany.

He gave us the usual briefing information – route to the target and back, flak, possible enemy fighters, escort, bomb run, target photos. All in all, it didn't look so bad. After getting material from weather and operations, we split up to get specialized briefings for additional data. Jack and I stayed with the other pilots to get information on taxiing times and position.

Together with the others again in the locker room. I went to the equipment room and asked Shorty to give me a 34-38 heated suit and gloves. The pants would barely fit as usual. We waited until everyone was ready, then a waiting truck took us to our plane. It took a while for everyone to make sure his individual equipment was in working order. That done, we assembled in the dark to talk

11

over the mission. All agreed it would not be so bad. The boys did their usual amount of fooling until starting time came.

At 6:15 we got into the airplane. After a few backfires all four engines purred smoothly. We ran the props through and checked the mags, making sure that all the instruments were in good order. Brakes off, and we taxied into position in the line of waiting planes. At 6:30 promptly the first 24 of the group lumbered down the runway, using most of the field's length. One by one, the others took off and started the climb to assembly altitude. Finally, our turn. Racing engines strained against the brakes, and we were accelerating down the runway. The plane rose beautifully into the air. Wheels up, then flaps. I increased the power to climb and get into formation, which is the most laborious flying of the whole mission. A single red flare identified our group. To save gasoline, we cut down the power again and got into No. 3 position of the low left squadron, then spent some time circling over England before heading for the North Sea, according to schedule.

We flew a straight course and made landfall. No flak at the enemy coast, so we felt pretty good. A heavy layer of low cloud formed a complete undercast. All the time we were climbing to briefed altitude, finally leveling off at 22,000 feet. The group formation really looked good today as we resumed our course to the target.

After 35 minutes we turned to the right to reach the initial point of the bomb run. Bombing was to be by pathfinder methods. All the squadrons got into formation. Finally a turn to the left, and the lead ship opened his bomb bay doors, a signal for all the rest to do the same. At this point everyone is at a peak of nervousness, expecting to see flak at any moment. For some reason my fingers got very cold, and I borrowed the radio operator's gloves to keep from freezing. I was flying the bomb run today, so I got into a close formation with the lead ship.

After what seemed like ages, the smoke bombs from the lead ship left and it was bombs away. The smoke streamers looked like rockets. We made a turn to the right and resumed our course out. Again I remarked how good the formation looked.

Everything was quiet all around for about ten minutes. Then suddenly the tail gunner of Isom's ship to our right fired at something, and our own plane started to quiver as the gunners opened fire. Small white puffs of smoke appeared throughout our formation. I had my radio tuned to the fighter channel, and called for escort. They answered immediately. I said we were being attacked by bandits, but before I could give them our position, we were hit in the waist and the radio went out.

To our right was just plain hell. Planes were going down, some in flames, others just exploding. The air was full of exploding 20 millimeter shells. I thought the whole German air force must be in the air at the same time. The tail gunner said later they were coming in 15 abreast, wave after wave, and I saw them as they broke away past us, iron black crosses standing out on wings and fuselage. The first pass they made took most of our squadron with them. Isom's ship and ours were left with no one to protect us from the rear, and still the Nazis came at us.

Our plane shook like a leaf in a good blizzard from the guns all firing at the same time. On the right, a B-24 with its No. 3 tank on fire blew up and three of the men got out of the waist. The others didn't have a chance.

The air was full of debris of burning planes and chutes. We saw engines torn away from their mounts on one plane. At least three of the boys pulled their chutes too quickly, the silk caught on fire and they plummeted to earth.

The enemy had a rough time of it also. On my right where the main fight was occurring I saw a FW-190 going down in flames. A German plane in a death spin crashed into another enemy fighter and they went down together. The whole scene was unreal and unbelievable.

Meanwhile our nose gunner, Ted Hoiten, was frantically busy keeping the fighters off Isom's tail. His plane was slightly higher than ours and a little to the right. FW's were coming up from beneath and trying to get him from the belly. When one of them stalled out in front of us I saw Ted's guns blazing and his turret shaking from the long burst that he gave the Nazi as he hung there trying to pump Isom's ship with 20-mm shells. Then the fighter caught on fire, fell over on its back and went down to disappear in the clouds.

Another fighter came up under the tail of Isom's ship but couldn't get him so he swung around hard to his left and came in at us at 2 o'clock, with all his guns blazing. It looked as though the leading edge of his wing was on fire. I thought that we had had it, but our engineer, Kenneth Kribs, turned his top turret violently and took on the attacking plane. Again our plane shook from a long burst. The Nazi plane kept on coming closer and closer and Kribs still kept shooting; then suddenly there was nothing in front of us but debris. Another attack came in from the left waist and I could feel several hits. That one destroyed our controls, damaged our rudders, hit the hydraulic reservoir, and broke several of the oxygen bottles in the waist. Jack switched on the automatic pilot, and we found we could still fly. Then we waited for another attack, but none came.

Ernst Schroeder

"A Storm Fighter's View of 27 September 1944" is reprinted from the 8th Air Force News of September 1989. It was the result of a request by Dr. Helmut Schnatz, and was translated by Donald Mathie of Boardman, Ohio.

On the 27th of September 1944, our group took off from Finsterwalde (our regular base was at Erfurt-Binderleben) in FW-190s at 10:00 a.m. for an enemy engagement against a bomber air raid consisting of perhaps thirty airplanes. We had, according to my memory, an overcast sky and had to climb through a relatively thin cloud layer at about 1,500 to 2,000 meters (4,920-6,560 feet) altitude in order to get to the Americans, flying at about 7,500 to 8,000 meters (24,600 to 26,240 feet). We were led to the bombers by the Y-Command of the fighter division.

Because we were flying over the clouds, we could not see the ground. The orders often changed our course direction, so we never knew where we really were. Normally, a pilot would look on his maps for locations which were radioed to us. But a pilot of a single-seat fighter could not do that; he had to concentrate on the flight of the group and the steering of the plane.

I remember that around 11:00 a.m. (German time, 1000 hours British time) we were flying farther and farther west. The ground commander became more and more agitated and said we now had to see the enemy planes in front of us. Indeed we did.

After a short time, we saw a large group of B-24 Liberator bombers, at our altitude, like a swarm of mosquitoes, flying right in front of us, going in the same direction. The silhouettes very soon became bigger and bigger because of our great speed.

Suddenly several of these big ships began to burn and to plunge down with fire and smoke – even before we had fired a single shot. A fighter unit flying ahead of us had begun the attack.

Immediately the sky was full of parachutes and wreckage, and we were flying right into it.

My squadron leader and I had installed (for trial in combat) a new aiming device. We had a gadget built into our airplanes that included very rapid running gyros that automatically calculated the necessary aiming allowances. Therefore, one could shoot rather precisely and effectively from a greater distance than otherwise. The result was impressive in my case.

Even before I had covered the remaining distance to my bomber, it already stood in flame as a result of my six machine guns. Both left engines of the bomber were burning. The airplane turned on its side and plunged. Also the neighboring machine was already smoking from a previous attack. I only needed to change aim to shoot again. Then this one stood in bright flames. The new aiming device was functioning astonishingly. I was so surprised and fascinated that I flew alongside my victim and stared at the meter-high flames which were pouring out of this Liberator all the way back beyond the elevator. Then this great machine clumsily laid itself over on its back and went down. All of this happened much faster than you can read in here.

In view of this surprising success, I naturally wanted to know precisely where my two opponents would fall. This was necessary because a double shootdown of two four-engine bombers (they were also my only ones) was for us in 1944 something exceptional.

Therefore, I circled the crashing wreckage of my two adversaries in large downward running spirals. But my intention was hindered in a most horrible way, because the entire sky was filled with fliers in parachutes, who had jumped, and small and large chunks of airplane debris which suddenly appeared in front of my windshield at my high diving speed of 600 to 700 km/h. I truly had to close my eyes often because I believed with certainty I would run into something.

Under me came the cloud layer through which here and there the surface of the Earth was quickly shimmering – closer and closer. Through this cloud cover rose ten to fifteen columns of smoke from the explosions of the crashing aircraft. I flew through the relatively thin cloud layer, which now spread itself out at an altitude of about 1,000 meters (3,280 feet) above the ground.

Below me lay a valley with forest covered mountainsides. Through the valley ran a stretch of double railroad tracks and on it stood a long train. The smoke of the locomotive climbed vertically. This image has clearly imprinted itself on my mind until today. When I close my eyes, I see it clearly before me.

Where had the two bombers fallen? Everywhere there was burning wreckage. The fields were covered with white parachutes, where American – and certainly also German – flyers had come down.

I arrived at almost 100 meters above the ground and could clearly see the crewmen who had bailed out running through the fields. When I flew over them, they stood and clearly raised their hands high. Also I saw people already – perhaps also soldiers and policemen – running toward them to take them captive. My intention to recognize the locality through some distinguishing landmark failed completely.

Something suddenly happened which quickly broke me away from my intention. I was, as stated, about 100 meters above the ground when diagonally from the front an airplane with a yellow nose shot towards me – an American fighter unmistakably of the P-51B type. In the wink of an eye we had raced closely by each other on an opposite course and hurried both of our machines again on an opposite course, so that we flew towards one another like jousting knights of the Middle Ages.

Both of us opened fire simultaneously with our big caliber weapons. The American immediately made a hit on my tail section. My weapons, on the other hand, failed after a few shots. When we had flown by one another, the maneuver began anew. Since I could not fire a shot, I began to fly with evasive movements the moment the American opened fire, so that he could no longer aim correctly. It was a strange feeling each time looking into the flash of his four 12.7-cm guns. After we had played this little game for five or six times, there was only the possibility to fly low over the ground immediately after his flight over me and to rush off immediately. I was successful. After his turn, in which he always pulled up sharply, the camouflage paint on the top of my plane made it difficult for the American to find my plane against the dappled ground.

I landed after minutes of fearful sweating at 11:30 a.m. at the Langensala Airport after a total of ninety minutes of flight time. On inspection my machine showed some hits in the tail section. A part of the covering of my rudder was torn off. The damage was so slight that I could take off again at noon. I landed at 12:15 p.m. at Erfurt-Bindersleben, where my bird had to be repaired in the hangar.

George Collar in his "war room" in 1999.

Chapter 2: Curse You, Red Baron

George Collar

Lieutenant George Collar was a bombardier on pilot Jim Schaen's crew, and was a co-founder of the Kassel Mission Memorial Association. This and later excerpts are from my interview with George in 1999

I was brought up during the aftermath of World War I, and we were always taught that that was the war to end all wars. All of us kids were kind of steeped in the heroics of Raoul Lufberry and Eddie Rickenbacker and Frank Luke, and we were a little bit sad there weren't gonna be any more wars, we wouldn't be able to get to fight. Boy, we were really wrong about that.

When the draft came out, I had a pretty high number, and the lower numbers came first. I had a cousin who was in the 75th Toronto Scottish Regiment. He was called to active duty in 1939 and went overseas. He was gone for six years. He was at Dieppe and he was down in Italy and he was all over, with the Canadian army.

My uncle, my mother's brother, had been killed in the battle of the Somme when he was fighting with the British army. We kind of had a military background and we were eager to go, especially when

19

everybody else was going. So one day another fellow and I drove over to Windsor, and when we went across the bridge, the customs man says, "What are you going to Canada for?"

We said, "We've got business."

He hollered down, "Two more!"

There were over 10,000 Americans who crossed the Ambassador Bridge to get into the Canadian army.

But when we got down to the headquarters, they said, "Go home and get your birth certificate and we'll take you."

In the meantime, there was a local garage that was recruiting for a special unit, and when you finish your training they'd give you a staff sergeant rating and send you to Egypt to be attached to the British 8th Army to repair those old tanks that went over on lend-lease. So another fellow and I went down and signed up. Quit our jobs. They gave us a paper and said we had to take it over to the induction center on Monday morning. So he took an early bus and I took a later bus, and I got there at 20 minutes after 12. I came in, and there was a great big master sergeant in this office.

"What can I do for you?"

I gave him the paper. He looked at it and he said, "You're 20 minutes too late. They filled that quota at noon."

I said, "What else have you got?"

He said, "We need a lot of people in the infantry."

"Is there anything else?"

He said, "If you can pass the mental and the physical, you can get in the Cadets."

I went down the next week and there were 60 of us. Out of the 60, about 25 of us passed the written test. Then I passed the physical.

I got notified on the 5th of January and reported to duty at Detroit, about 250 of us. They marched us in a body down to the station. They had a band there, but it was 25 below zero and the horns froze up and they couldn't play.

I went to Nashville. They gave us all kinds of tests. And I passed. I could either go to pilot training or to bombardier school. I said, "I want to be a pilot." Everybody wanted to be a pilot.

They sent me to Maxwell Field, Alabama. I went through pre-flight there, and I ended up at Carlston Field in Florida in primary. And I washed out on a check ride. They washed them out like mad, because they had more than they could use. But they didn't have enough going to bombardier school.

I was disgusted when I washed out because I knew I could fly but I screwed up a couple things. On an S-turn I lost 50 feet. I didn't do too good on a forced landing. I did pretty good on the spins and stalls, but I felt in my own mind I could have passed. Anyway, that's neither here nor there. I flunked out. And that was one of the lowest points in my life, because everybody at home thinks you're gonna be a pilot and all of a sudden you're letting everybody down, including yourself. So I had to meet a board. And they asked me, "What would you like to do?"

I said, "I want to go to ordnance OCS."

"Well, you can have that for second choice. We're sending you to bombardier school."

That's how I became a bombardier.

Doye O'Keefe

Sergeant Doye O'Keefe was the radio operator on the Pearson crew. This and later excerpts are from a memoir he wrote in 1981 at the urging of his son Mike.

It was fairly late in the afternoon. It had been a great day. I had spent the day with "Pop" Stonecipher and my friend Wilford Stonecipher and his brother "June" hunting quail east of Devide, Illinois along Horse Creek, and we all were on the way back to Aunt Dieds' house. As we walked along over the fields talking about the happenings of the day we walked uphill out of the creek bottoms. We could see Aunt Dieds waving frantically and hurrying toward us from the barn yard.

I wondered what in the world she could be so excited about to run out to meet us. She had never done that before.

I had just spent the day with close friends hunting quail in good country with a good gun dog. I had that good warm feeling you get after a day in the field with several quail in your game bag. It was a good hunting day, a little chill, overcast, it had been a great day this Sunday, December 7, 1941.

As we came within shouting distance she called, "We are at war! Japan bombed Pearl Harbor!!" over and over. At first we all were in disbelief.

For years, news came over the radio and in the newspaper about the war in Europe. My senior year in high school, September 4, 1939, war had been declared with England and Germany. War news was not new, but were you sure about Japan?

Wilford and I were the same age, both had turned 20 and single. When we got to the house, a log cabin actually, I made some comment that I probably would not be back for some time, or some such weak statement. Wilford could hardly believe it. Pop said, "This will probably change the life of every person in the world." How very close he was to being right. Going home we were rather silent with disbelief and talked about earlier trips together and Pop tried to assure us all, including himself, there would be more times together.

When I got home my mother didn't say much but we talked about it. In my early teens I often overheard her comment with the news of the war during the past years. She felt she was raising her boys to fight a war. I knew she felt bad. Every mother of every combat age young man felt bad. I knew then I must always remember that. Already nothing was the same.

Glen McCormick

Glen McCormick, the waist gunner on the Chilton crew, was at Hickam Field when Pearl Harbor was attacked. This and later excerpts are from an account he wrote about his military career.

December 7 was a day I shall never forget. I was in the mess hall and just finished breakfast when the first bomb or torpedo hit Pearl. Our first reaction was, "What's the damn Navy doing at this hour on Sunday morning?" We went outside and saw the torpedo airplanes flying over with those big red assholes painted on their wings and fuselages. We ran back to the barracks to get whatever we could. I got a gas mask and an empty .45 holster. We all headed to the flight line on the dead run. I had just got to the edge of the ramp and saw some planes, three of them, strafing the field. I ducked under a heavy roller they used to roll down the ramps and that saved my old skin.

December 9th, we moved to Bellows Field, an outlying field, and were there for about a week, and then to Wheeler Field, still on the island of Oahu. We spent the next year patrolling the islands, all eight of them, to see if there were any signs of landing craft or submarines.

The Japs really hit their mark on the 7th. We had two of our A-20s in the Hawaiian air depot for some major work, and they were completely destroyed. The planes on the line were strafed and some were badly damaged. Our airplane came through without a scratch. In fact, our airplane and two others were the first airplanes to take off from Hickam after the attack. We fanned out in an attempt to find the Jap carrier or carriers. The guys in the big central barracks, not us, would run out of the building and then they would strafe them and they would run back in and then get bombed. They killed a bunch of them that day. I went up to the hospital ground to help identify the dead. That was a tough chore, but I did see some I knew.

The Jap attack on Pearl Harbor was a significant chapter in my military career, but I believe the flying over Germany was far more significant.

Frank Bertram

Lieutenant Frank Bertram was the navigator on the Miner crew. As I was unable to travel to San Francisco, he recorded a tape of his experiences.

I knew nothing about the Second Air Division Association until about 20 years after the war, when a friend of mine who lived right around the corner from me in Stockton told me he belonged to it. I thought that sounds interesting. I joined this organization and they're sending letters and newsletters, and it was interesting; you'd run into names you knew, people you might know what happened to them, etcetera. But it was always in the back of my mind and every once in a while I'd think, "Gee, you know, what happened to me, I'd like to go back there and find the area where I was shot down." My wife, Mary, and I did take several trips to Germany, but I could never find it, and me, a good navigator, I didn't know where the hell I was. I knew the approximate area, but I couldn't pin it down.

As I went through life, I kept in contact with a few of the fellows on the plane, but never anything personal. Until one time, in February of 1986, I came home from work and my wife doesn't say hello, she doesn't give me a kiss, and she says, "What was the number of your plane?"

I looked at her – now this is 40 years later – and I said, "What plane? I drove home."

She said, "No, no, no, the plane you flew in the war."

I said, "You want to know the number? All I remember is it was a B-24." I didn't even remember they had numbers. So I said, "Why?"

She said, "Wait till you see this package."

Well, this packet was from Walter Hassenpflug. It had letters from the 8th Air Force Historical Society and from the 19th Armored Division, which was in the town of Bad Hersfeld where one of Walter's interpreters worked. And it said that Walter was researching what happened on this particular day over the town of Bad Hersfeld.

Walter's letter stated that as a boy of 12, he witnessed an airplane explosion in the air, and then he witnessed some parachutes coming down, and he said two days later they were walking through the forest – and maybe they were there picking up leaflets that the American bombers had dropped – and they came across this man lying by a creek. And I thought, "My God, that's me!"

His letter stated, "All I remember is that he was a first lieutenant from San Francisco."

I immediately wrote to Walter. Then we got to writing back and forth. In August we went to Germany and met Walter, who much to my surprise did not speak a word of English, but he had a fellow named Carl Lepper who was the interpreter.

And Walter identified himself, as he did in the letter, and said he was the one that found me in the ditch.

You mentioned something the other day about post traumatic syndrome that apparently a lot of the veterans from Vietnam have had, which was not even heard of in Korea or in World War II. However, it must have been there to a certain extent. It is my opinion that nobody that went to war, particularly if they went overseas and more particularly if they got into combat, when you came back, you were not the same person. For guys who were prisoners of war it was even worse, because you actually felt that you were looked down upon. It's very demeaning to be a prisoner in war. You're stomped on to a certain extent. You try to forget about it, but every once in a while something snaps and bingo, you start thinking. Things like that happen to me where I actually relive every moment I was in that plane that day, after coming under attack.

Erlyn Jensen

Erlyn Jensen was the kid sister of command pilot Donald William McCoy, whom she knew as Bill, although in the Air Corps he was known as Don.

"I'm going to fight!" That was Bill's reaction when Pearl Harbor was attacked. He went right down and signed up. I know my Dad was very proud of him and I'm sure Mom was too but she didn't want him to go. And somewhere at home, I've got a picture in the Seattle Times, it's a whole group of young men in suits and ties getting ready to go off to wherever they went off to for the war. It's got a line down at the bottom, and my brother's head is circled in this group of people and it said that Don McCoy was selected to lead this group. I think it was to Kelly Air Force Base in Texas. And that was when I first realized that he was leaving and wouldn't be back for a while.

I remember the one and only time that he came home on leave right before he left for England. He and Carmen, his wife, had told Mom and Dad that he was going to be able to come home but he couldn't give them a definite date. I had gone to school, and I was in my classroom in the fourth grade, and the buzzer rang for a message – this always makes me cry – for a message that someone needed to run down and get the message in the office, and my little neighborhood boyfriend was the messenger for that day, so he ran down, and I could hear him yelling all the way back down the hall, "Erlyn! Erlyn! Bill's here! Bill's here!" I got up from my seat, didn't even ask the teacher if I could be excused, and I opened the door and went out and there was my brother and Carmen walking down the hall. They had come up from the house to pick me up, and I got to leave school that day and go home and be with him.

I don't remember how long they were there on leave, and then, if I remember rightly, he went directly to Florida, and he flew out from Florida. And I remember very well him calling my mom and dad and saying, "I'm going to be shipped out. I can't tell you where, but just keep in mind that I'm with Jimmy Stewart." Well, that was a dead giveaway, because everywhere Jimmy Stewart went was in the newspapers, so Mom and Dad never had a doubt about where Bill was. And about a month before the Kassel Mission Bill wrote home and said, "Mom, will you please send some of those little juice glasses that we used to have with the clamp lid on them, and please send some Ritz crackers. We're going to have a surprise birthday party for Jimmy Stewart at the end of the month."

Now, one of the fellows here last night [at the 2004 2nd Air Division Historical Society reunion] said, "Your brother and Jimmy Stewart were very, very good friends." I've been told by many people here that oh, everybody wanted to say that they were friends with Jimmy Stewart. And I've often thought that had Bill come back home, he would have probably gone the route that Jimmy Stewart did to continue flying, or, rather than becoming a lawyer, I never could see him as a lawyer, possibly going into commercial flying, because flying was his life from the time he was a little boy.

Colonel Jimmy Stewart and Major Don McCoy

Chapter 3: Ragtime Cowboy Jim

The actor Jimmy Stewart was the original commander of the 703rd Squadron of the 445th Bomb Group. By the time of the Kassel Mission, he had been promoted and moved to a different bomb group. He was very shaken up by news of the battle, and took part in debriefing the few crews that made it back to Tibenham.

Gene Crandall

Sergeant Gene Crandall was a maintenance crew chief in the 445th. I interviewed Gene and Floyd Ogilvy, who joined the bomb group immediately after the Kassel Mission, at a Cracker Barrel in Battle Creek, Michigan, in 1999.

My son wrote him a letter and said that his dad was always talking about Jimmy Stewart, and he told Jimmy Stewart that he really enjoyed "It's a Wonderful Life" and that his dad was always talking about it, so Jimmy Stewart sent me a letter back. I didn't know him all that well. I talked to him about half a dozen times.

When I was at Sioux City, he was doing practice takeoffs and landings in a B-24 at night, and there was a bad thunderstorm. He came in to land, and he must have been a couple of hundred feet high, and a bolt of lightning went right across the front of the canopy, and he dropped it down and snapped off the nose gear, which was the weakest part of the landing equipment. And then the whole airplane went down the runway at like a 45 degree angle and the sparks flew out from the landing gear strut, just like a dragging wheel. So I went out there with a couple of other guys in a jeep, and Stewart got out of the plane and he was shaking and trembling and all shook up, because he just damn near died. And the colonel was there. The colonel says, "You didn't see anything, did you?"

We said, "No, Sir. We didn't see a thing."

That was when we were in training at Sioux City. Then we went to a satellite field in South Dakota, and from there we went to New York, Camp Shanks, and then we went over on the Queen Mary.

The chief inspector and I went over to Cambridge. They told us we were going to school. What we did was re-work these patrol airplanes that were working on these submarines. They were all painted blue, they had sea waves on the bottom, and the spark plugs hadn't been changed for 400 hours. That's a no-no. You should never, never let an airplane like that get more than a hundred hours, and the spark plugs were snapping off right into the cylinder head. We had to take little hacksaw blades and cut the shredded part out, and then we took a nail and put a wire around it with a battery and made a magnet and we reached out two sides of the cylinder and got the filings out.

Anyhow, I was over there and this airplane lands, and it's a B-24, this Ten-Uv-Us lands, and I said, "Damn, that must be some kind of a Latin name." And it struck me eventually that that was Ten Of Us" in a crew. And that was Jimmy Stewart's airplane. He got out, and I went over to it, and he looked at me and said, "What the hell are you doing here?"

I said, "We're over here fixing these patrol bombers." They were using them for the submarines."

And he says, "You won't be here long." And within two hours, a 6-by-6 came and got us and we went back over to Tibenham. Then on Thanksgiving, he came down to the mess hall and he was the O.D., the officer of the day, and he said, "Sergeant, can I sit with you?"

I said, "Yes, Sir." He was the squadron commander. And he sat down and he said, "How do you like the turkey?"

I said, "Well, the outside's all right, but the inside's all frozen."

And he said, "Oh my god." And then he got up and went back, he found the mess captain drunk with a bunch of bottles around. They broke the mess sergeant down to private. Stewart didn't do that. And they broke the captain down to second lieutenant and put him on the China Clipper, you know, the dishwashing machine. And he had to stay on there a whole month. So Jimmy Stewart wasn't exactly soft.

The last time I saw him, he'd been on one of those 12-hour missions, and I was checking him out when they hit the ground, because he was flying our airplane, a 700th Squadron airplane. I think he flew the 700th Squadron's planes because the Germans were after him. It would have been a great coup if they'd have shot down Jimmy Stewart.

John Knox

John Knox was the tail gunner on the Baynham crew. I interviewed John and his wife, DeDe, in Florida in 2010.

When we went over to England in 1990 he was supposed to be there, but he was getting pretty old and his health prevented it. We were hoping we'd meet him then. I've got his book. Beautiful book. Just his military life. He was always a favorite of mine. I guess he used to come to the enlisted men's barracks and talk to them. Between the two groups, he was with our group and then he went to the 389th. I think he flew about 20 missions altogether.

Reg Miner

Reg Miner was the pilot of the plane on which Frank Bertram was the navigator

I didn't have any personal contact with him. I saw him over there from time to time. He was a great friend of Colonel Terrill, who was the commander of the 445th when I arrived. And he would be at our parties at the officers club. I remember him playing Ragtime Cowboy Joe and singing it on the piano. But I never talked to him personally. Omick, my bombardier, asked him for an autograph, and Stewart laughed him off. I don't mean he did it unpleasantly, and I thought, Jesus Christ, that was uncharacteristic of Omick, in my opinion, to ask for an autograph, I couldn't believe he did that. I could understand it, what the hell, it is a noted guy, an opportunity to get an autograph. But Stewart was not in our group at the time, I don't know what his job was, I think he had a wing job in the 453rd Group, which was a sister group. We had the 389th, 445th and 453rd in our wing.

Web Uebelhoer

Web Uebelhoer was the pilot of the deputy lead plane on the mission. His was one of only four of the 35 bombers to return to its base at Tibenham.

You know, when an aircraft was shot down, the ground personnel came in and got their personal effects and sent them home. And they came into our barracks, they were gonna take my stuff and send it home. And Jimmy Stewart was no longer assigned to the 445th, but he was aware that something had happened and he drove to the base. I don't know where he was assigned. And when I got out of the briefing room, about 10 or 12 people were standing around, "Hey, Uebelhoer, we want to talk to you. What the hell happened?" And I talked to them the same as I'm talking to you. And while I was talking to them, Jimmy Stewart – my god, that's a big movie star – came by, and he did not try to take over. He stood on the outer edge and listened intently. And I think that he almost became ill listening to what had happened. And of course I was watching him because he was a big movie star. He didn't ask a question. He listened.

George Noorigian

Jimmy Stewart was connected to the 445th. I used to talk to him. Every once in a while they would have a dance in the officers club, and he would always be there. The Red Cross would get a bunch of girls from town, and they'd get a GI orchestra to come in. And all the girls would be there. But then you would talk to him there. He was a regular guy. I never forgot the day he stuck his hand in his pocket and he came out with a knife. He said, "You see this knife? This is my good luck piece. I always carry it with me, and I never have a problem." From what I understand, he flew about 13 or 15 missions. When you're up high you don't fly every time.

Ira Weinstein
Ira Weinstein was a bombardier who became a prisoner of war.

Early in the game Jimmy Stewart flew as a command pilot in our airplane. We were all pretty excited about it, and a little nervous. I had flown other missions where we had a command pilot on board, and they just sat between the pilot and the co-pilot on a little box; they didn't fly the airplane. They were there as observers, or to get the flight time and another medal. So Stewart was up there. Other guys would be on the intercom, "Lieutenant, is everything all right down there? Have you got your bomb sight set? Do you know where we're at?" This would drive me crazy. Stewart never said a word. Before we got on the initial point, he called down and said, "Lieutenant, are you all set? Everything all right down there?"

"Everything's fine, Colonel."

"Go get 'em."

That's all. As soon as we said "Bombs away," he came on the intercom and said, "Good show, boys. Let's go home."

George Collar

One night we had a party at the officers club, and he came in with General Timberlake. Of course, being a second lieutenant I'm not about to go up and start talking to Jimmy Stewart, who was a lieutenant colonel then. They were standing at the bar, and all the girls, there were a lot of nurses and there were English girls, they circled around him like flies around a horse biscuit. You couldn't get close to him.

He was a good friend of Captain Steinbacher. After they finished their missions Captain Steinbacher and Neil Johnson both went into P-51s. They came over one night and gave us a little buzz job. And then the night that Jimmy Stewart was there, Steinbacher came back from a raid to Munich that day, and he had shot his first FW-190 down. He was celebrating that. Later on, after I got shot down on the Kassel raid, one night he did a buzz job over Tibenham and he pulled up and went into a high speed stall and crashed, it killed him. I talked to a guy that was in the medics that went out and dug him out of the plane.

Bill Dewey

Bill Dewey was a pilot and a co-founder, with George Collar, of the Kassel Mission Memorial Association, which later became the Kassel Mission Historical Society.

My only contact with Jimmy Stewart was one mission I briefed that he flew as a command pilot, in April. After the main briefing they broke up into the specialist areas; the pilots stayed together, the gunners stayed together, navigators and bombardiers, all went to different places. I went to the navigators' briefing, which was in the war room, and Colonel Stewart – he was a lieutenant colonel by then – was there. After the navigator briefing I asked Colonel Stewart, "Do you have anything to add?" And he said "No." That was my only conversation with him. But I guess he was a pretty good guy. He used to come back to the base and play the piano, and they said he was just a regular guy. He didn't put on any airs at all. You know, he enlisted as a private. Then right away, because of his experience, he was promoted.

Malcolm McGregor
Malcolm McGregor was the bombardier on the Sollien crew.

I was with Sollien's crew for at least 12 missions, and Kassel was my 34th. It was his 26th mission when he went down, so I had eight missions ahead of him. I flew with six different crews. But I flew most of my missions as a bombardier with Carl.

Carl loved to play the piano. Before the war he had been a sign painter. And he had a wife, and several kids. I really enjoyed him. We had a kind of bonding. It happened quickly. It always happens quickly. You go into a barracks and heck, within a day or two you're bonding with two or three of the guys that you like and you go out and you're with them. I liked Carl, and we actually went on leave together once in London. That was fun. Typically I wasn't with him. But he was a good piano player. That's why Jimmy Stewart came over and hung out with us sometimes in the officers club.

The first time I met Jimmy Stewart, he asked me – he was just being friendly to a second lieutenant – and he asked me how many missions I had, and I said I had five. And I said, "How many do you have, Sir?" and he said, "I have 13." Then we each went our own way. And the next time we met was in September. He was back at the officers club, and he said, "How many missions do you have now?" And I said, "I've got 30." I said, "How many have you got?" He said, "I've got 18. Those sons of bitches don't let me fly anything but a desk up here."

Then he said to me, "Lieutenant, do you like bourbon?" And I said, "Oh yeah, but I can't get any at the bar here." And he said, "Come with me." So he took me back in the part of the officers club that was the senior officers club, that's where the Red Cross girls were and the majors and colonels, and he had a bottle back there, so he gave me a drink of bourbon. And we sat there and talked a little bit, then I went back. But he was very down to earth, extremely friendly. He wasn't like you think of wild entertainer kind of things, that wasn't his personality. I met somebody on the bus the other day who was with Jimmy up at wing, he was one of the wing navigators, and he said he always tried to beat Jimmy to breakfast and never succeeded. He said Stewart really worked hard at his job, and he wanted to be a combat pilot, and he had no reason to do any of that because he could have easily gotten out.

Chapter 4: Prelude

Ralph Pearson

Pilot Ralph Pearson was interviewed by Rolland E. Kidder for the book "A Hometown Goes to War" about veterans from Jamestown, New York.

Our first mission was on June 29, just three weeks after D-Day. By that time we were flying far into Germany. We were on daylight raids and sometimes there would be 800 to 1,000 planes on a mission. We would circle and get lined up over England, and then off we would go over the channel.

We would usually get our first taste of flak from German anti-aircraft batteries on the French coast, but it was nothing like the flak we ran into over Germany. It was especially bad over Berlin. I remember my first mission over Berlin. There was a cloud of flak about five miles around with thousands of red explosive bursts going off inside it. One of the fighter pilots providing escort must have been on his first mission. He called his leader and asked, "Little Red, this is Little Red One, are they going to fly through that stuff?"

"Yeah," the answer came back. "They [the bombers] are but we're not."

And then into the cloud we went. We lost a few planes but most of us made it back. How? I still don't know how most of us got through that stuff. You ask yourself now how you were able to keep going up and flying back through that flak two or three times a week. It's hard to say, but for most of us, we believed in the need for the war. As far as we were concerned, Hitler was a madman and we had to do our part to get rid of the sonofabitch.

We had to abort one mission. Right after takeoff, when we were rendezvousing for the mission, the No. 1 engine went into reverse pitch. The governor must have broken or something because I couldn't control the engine. It pulled us out of formation and was vibrating the whole plane. I was so busy that I couldn't talk to the crew but they knew something was wrong. We started to lose altitude and the only way I could keep the plane under control was

35

with full right rudder and ailerons. My other hand was on the throttles because I had to reduce power in the No. 3 and No. 4 engines and goose the No. 2 engine in order to keep us from flipping over. My hands were so busy that I couldn't use the mike. In the midst of all this, the flight engineer came into the cockpit. I nodded or something and he interpreted it as an order to bail out. All of a sudden, the tail gunner called in, "Hey, there's two chutes out here!" Those guys must have thought I'd given the order to bail out.

I couldn't think much more about that problem because I was in a fight with the airplane. I figured the only way to bring the plane back was to ride it down to 10,000 to 12,000 feet or more and see if the engine would finally burn itself out and freeze up, which it eventually did. Then on three engines we went out over the channel, dropped our bombs and headed back for Tibenham. By that time I was exhausted, but we got a clearance for a straight-in approach and I landed with no problem. Because of the crisis, I had forgotten about Johnson and O'Keefe bailing out; and, just as we pulled in to park the plane, here they came in a jeep, carrying their parachutes and eating candy bars. Can you believe it, they got back to the base before we did.

Doye O'Keefe

We had started the morning like any other mission. Up at 3:00 a.m., breakfast, briefing, dress and takeoff. Don't remember where the target was supposed to be but we had started to fly in formation at about 18,000 feet and all of a sudden there was a terrible roar from our No. 2 engine. The plane began to shake. We had a runaway propeller. The engine had lost all power and the wind was spinning the motor at a terrible rate. The pilot couldn't feather the propeller to make it stop and signaled over his shoulder to the engineer, Johnson. Johnson came to me and over the noise yelled to me, "Bail out!" It did feel like the plane was about to shake apart and I didn't question him. So I opened the bomb bay after snapping on my chest pack, looked again and he pointed down so I jumped out. I counted to ten to clear the plane and pulled the ripcord. Out it comes and streamed up above and suddenly gave me a jerk that I thought about pulled me in two.

Suddenly, all was very quiet. I could hear the plane's engines. I could see our plane still flying. Lieutenant Pearson now had the prop feathered and was flying on three engines. He came by fairly close and I waved to them. I looked around and Johnson was also floating down, chute open. I yelled at him, "Hey, dummy!!" Don't think he heard me, though. We had been trained how to jump as a life saving protection but never had jumped. It was a long trip, floating down with a chute open. Finally, I went through the clouds and could see I was yet above land. I slowly came down and I landed in a wild rose thicket in a church cemetery. I was really concerned I might hit a large headstone. I'd no sooner gathered up my chute and two M.P.s in a jeep were there. They asked what outfit I was from and took me back to the 445th Group. We had only formed up our flight so it wasn't too far away.

When I arrived, of course, the first thing I was asked was how come I had to jump? All I said was, "My engineer instructed me to." Johnson now had been brought back also. When asked to explain he said he had misunderstood the pilot's instruction. Lieutenant Pearson had signaled him to go back and cut off the gas to the runaway engine. Johnson thought he meant to get out of the plane, so we did. All a big goof up. Of course, our plane had to abort the mission, short two men and on only three engines. They had to go way out over the North Sea, drop all the bombs for safety when landing, and return. Sure enough, when they landed and pulled up to the pad Johnson and I were waiting for them. When they stopped and unloaded we all got a good laugh out of it. We'd never let that happen again.

I learned several things. If ever over enemy territory, delay the opening of the chute as long as possible. Every German in the country could be waiting. I don't want a chest pack that I'd have to find and snap on. I want a backpack, one that when put on is always on and ready. If ever in real trouble, you may never have time to find it and snap it on. I'm sure many lost their lives because of a few seconds to find the chute. I went down to flight supply, explained my feeling, and they issued me one. Only pilots and co-pilots were supposed to have a backpack, but they were understanding and fitted me for one. It would work out right for me later.

Another thing I discovered was the heavy flying boots, for high altitude warmth, were not for walking when you came down.

So I tied up in a roll a pair of my GI shoes, attached a small bomb holding wire loop with a snap on it, tied it on very secure with extra shoelaces, and would snap them to my parachute harness. This also would prove right. You must think ahead. If ever I had to jump out over Germany, I was making plans to return home. Delay the opening so no one would have time to be waiting for you on the ground. Have the right shoes to change to. And I'd stick a box of K-rations in each pocket. It was food, enough for a long time, rationed out right. It would hold for several days or longer. My bailout was quite an experience. It taught me many things.

Bill Dewey

I didn't get to Tibenham until August 6 of '44, and ten days later, after training and flying practice missions, we flew our first mission on August 16. That was the same mission, the Dessau mission, that George Collar was on, and we lost a couple of planes from the group. Two of them came together. I had no way of knowing because it was my first mission, but it was a tough mission because Dessau is about 150 miles south of Berlin on a main railroad line, and the way it works out, each group makes its turn at the initial point of the bombing run. They get spread out.

By the time it got to us, and we were fairly far back in the bomber stream, we were going right over the main line of this railroad that runs south from Berlin, and all the way along they had flatcars with 155-millimeter guns shooting at us, and we just took a tremendous amount of flak. That's what hit those two planes that came together. If you talk to Ray Lemons and Jack Knox they'll tell you about the Dessau mission. That's when their plane made a roll. It rolled right on over.

Jim Baynham

At 19, Jim Baynham likely was the youngest pilot on the Kassel Mission. On the mission to Dessau, his plane flipped over when two planes collided nearby.

The Dessau mission wasn't anything eventful until this plane up above us got hit by a direct hit of flak and dove into the one in front of us, and when it did, we went right into the fireball. We had serious damage to that plane. The left wing had a big hole in it. The canopy over our heads and the flight deck was crushed in, and the fuselage on the right side was crushed. The bomb bay door was messed up.

John Ray Lemons

John Ray Lemons was a waist gunner on Baynham's crew. In 2010 I interviewed Baynham and Lemons together, whereas I had interviewed Lemons individually previously.

It wouldn't close.

Jim Baynham

We still had our bombs, and some of them broke loose. It damaged the hydraulic lines and all kinds of stuff. So it was a pretty fierce day. And then, all the guys, Ray said in the back that they thought we were going down so they grabbed their escape shoes. All we had was those felt things to try and keep our feet warm, so we carried regular shoes with us so if we bailed out we'd have a chance to do some walking.

John Ray Lemons

There were supposedly three planes that went down that was noticeable to the rest of the formation. In fact Bill Dewey was on that mission, and I think he wrote up a story about that later on, but we were the third plane, which, I think, what did you say we pulled out at?

Jim Baynham

Ten or twelve thousand feet. When it happened, we started trying to turn and it blew us on over, so we went straight down, and it took a long time just trying to pull back out. But we finally did, and went home by ourselves and nobody got us. It's amazing somebody didn't knock us off.

John Ray Lemons

Jed Lord was waiting [the ball turret had recently been removed, so one crew member would stay behind on a rotating basis], and we weren't there. And they'd already said there's three planes went down, so he was sure it was us.

Jim Baynham

They reported us as down. We never caught the formation. We went home alone. We were a sitting duck if a fighter had seen us, they'd have come after us, because that's what they did is pick off the easy ones. But we got back, and I don't think that ship ever flew again. It was like warped 20 degrees, the fuselage was. But it got us home, that's the main thing.

John Knox

John Knox was the tail gunner on Baynham's crew. I interviewed John and DeDe Knox together in 2010.

We were going to Dessau, and we were in formation. Of course I'm always looking the wrong way in the tail turret. But a plane above us in the next layer got a direct hit of flak and flew up, kind of, and peeled over and crashed into another plane right over us. And that came down and blew up in front of us, and flipped our plane over. The B-24 is not supposed to recover once it's out of control but Jim Baynham and Charlie Bosquet [the co-pilot], because of centrifugal force we couldn't move back there, because we were going straight down I guess. And we were pinned to the airplane. And finally they pulled the thing out, and we got back okay. And I looked down in my turret and there was a piece of shrapnel laying right beside my leg, about three inches big with jagged, sharp, it looked like maybe fifty or sixty razor blades glued together, just terrible. It must have just run out of steam after it broke through the aluminum, and didn't touch me. I can picture it. But being back there where we were, we didn't really get to see much of what happened, we just knew we were pinned to the floor. But that was a bad one.

DeDe Knox:

Jim said that made him realize that war is scary.

John Knox

That was the second mission. I figured how the hell are we going to do this 25 times? And shortly after that they bumped it up to 35.

George Collar

The day we went on the Dessau raid it was the 16th of August. That was a tough target. It was down not far from Magdeburg. It had a lot of flak and stuff that day. And our old plane, whatever we were flying we had supercharger trouble. The pilot couldn't keep it in formation. So before we got to the target he got permission to leave the formation and head back to England. So he called me up and said, "Get on the bomb sight and pick out a target of opportunity before we get to the Dutch border."

In the meantime, we had a guy by the name of Frederick Jacoby, who lives in New York City, he's retired from Columbia University. Lives on Central Park West. Frederick Jacoby was an intelligence officer. Donald S. Klopfer was our intelligence leader, he was a major, and he was the boss of all these intelligence guys. He was a partner with Bennett Cerf and Alfred Knopf and they started Random House. He died in his eighties a few years ago. He was a good friend of Jacoby, and after the war Jacoby worked for him for a while in the publishing company, then he eventually went into television. He was one of the guys on the Howdy Doody show, one of the original people that ran it. Then he eventually became a publicity man for Columbia University.

Jacoby always was pushing to try to get on a mission, so they finally let him go, and he was riding up in the nose turret that day. And after we started back for England, we called for some fighter escort but it didn't show up right away.

Here we are stooging across Germany all alone in real good weather, and I had to get on a target. I saw the Dortmund-Ens Canal coming up, and I'm going to hit a bridge on it. I picked a bridge out, and I'm on the bomb run. I've got control of the plane. Everybody's supposed to keep their face out of the intercom. Old Jacoby's real excited because he thought fighters were coming after us. "Oh, my god!" he says, "There's an airfield!" He screwed me up and I knew I was never gonna hit that bridge. So I thought, "Jesus,

I've got to do something quick because the Dutch border isn't very far away." So I hurried up and you've got to remember, on this autopilot, it was a Sperry that you've got on a B-24, you can rack that baby clear over to 45 degrees back and you won't tumble the gyro. On a B-17 it had the Norden autopilot, it'd only go about 18 degrees back and he'll tumble the gyro, then you're really screwed.

Anyway, I racked that baby, I tilted everybody about 45 degrees. I went down and got on that bomb run on that airfield that he's pointing out, and I've got the course killed with the one knob, and I knew I wasn't gonna get it killed in time and sure enough the bombs went over the top of the target and hit in the woods. And I was mad. Jesus, I was mad at Jacoby. You dirty bum. My chance for being a hero here, and you screwed it up. I thought if I could have only got that bridge. I kind of barked at old Jacoby a little bit.

We got back to the base, and he rushed right into the intelligence office. He comes running out, all smiles, and he had a folder full of maps. He said, "You know what that was? That was a night fighter base and they had their planes stashed in hardstands in the woods." So we got credit for the mission.

Bill Dewey

Kassel was my eighth mission. On our fifth mission, we lost the No. 2 engine as we were climbing in formation and I couldn't feather it. We lost all our oil pressure and it was windmilling, and I was concerned that it would come off and come through the cockpit because we couldn't feather it with no oil. So we dropped out of formation and dropped down after we made landfall, and dropped down to about 5,000 feet and we found an open field. We circled a couple of times, made sure the bombs were on safety, and we salvoed them in an open field.

Herb Bailey, the navigator, picked up Paris, so we headed for Paris. This was eight days after it was liberated, and Le Bourget – that was the field where Lindbergh had landed – the main runway was all cratered from bombing by our troops, but C-47s were flying wounded out of there. But there was a grass field 2,700 feet long. Normally a B-24 lands and takes off on at least 3,500 to 6,000 feet. This was 2,700 feet I found out later. But we only got one shot at it with three engines, so it took both the co-pilot and I because of the yaw you get with one engine out and two on the other side.

We had to put it down on the first third of the field and then as soon as the nose wheel came down we put the brakes on and we skidded right to the fence, and a jeep came out with a big Follow Me sign. We parked the plane and jumped in a 6-by-6 and went into Paris. There was still fighting in the streets, and the FFI (the Free French of the Interior) and the Maquis had these squads that were going down and mowing down collaborators. Charlie Craig, our aerial engineer, and I stood in a park on this road, there were apartment buildings on the other side, and we saw three cars pull up with big FFI with white paint on the side of them, and a bunch of guys with tommy runs run into this building and we heard machine gun fire.

We walked all around Paris because there was no transportation, and a lot of the power was out, but we saw the sights. It was getting late. We went up to an apartment building, knocked on the door, said we were looking for someplace to sleep that night. This woman came to the door, a Frenchwoman, she couldn't understand what we said, but a man came up behind her and he was an American, a World War I vet that had stayed over after the war. They invited us in, and gave us a room, fed us and gave us breakfast the next morning.

Then we took off back for Le Bourget in a 6-by-6, got on a C-47, and went back to England. And right next to me going back was a fighter pilot who was going to London on leave. He was bragging about having mowed down a whole bunch of civilians coming out of a church. And he was bragging about all the souvenirs, he had a P-38 German pistol, one of those beautiful pearl-handled officer's pistols, he had all kinds of souvenirs he was gonna bring back. He bragged about drinking cognac and kummel. I'd never heard of kummel. He said that was the greatest drink of all, you'd get drunk faster on that than anything else.

You know, our whole mission was the pinpoint bombing of military targets. This wasn't. I didn't go for that at all.

Reg Miner

I was shot down on the Kassel mission, but I had one mission that was worse. That was over Saarbrucken. We were leading our high right squadron, and we got hit badly by flak over the target. The radio operator, his job was to hold the bomb bay doors open, with the lever, and he got hit in his right foot, and it took his big toe off. And the plane had significant battle damage, a couple of engines out. So I got the deputy lead to take over, and we went back by ourselves.

We threw all our little stuff out over the Channel, and I dropped down below the cloud level as I approached England, so I wouldn't have to make an instrument letdown if there were heavy clouds. There were broken clouds at 3,500 feet, so we're flying under that, heading for Tibenham, and all of a sudden another engine let go. So I told Bertram to give me a heading for the nearest airfield, which he did, and we headed for it. I went over a bunch of woods.

We checked the flaps over the Channel, and the indicator was out. I asked the co-pilot for ten degrees of flaps, which improves your slow speed performance, it keeps you from stalling out. But he'd forgotten that the flap indicator was out and he dumped them all. It was like, oh, Jesus, like hitting a frigging stone wall. Not a stone wall, but a soft wall. Holy Cripes, I look down, and there's just woods under there, so I've got to go into those woods. Holy Jesus. So I looked out of the corner of my eye and I saw a field, looked over, threw the landing gear lever down, and flaps, and headed into it. I went through the tops of some trees to get into the field.

The field was in the shape of a hill going to the level part, and I went through the tops of the trees to get to where I wanted to go. Bertram was going through the bomb bay when we went through the trees, and he just got back into the waist and the guys dragged him down into their ditching position, and he still bounced around a little bit.

I landed, and went back to check the tracks that I landed on. The left wheel was still up in the wing. And then it eased down on the nose wheel, and we finally stopped. We lost rolling speed, and the left wing dropped, and it tore the right wing off. The landing gear acted as a pivot and ripped the right wing off. And we eased to a stop. I looked out the top hatch and the crew was all out in the field already, sitting there looking over and waiting for the thing to burn. So my co-pilot and I hopped out and joined them.

As I was looking through the bottom of the plane I happened to find the radio operator's toe. He said "You should have given it a decent burial." Jokingly. This was after the war.

After it was all over, I had kind of nightmarish thoughts about it, because it's a what-if kind of a deal. What if I hadn't done this or what if I had, Jesus Christ, I mean I was looking at disaster going into the woods. Because the woods may look kind of leafy from up above, but they're nothing but big hunks of wood there that are sticking up waiting to spear you. It would have been a big mess if I hadn't spotted that field. That was the thing that scared me most. If I hadn't seen that in time, Jesus, it would have been nasty. And it gives you the chills to think about.

It's like George Collar's older boy asked me, we were together out at Wright-Paterson having lunch in the officers club, he asked me a question, I can't remember just what it was, but my answer was that I was glad I never did anything stupid that killed anybody. I was able to look back on my flying career and say I never did anything that hurt anybody and was wrong and ended up bad. If I did anything wrong I was lucky and nothing happened that was significant. But that would have been really bad, if you did something that you know was stupid and wrong and dumb and you killed a few guys. And it happened a lot. Airplanes colliding in midair. One time we were flying into Europe and way up ahead, in the group ahead of us, I saw two guys come together in formation and go down. Jesus. An error like that, holy Jesus. Of course it could have been with equipment failure, because usually a pilot is the key guy and if he screws up, it can be a disaster.

Frank Bertram

On a previous mission to the Kassel mission – six missions before – we had flown one that was scarier than the Kassel mission, but with not quite the same results. We were shot up very badly over the city of Saarbrucken. Our plane took a thumping that you wouldn't believe from flak. We must have taken five or six damn near direct hits. You could see the red interior of the shell. Our radio operator had a piece of his foot blown off.

We lost one engine over the target, and another one was windmilling. We couldn't feather it, and we dropped like a wounded bird. The group had us going down in France. They had us down in the English Channel. They had us down in England. They gave up on us. We were all by ourself, and we fired off some flares, and within thirty seconds we had an escort of P-51s. They would circle us and talk to us and no German plane would go near us. We went all the way across the Channel. We ended up throwing stuff out of the plane into the Channel. We even threw our parachutes out to lighten the plane because we were down too low to jump.

We threw everything out except the bombardier, he was next. And for one reason or another, we didn't make it, and we crashed. The pilot again did an inspirational job. But we crashed and it was quite an experience. We bounced around, very traumatic. The next day I was so stiff and sore I could hardly move.

On that particular mission, George Collar had been taken off our plane and we had this guy Omick as our bombardier. And in the nose turret we had a first lieutenant, Richard Aylers, and he only had two missions to go. So he was in the nose turret, and the pilot said to me, "Give me a heading for the closest airport, quick!" I looked out and right in front of us there was a runway, and I said, "Straight ahead!"

He said, "Clear the nose and get out of there!"

I opened the nose turret door and tapped that guy on the shoulder and tried to pull him out. He got mad, he didn't hear the conversation, and he was gonna take a swing at me because I jolted him. I got him out and got him in back, and I didn't quite make the bomb bay when we hit the ground. I was still in the waist and got thrown into the bomb bay, or out of the bomb bay into the waist, I kept bouncing around like a rubber ball. All the other guys were strapped in. And Miner brought us to a safe, healthy conclusion.

John Cadden

John Cadden was the radio operator on pilot Stanley Krivik's crew.

The Kassel Mission was our second experience with a crash. I flew 19 missions and the first 11 or 12 were on a plane called Fearless Fosdick, and we used to have all kinds of trouble with the gasoline tank readings on that plane. We thought we were running out of gasoline over the Channel on one of our missions, so as soon as we hit the English coast there was an air base at Manston that had extra long runways, and we put into that. And it turned out, we thought we were just about out of gas, it was reading empty, and we had 200 gallons left. So they recalibrated the gasoline gauge, and it was shortly after that, maybe the next mission, that we thought we had a lot of gas and we ran out.

We were over England at the time, and we're flying about 1,500 feet, and all the engines conked out. Fortunately we were in a farming area and we crashed in a corn field. They call them corn fields it was like a wheat field. Nobody got hurt, but the plane was totaled. After that mission, that's when we started flying Percy. That was the plane we were on on the Kassel Mission.

I got in hot water because of the crash of Fearless Fosdick, because up until then intelligence gave me this camera and I was supposed to take pictures of the bomb hits out the bomb bay doors. It's a great big thing that you hang out the bomb bay doors, and I did a good job of it so they kept letting me take pictures. But after that crash, I took that aerial camera and I took pictures of ourselves, all over the plane, waving, and when I got back, it never dawned on me, I forgot that this thing would be developed, and they got mad. They didn't say anything to me, but they raised the devil with Krivik over it. And after that they never assigned me the camera again. I didn't enjoy hanging out the bomb bay anyway.

The Krivik crew after the crash of Fearless Fosdick, prior to the Kassel Mission.

Chapter 5: The Polish Slave Laborer Theory

George Collar

On the day before the Kassel mission, I flew to Hamm, which is a railway yard. They had been hit quite a few times, but the Germans always were able to have it running in a couple of days. They had big trainloads of Russian prisoners whose sole job was to fix those railroads and get the main line going.

The next day I was scheduled to go on a three-day pass. Normally, you'd go down to Tibenham station and catch the train the night before. But I didn't do that. I thought I'll take my time. I had it coming, too, boy, I'm telling you. I hadn't had a three-day pass for about 17 missions.

About 3 o'clock in the morning, there was a jeep that had a squeaky brake. In the middle of the night you'd be sleeping and all of a sudden you'd hear a jeep coming, you'd get about halfway up, and you'd listen. If you didn't hear any squeaky brake, you knew you're okay, you could go back to sleep. But if you heard a squeaky brake, oh my god, he's coming in our hut.

So he'd come in and you'd just lay there hoping he wouldn't come over to your bunk. Or he'd grab you and shake you, "Come on, Lieutenant, you're going on a mission." And hey, he woke me up.

I said, "No, I'm not going. I'm going on a three-day pass."

"I've got your name here on the list," he said. "You're going to take a guy's place."

It was Lieutenant Aarvig on Schaen's crew. Schaen and Aarvig and his co-pilot Bobby McGough and his navigator was Corman Bean, they were all in our hut. Aarvig had failed to come back from London on his three-day pass. So I'm taking his place.

I was mad. I didn't want to go. I had my heart set on going to London. Well, okay. So I went down to the briefing. And I remember distinctly, I think that was the morning that Major General Kempner, he might have been in command of the 2nd Air Division at the time, at one time he was in command of all the fighter groups. He was a real good guy. And he came down to the

49

briefing that morning. I think it was that morning, but sometimes I get mornings mixed up. It seems like he was there and he came to the bombardiers' briefing.

Then I went out and got in the plane and we took off. I think we talked about coming in to the IP (initial point) and making a wrong turn. We dropped the bombs at Goettingen and then instead of turning around and getting the heck out of there they made the same old pattern that they originally had for Kassel only about fifty miles too far west. Made a right turn, and in the vicinity of Eisenach we made another right turn, and at that point we got hit by about 150 FW-190s. They came in sort of like on a broad front, in three waves, and were just totally unexpected. They hit us, Bang!

The first inkling I had was when I heard something hitting the plane. It turned out to be 20-millimeter shells. Oh, before we got hit, I saw these small flak bursts in front of us, about the size of a basketball, and they were very close. My god, I never saw flak like that. It didn't dawn on me that it was fighter cannons coming from behind.

I didn't know what it was, and I'm looking all over the sky. I couldn't see any fighters because they're coming from behind. And then I started feeling jolts hitting the plane. There was one underneath the turret and there were some on the left wing and the next thing I knew the left wing's on fire.

About that time this fighter plane came over the top of the plane. It couldn't have been, I'd say, maybe ten or fifteen feet above us. I tried to get the turret trained on him and nothing worked. The turret was just dead.

After that fighter plane went over, I looked out and saw the wing on fire and we started nosing down. I looked over toward the lead squadron and I could see at least two planes flying along on fire, and finally they dropped off. One of them I think was the lead plane of the lead squadron. The lead squadron was actually the 700th Squadron. The high right squadron, which we were in, was the 702nd. The high high right was the 701st, and the low left was the 703rd. Now, what confused a lot of people later on trying to figure out who was leading was the fact that Captain Chilton, who was the lead pilot in the lead plane, was from the 703rd. They'd borrowed the 703rd lead plane to lead the group. And Major McCoy was flying in the co-pilot seat with Captain Chilton. In the deputy lead was Captain Uebelhoer, who was also a radar plane, and in the co-pilot seat was Captain Jim Graham.

You couldn't wear a parachute in the front turret, so I had it sitting someplace near where you got out of the turret. When I got out it wasn't there. Bean had it in his hand. He had his on already and he snapped mine on me when I got out of the turret. And he bent down and opened the nose wheel door. He hesitated, and I found out later he was looking up. He could see the feet of the pilot. I thought he didn't want to jump, so I gave him a little boost. He gave me heck about that later. He said, "I was looking up to see what they were doing."

Then I went out right after him, and "my god," I thought, "I'd better make sure this chute's gonna work." So I hadn't fallen very far when I pulled the ripcord and Bom! My boots took off.

When I bailed out, it was just like the battle in "Wings." ["Wings was the 1927 World War I movie that won the first Best Picture Academy Award.] You'd hear those guns shooting and you could hear stuff blowing up and planes blowing up and bomb bay doors come floating by, oh, Geez, and to look at it you could see the fighters sailing in on these guys. It was just like in the movies. Better than the movies. More realistic.

Everything happened so quick. It seemed that there had to be about 40 chutes in the air, and there was bedlam. But gradually, as you went down, the battle faded away. Pretty soon you could hardly hear it. And by the time I got into the clouds – the clouds had tops at about 6,000 feet – it was deathly silent. I could see nothing and hear nothing. The most eerie, quiet feeling you'll ever hear. Especially after leaving a din like a battle. It seemed ethereal.

When I broke through the clouds at about 3,000 feet, I could see everything on the ground. There was a panoramic view. Beautiful scene. Little village. Ruined castle on a hill, and a little river. I heard a plane coming and I looked up, and here comes a fighter plane right about my level, right towards me. I thought, "Oh boy, I wonder if it's a German." When he saw me, he banked around, probably the length of a football field away, and I could see it was a P-51 with a yellow nose. And he saw me, he knew I was American. He waved at me and I waved at him. And then he went on and his prop wash hit me, and I swung as high as the Eiffel Tower both ways.

When that settled down, I began to see more clearly on the ground. They told us when we're gonna hit the ground to kind of relax like a tumbler.

Before that happened, I could see a guy coming up a lane on a bicycle. He was looking up at me. I thought – I was stretching things but I thought, "He's probably a Polish slave laborer, and I can talk him into hiding me out." He turned out to be the burgomeister. And when I landed I lit hard on my feet and I twisted my left ankle, and fell heavily on my left shoulder. It knocked the wind out of me, and the chute was dragging me across this field. I reached out and pulled the shrouds and collapsed the chute. I'm laying there trying to get my breath when the guy on the bicycle came up and he had a luger pointed my head. I thought, "Well, that's the end of that Polish slave laborer theory."

Corman Bean
Corman Bean was the navigator on the Schaen crew.

I'm sure George mentioned to you that he flew as a substitute on our crew the day we were shot down. Our regular bombardier, Richard Aarvig, had been on a three-day pass and didn't get back in time. The irony of it is that he was shot down and killed in a subsequent action. If he had flown with us he'd have probably been a POW and survived the war.

It just so happened that the crew I was on and Reg Miner's crew were assigned to the same Quonset hut, so we spent a lot of time together in England.

My pilot was Jim Schaen. I think of him as being a damn good pilot. He took us through some scrapes that we owe him a lot for the way he handled an airplane. One night when we were in Casper, our crew was assigned for a nighttime bombing practice. For me, the navigator, it was supposed to be a milk run because we were just a few miles from base and the pilot was navigating by radio and that was all there was to it. Until our electric went out. And he didn't have radio to guide him back anymore. So there we are flying in a light snowstorm up in mountainous territory.

Casper is right in the foothills of the Rockies. And he didn't know where to go. So we circled around, and kept our eye out on the ground, and finally we saw a couple of rows of dim lights, which we knew would be an auxiliary field, probably an emergency field for an airline. And he took us down and landed on that in pretty soft mud. It was a doggone fine job of flying. We got up the next morning, I think we spent the night in the airplane, and when dawn broke we looked around and there were mountains on three sides and the side we came in on was the open side. That night we owed an awful lot to Jim Schaen for getting us down safely and taking care of that airplane.

The Kassel mission was my 16th mission. I don't recall anything out of the ordinary until we got to the initial point. And a couple of minutes after we hit the IP and made our turn supposedly toward the target, we could look out to the right and see the main bomber stream, the hundreds of airplanes, in a line, headed down that way, and here we were headed over this way.

There was a lot of communication once everybody realized we were wrong. I think everybody knew it except the command pilot, and if he knew it he didn't do a damn thing about it. And they never had a chance to interview him because he died on the mission.

I was not among the first to see the fighters. The navigator was bundled up in that little tiny hole in the front of the ship with a desk, and while we didn't have much to do on the bombing run, we didn't have a very good observation point either.

I'm sure we knew we were under attack before we were hit, because one shot doesn't bring you down. You get shot up pretty badly before that airplane falls. But during the air battle I could look out through that little bubble and I did. I looked to the rear of our airplane, and from the bomb bay back it was solid fire. So you know then it was just a matter of seconds before the bell rang and it was time to leave. I thought at the time that there's no way those guys in the back could ever get out; if they're not dead already they're gonna die with the ship. And they did, all three of them back there, the two waist gunners and the tail gunner, all three were killed.

The tail gunner was Hurd. The waist gunner was Johnson, and another guy was Parsons. Dick Parsons. Those three and Jim Schaen were the four that died. But when the bell rang to leave the ship, I was up in the nose, and Collar was riding the front turret, and there's no way a guy can get out of that quickly. Usually you're gonna squeeze your way out if you've got a lot of time, but if you're in a hurry you can't. So I distinctly remember opening those doors to the turret and grabbing Collar by the neck and pulling him ass over teakettle backwards into the little navigator's quarter, and then we got our parachutes on, and I went out first and he followed me.

Chapter 6: "I See Flak. I See Fighters."

Bill Dewey

My first indication that anything was wrong was when our tail gunner said "I see flak. I see fighters." The flak he saw was the gray tracers from the 20-millimeter cannons that were right next to us. And then all the guns opened up, and the plane started to shudder and shake, not only from our guns but also from the hits from five planes that were converging on our tail.

I didn't see any of this because I was in the left seat, and we were flying in the high high right squadron. This was a maximum effort. We were supposed to have 40 planes, and at that time we flew in 10-ship formations. Originally I think the group had flown 12 ships, and they cut it down to ten because it was much more maneuverable. So we had a three-ship lead element, a three-ship slot element, a high right element and a low left element.

That would be the ten planes in each squadron, and there would be four of those. There would be a lead squadron, a high right squadron, a high high right squadron and a low left squadron. And when you make a turn, there was always a tendency for the higher squadrons to overrun the lower, because of the variation in elevation. So we had dropped our bombs and we were turning, and we had swung our squadron, instead of being high high right, we were way off to the left.

Now these 150 German planes coming up, six to thirty abreast, came up from the clouds, below and behind us. So I didn't see any of it. But our plane was shaking. Bill Boykin, my co-pilot, was looking out, and he said, "There's another one going down. There's another one. All over the sky, they're all going down. Everyone's going down." At the same time, all the guns, the twin .50s in the tail, the two waist .50 calibers are going off, and our top turret. Of course the nose gunner had nothing to shoot at, Charlie Craig, and his twin .50s, he was shooting too.

It all took place in two or three minutes. It was a very short period of concentrated, intense activity.

55

The tail gunner shot a plane coming in and then his tail turret exploded and caught fire from hydraulic fluid, and he had to get out of it. He was wounded from the Plexiglas, because they had made a direct hit on the tail turret. Both of the waist gunners were hit with 20-millimeter. Both went down, and both got up, and there right next to them were FW-190s. All Walt Bartko had to do, he said, was just open up. When he got on his feet there was the plane. He just pulled the trigger and this plane exploded in an orange ball of fire. The same thing for George Johnson, the right waist gunner.

By that time there was a hole ahead of the right waist window about seven feet in diameter. In fact, when we landed, they took the wounded out right through that instead of coming out through the bomb bay or the hatch.

At that point the plane was flying okay. We had no problem with the engines, although I could see the big hole in the upper surface of our right wing, about a three-foot diameter hole, with hundred octane gasoline coming out. But we were flying okay even though the plane was shuddering and shaking.

Our intercom was out and that's when I asked Bill Boykin, the co-pilot, to go back and check on what's happened back there. He came back five or ten minutes later and said, "Bill, we're in bad shape. The plane's not gonna make it."

At that time we didn't have hydraulics for our controls, everything was on cables and pulleys, and he said that the cables were all frayed, and the tail looked like it was going to come off at any time. Both of the waist gunners were down, and Montanez wasn't in good shape, with blood all over his face. He was the tail gunner. Les Midlock was our nose gunner, and I asked him to go back and administer to the wounded. They were out of oxygen back there, so he carried oxygen bottles from the front of the plane through the bomb bay, and made about three trips with that, and covered up the guys as best he could, with all this freezing cold air coming in, and administered to the wounded.

This all happened about five minutes after all of the action had stopped. But Charlie Craig, the top turret gunner and aerial engineer, told me later that one plane came right up next to us, so close he could look in and see the oxygen mask of the fighter pilot, he could see his goggles, almost see the color his eyes and see the instrument panel, but he couldn't lower his guns enough to shoot the guy. So this plane evidently just came up to take a look at us, then it dropped down 150 or 200 feet below us and kept watching, expecting us to go down because we were in such bad shape, I mean the tail was almost gone.

At that point there were about seven planes left. I tried to keep up with this loose formation and couldn't. The plane was just shaking, at 160-mile airspeed, I had to cut it back. I called the leader and asked him if he could slow down. He said we'll try, but he didn't try very hard. He wanted to get home.

Charles Graham
Charles Graham was the radio operator on pilot Carl Sollien's crew.

My pilot was Carl Sollien. He was a professional photographer in Hamilton, New York. And my bombardier was a boy by the name of Hudelson. He was from California. And my top turret gunner was Ammi Miller, he was from Blackfoot, Idaho. Today he's a preacher in New Mexico. And my engineer was Stephens, he was from Detroit.

My one waist gunner was Jimmy Bridgeo, and he was from Boston, Massachusetts, and the other waist gunner was – actually, what happened, Stephens and Bridgeo were pretty good buddies, so Stephens instead of flying the top turret, which the engineer's supposed to have done, wanted to get back in the waist to fly opposite his buddy Bridgeo, so consequently, Ammi Miller was in the top turret and Stephens was on the waist.

And the tail gunner was Tommy Imhoff, he was from Spokane, Washington, so you can see we were from all over. I was from Decatur, Illinois.

Five of the crew were killed in the battle and five were prisoners of war. Tommy Imhoff from Spokane just turned 21 that day that he was killed. Bridgeo in the waist and Stephens in the waist were killed, and the nose navigator was also killed. The co-pilot was the only one that had on a back type chute, and the chute never opened when he bailed out.

On the plane, the No. 4 engine was on fire. I saw this one fighter coming in, I could see the fire coming from his wings, coming right at us. We were flying deputy lead that day and our lead ship blew up in front of us, so we had to take over the lead. And as I looked from my position up toward the pilot I saw Carl Sollien pull the control back and it all came right back in his lap. So he had no control over the ailerons or rudders, and he blew the thing for bailing out. And for some reason or other, the lead navigator was about 25 miles off his course, so we did not hit the target that we were supposed to have hit, and that was the disappointing part of it.

I'd never used a parachute before, so I got down, preparatory to getting on the catwalk to bail out the bomb bay doors, and something hit me in the back. It was my top turret gunner, Ammi Miller's flak suit. He had loosened it and it had fallen out of the top turret, so when he got down, I put his chest type chute on. I already had mine on. And we both bailed out about the same time. So Ammi and I were the only enlisted men that were prisoners of war, whereas the pilot and navigator and bombardier were the only other three members of the plane that were prisoners.

When I hit the ground I really didn't hit the ground. I don't swim, so I had my Mae West on, and I thought, if I go in the water, I'll drown, and I'd probably forget to pull the Mae West anyway. And I passed over this little body of water, and then all wide open fields and one tree. And I lit right in the middle of that darn tree. I undid my parachute and it dropped to the ground. It was only about four or five feet.

At that time, a man and his wife came out, buried my parachute, and took me into their home. There were several other American boys in there, and they were getting a meal of fried apples ready for us when a knock came on the door, and here stood two great big German officers and they were on big white horses. And they came in and said, "For you the war is over." And that's all. Then we were divided into different parties. I went into a party going around checking on the wounded, and my pilot was on one going for the dead, and that's the reason, as I found out later at transit camp Dulag, why Sollien got to me, and he was wearing Bridgeo's overseas cap. Sollien always was immaculate with his uniform and always wore the visor type officer cap, so when I saw him with this little overseas cap, I knew that he was trying to relay something to me. And he finally got to me and told me that was Bridgeo's cap, and he had been killed in the battle as well as the tail gunner and the other waist gunner.

Malcolm MacGregor

Kassel was my 34th mission. I didn't know anything about it. I had no reason to think it would be any worse than any of the others we had. And one of the navigators was fairly new.

This was his first mission with us, Jack Dent. I remember him saying, "You guys don't have anything to worry about. This is my fifth mission. I've never had any trouble." That's kind of interesting. But I didn't say anything. I just listened, and he went off to his nose turret.

When we got shot down, Wes Hudelson unplugged all his stuff and tried to get the nose wheel door to open. He told me, "I remember Jack as being out of the nose turret and waiting for me to get the door open and the door was locked." It was probably frozen. So Wes was jumping up and down and finally it broke loose but it didn't break loose until about 5,000 feet, he said, before he got out of the plane. So he was in the plane when it was going down from about 23,000 feet to about 5,000 feet before he got out. And Jack never got out of the plane. He was still in the nose.

You can speculate, but it could be that there he was, he didn't have anything to do, nothing to occupy his mind, just watch this guy trying to get the door open, and the thoughts going through his mind. I think both of us thought that he froze and just couldn't get himself going to get out of the plane. He'd have had enough time if he jumped, but who knows, he could have been shot, we didn't know. But he never got his sixth mission.

As we approached the initial point, Carl talked to me through the headset and he said, "Mac, there's no sense in your setting up your bomb sight because we don't have any radar and you're never going to be able to see anything." And that plane we were on had a little couch right behind the pilot. That's where I was. It didn't have any arms, but it was nice and comfortable.

I had left my parachute, my chest pack, down in the front of the bomb bay. There was a tunnel on our plane that went up beside the nose wheel so you could get up comfortably and get into the front of the plane. I'd left my parachute right there because my expectation was that when it came time to go set up, I'd go through there and I'd pick up my parachute as I went and I'd have it up front in case something happened. So I was up on the flight deck without my parachute. And then things started to happen.

All of a sudden the top turret gunner started firing. That was Ammi Miller. He shouldn't have been up there. He was supposed to be a waist gunner, but the engineer, Stephens, who was supposed to be up there because that makes him closer to the controls, he got claustrophobic being in the top turret, so that cost him his life, because he was in the back of the plane, and all those guys were blown to pieces back there, all three of them.

The first thing that went through my mind, I said, "What the hell's wrong with Ammi? Why is he clearing his guns?" We were at 23,000 feet. And then I realized that whoops, maybe he's got a reason. So I looked out, there's a little window that goes right above the top of this couch, and here was an FW-190, beautiful plane, all painted red, the bottom of it anyway was red, it was just split-S-ing over the left wing. And I swear I thought I saw bullets bouncing off the bottom of it. I think they heavily armored those planes.

So then I said, oops, I'm up here and my parachute's down there, I'd better go get it. So I jumped up and unplugged myself from my oxygen, headset and all that stuff, and jumped down in front of the bomb bays and got my parachute.

At about this time I started seeing exploding shells coming up through the bomb bays. The last one went off three or four feet from my right side, and I picked up a little more than a dozen pieces of shrapnel in each of my legs. The worst one is about halfway through my calf, and that one has bothered me ever since, but the rest of them don't bother me. The Germans told me if they took them out they'd do more damage than leaving them in. And in general they were right.

So then I put my parachute on, and I looked at Carl. He was standing up looking over the back of his seat, and his eyes were about twice as big as usual, and he was pointing. He had no intercom, but I knew what it meant. So I turned around and went and opened the bomb bays. The right bomb bay, which is where the shells were coming through, didn't go at all. The left bomb bay came up about halfway, and I don't know whether the back bomb bay came up at all, but the left front bomb bay came up about halfway, and as soon as it did I dove for it.

I landed on the upper half of the left bomb bay and there was gas and fuel running out so I got soaked, but I was on a nice and flat surface, and I just rolled out.

I remembered that they told us you should make damn sure you're out from under the airplane, and that's what I did. I waited until the airplane cleared away from me, and I opened my parachute, and I do not remember the jerk or anything, but of course I was running on adrenaline and I hadn't had oxygen for quite a while, but I can distinctly remember the plane going away from over the top of me and I pulled my chute. I don't remember any sudden stop but both my boots went off and the shoes that I'd tied onto my parachute, they broke loose and went off, so it must have been a pretty good jolt. But I didn't hurt or anything, and then all of a sudden the air battle was gone.

I didn't see anybody else in the air. There wasn't another parachute. The planes were all gone. And there I was, all alone, in the middle of Germany, probably 18, 20,000 feet above the ground and going down at a very slow rate. I think it took me 15 or 20 minutes to get down. And I was terribly lonely. Here I am, all my buddies and all the rest are gone, and they're probably mad at me anyway. I wouldn't call it fear but it was extreme loneliness.

I was probably a little more than halfway down when two fighter planes came toward me, and what crossed my mind was oh, jeez, that's the Germans and they're gonna shoot me in the chute. Fortunately they were P-51s. Of course they couldn't do anything for me, so they just went around me and went on. They were looking for German fighters. And the next thing I remember is here was the cloud layer.

I came out the other side and I looked over along the edge of this plowed field, and here was a little car coming down the road, and I looked up at my chute, and while I looked up I hit the ground. And I sprained my ankle very badly. So I was still lying there on the field and the Germans, two guys got out. They were Wehrmacht, and one of them had a little pistol. He waved it at me. I waved back at him to show that I wasn't about to start a war in the middle of Germany. And they came over and helped me out of my parachute, and helped me walk over to the car, and they put me in the back seat. It was a two-door car. They got in the front seat and drove me down the road until they came to a field that had a bunch of prisoners in it. Then they took me out and put me in with the rest of the prisoners.

I thought I might have been the only one that got out of the plane. I did exactly what I should have done. As the bombardier, I had nothing else to do, the main thing we needed to do was get the bomb bays open, and I got the bomb bays open, and that made a space for Carl and Ammi and Chuck to get out, so I'm happy with the role I played. Dent should have gone out the nose wheel door with Hudelson, and the three guys in the tail were all dead.

Frank Plesa

Staff Sgt. Frank Plesa was the tail gunner on Hot Rock, piloted by Lt. William Mowat. Plesa was one of only two survivors from the crew of nine. This account is from a letter Plesa wrote in 1986 to 8th Air Force historian Mary Beth Barnard.

I appreciate the group and squadron booklets you made up. There sure were a lot of reports on Sept. 27 - '44, That is about the way it happened only it seems to me that most of the damage was from under at first.

I recall seeing the small size bursts of orange with white or grey puffs of smoke like flak all around us for at least thirty seconds before I saw fighters firing at us from the rear or 6 o'clock level attacks.

Our plane's antenna cable was dangling behind my turret and the intercom was out. I could hear but no one could hear me call when I did see the fighters. I heard the navigator ask the nose gunner "What's wrong Lello?" Then Johnnie, right waist gunner, asked me "Frank, what's wrong?" I heard T.J. Myers, engineer top turret, "What is that, flak?? Then he calls "Fighters 6 o'clock." I fired several bursts at a FW-190 at 6-level around five hundred yards or more only it and the others turned belly up and went down, I would guess for another attack. I could hear and feel a waist gunner firing and the Martin upper (Myers) as I was firing. I never heard the nose or right waist guns fire. As you might know we had no belly or Sperry ball gun turrets that I knew of in our group or plane.

When the first attack of FW-190s turned over and down to their right for about ten seconds I didn't see any more enemy fighters – then I noticed a FW-190 to my right. It seemed as if it was fifty feet to his wing tip. I was amazed at him being so close and I don't know how he got there throttled down and firing his guns (cannons) at the bomber in front of him and us, I assume. I didn't know how to fire at the fighter at such close range. I could see his blue eyes or possibly colored goggles, not sure, only I recall blue color above his oxygen mask, and the big black cross on top of his right wing, and his guns blazing yellow fire.

I put my optical sight on his engine cowl and fired and raked his front fuselage and possibly his cockpit with bursts of about three to four seconds, when I felt a shell hit under my turret near my right foot, then another a split second later on the left side of my turret, bending the left gun up – blown out plex top front heavy bulletproof window, and me all going out at the same time as if a horse kicked me in the chest.

My turret was facing around 8 o'clock. I was blown all out except my right leg and foot which was tangled up in hydraulic lines. Most of myself was sort of sitting on the right side of the catwalk and against the fuselage. You could smell octane gas through the oxygen mixer. After seeing the B-24 on our left side burn for a while then exploding, I wanted to get ready to bail out – only my right foot which was hit and trapped – also wounded in left forearm – right side of chest, only I could still get around.

I looked back for Johnnie Neher – right waist – only couldn't see him, seems as if I could see him down in a black sort of object (heated flying suit). Willie, the left waist gunner (his last mission!) was wounded badly on the left upper side only still firing down with his right hand – his heated suit was blood soaked along his left arm which was limply hanging. I tried to get his attention only to no success, he was fighting back. I heard no other guns now.

Then what I feared came – the plane was on fire and burned through the door and here came a flame like a blowtorch. Willie's gun is quiet, it gets hot, the flames come through the tail which is open. I cover my face, feel intense heat, think of my parents and loved ones and God – recall myself screaming in my mask. I could still hear it. I feel a hand on my right shoulder and a vision of white robe, then I felt and heard a big puff, everything goes black – could feel cold air and tumbling about, it felt sort of good compared to previous heat – only helpless.

I regain senses, look around – our wing is right next to me, fifty feet, flip flopping over whooshing with fire from its tanks. I look down and recall I was just issued a back type parachute two weeks ago. Pull the ripcord with right hand which was burned. Look up and it opened. Then I started looking down at the ground – it's real quiet and in about ten seconds the ground starts coming up to me and fast. I hit hard next to a farm house in sort of a pasture next to a forest and high electrical lines.

Hitler youth greets me, asks if I am American or English. We take off parachute and I hobble over to the farm house with him – quite helpless and burned. His mother comes out, they put me in a barn on hay and ladder – she checks my chest wound and replies "goot," gives me an apple and tells me she will get help. The German G.I.s come in a horse and buggy to pick me up and take me to Hersfeld – train station, wait for hours there on stretcher, then that evening was I believe in Frankfurt in a hospital with nuns in white giving first aid and comfort to many wounded in hallways and aisles in the hospital.

They gave me a shot and removed the biggest parts of shrapnel and wrapped my burns and wounds. I woke up the next morning feeling better and was then transported by train to an allied POW hospital near Menningen. British doctors stitched close my chest wound, with a rubber tube left in for penicillin the American Red Cross furnished, as well as many other supplies and food parcels.

I healed slowly and several places of burns required skin grafts. Was there until about the middle of December, then to a convalescent home for about a month, and then to Luft IV around the first part of February. Then a forced march to keep away from the Russians, which was really the most hungry and difficult part of POW life – liberated May 2 – by the British 2nd Army. The happiest day ever for me and I'm sure the others.

I saw T.J. Myers in the POW hospital. He wasn't hit too much and went to IV in about a month – never saw or heard of anyone else in our crew and their fate until I got home. I was afraid the other seven went down with or around Hot Rock. I was a very fortunate and lucky 19-year-old airman and will never forget the crew.

Well Mary, I didn't think I could ever write this much at one time. Hope you can make it all out, and helps you in your future stories and books you intend to do. There is more I could write you later on if we didn't describe most of my side of the Kassel Mission. We always forget and don't describe too well at times.

Theodore J. Myers

T.J. Myers was the engineer/top turret gunner on Hot Rock. He and Frank Plesa were the only survivors of the nine-man Mowat crew. This account was included in Missing Air Crew Report #9572.

We were on our way home after having bombed Kassel, flying at approximately 10:15 a.m., somewhere in central Germany.

I flew in the top turret. I was the first one on our crew to see the fighters and to report them to the crew. They were lined up, wing tip to wing tip, and were coming in low at 5 o'clock (I guess this was because we had no lower ball turrets in any of the planes).

We were one of the first four or five ships of the group to go down in flames. I saw several chutes in the air while I was firing. I fired my guns until they became so hot that they kept jamming until I finally couldn't charge them anymore. A shell exploded near the top of my turret and it looked like one of my guns was bent. The smoke of that shell got on the glass and I couldn't see out. I pressed the interphone switch to call the pilot and found that it wasn't working.

When my feet touched the flight deck I felt a heavy vibration in the plane. I looked forward and saw the pilot and the co-pilot. The radio operator was sitting on the floor with his flak suit and helmet on. They all seemed all right at that time.

I looked into the bomb bay and saw several large streams of gasoline shooting down against the bomb bay doors. A mist of gasoline was floating forward onto the flight deck. The first thing that entered my mind was to try to stop the gas flow. If those shells ever entered the ship, with all that gasoline squirting around, that ship would explode. So I climbed down into the bomb bay to look at the holes in the gasoline tanks, hoping they would seal themselves.

The holes were too large to seal up, so I decided to open the bomb bay doors to let the slipstream blow it out of the ship. During that time I got soaked from head to foot with gas. The slipstream started to clear up the inside. I turned around to get on the flight deck (all of this took less than a minute) to tell the pilot we had been hit bad and were losing gas fast. Before I could move, one or more 20-mm shells went off under my feet, wounding me in the right foot and both legs. The blow lifted me up and hurt my back and I fell on my back on the catwalk. Then I saw a blinding flash and I was on fire from head to foot. I felt my face burning and that was all I remembered as I thought I was dying.

I guess I had just lost consciousness. In a minute or two I awoke to find myself hanging in my parachute. The slipstream had blown out the fire. My face was so burned that I could only see out of my left eye. I saw a big streaming mass of fire go by me about 200 or 300 feet away. I am sure the ship exploded about that time.

I met the tail gunner, Frank Plesa, who was badly wounded and burned, five or six hours later in a German hospital. He said he had been blown out of his turret. He saw the wing of the ship go past him. Then he lost consciousness and came to about 800 feet above the ground and pulled the ripcord.

Plesa said that just before the ship caught fire he saw the left waist gunner, Everette L. Williams, a fellow who was flying his last mission, get badly wounded.

Chapter 7: Here They Come

Herb Schwartz

Herb Schwartz was the tail gunner on pilot Jack French's crew. This is from a diary Herb kept

I am about to relate the facts about Mission No. 21. Quite an unusual mission and by far, one of the hardest I have ever encountered. Awakened at 2:30 a.m. for a 3:30 briefing and a 6:15 take-off. Going through identical procedure as previous missions, I ate, dressed, briefed and started to the ship to check her over and look at my guns and turrets. We were flying a comparatively new ship: a lead ship belonging to Capt. Merrill. Lt. French, Lt. Cochran and Greenly were flying their last missions. Our target, Kassel, Germany. Our escort, P-51s in and over the target, P-38s to carry us home. P-47s strafing ground installations before our arrival. Forming at 11,000, bombing at 25,000.

We were to hit the same target at Kassel that we hit just a few days previous. Major related to us all the facts and told us everything in detail. We were told that we might encounter the Luftwaffe, but if we did, in all probability, we would hit them before we reached our objective. Major McCoy was leading; Heitz flying lead of the slot; Lt. French leading high right squadron with Lt. Bruce and Lt. Pearson flying off right and left wing respectively.

We formed, started for our target – weather fair until we hit target and target, 10/10 covered. We ran into scattered barrages of inaccurate flak to the target and over the target, not one burst of flak yet. I could see planes flying through heavy accurate flak behind us and I immediately told our navigator. We later learned that we were 23 miles off course, we had bombed the wrong target and we were flying the wrong route.

Fighter escort of P-51s was excellent being recognized by white contrails they left. We always had 15 to 20 on our tail. After leaving the target and starting for our base, Cochran said the roughest part was over as we were not scheduled to hit flak areas on the way home. I test fired my guns and all my equipment was in good shape. Twenty minutes later, Corman, left waist gunner, called out P-47s in large groups that he saw at 10 o'clock low. Everything began to happen fast. Waist gunner changed his call from P-47s to FW-190s, one of Germany's fastest and best fighters. We had it! Interphone was noisy and I couldn't get a word in.

These fighters were coming in in groups of 15 and all ready for the kill – which was us. We were flying damn good formation and in a good position should we be hit by fighters. They looked to me to be attacking from the north but I was wrong. Everyone started firing and before I knew it, they were in on us. 100 Focke-Wulfs and I was half scared to death.

They were through us and started to re-form for a tail attack and I knew it was my job to hold them off. I pulled my flak suit off, threw my helmet off, and turned on my trigger switch and was ready for what may come. They headed for Bruce and Pearson, flying off our wings, before they hit us in numbers.

Everything started to run thru my mind. Pilot said to be careful and take it easy. An FW came for me and I started shooting. Every attack but two were at 6:00 level and a dead-on shot. I let him have both guns and he started smoking and peeled beneath us. I looked up and saw Lt. Bruce's ship being attacked in formation by seven fighters and at the same time, a fighter coming in at his waist. His guns were all firing away, and at that split second, another fighter came in at his topside of fuselage.

He was on fire, and his plane got out of control. Another fighter started at his left waist and after throwing quite a bit of ammo, turned and headed for my tail, his engine already smoking. Fleming, left waist gunner, had hit him and now not knowing he was in trouble he came in on me.

I let go and after firing about 30 rounds, he blew up about 50 yards away from my turret. He had it, and Fleming and I were responsible for the kill. Lt. Bruce was completely in flames as I was later told by the right waist gunner. No chutes emerged and the ship was out of control. His ship started towards us, but French was on the lookout for same. Another FW came in. I fired but he peeled off to our left.

Before I go on, I want to say that my left waist gunner scored three kills and my right waist gunner scored one. So these ships may have been downed by them on the peel off from the tail. I did not have time to keep watching them.

Immediately following this another FW came in. I let loose with both guns and I could have sworn I got him. We can take credit only for ships we see break up or completely on fire, or where the pilot evacuates his ship. I had to hit him – he came in so close that I could have thrown a rock and hit him. I even believe I could have seen his facial expressions if I had had time to look. He peeled off and I guess the waist gunner made the kill.

Planes coming at tail either peeled off to either side or under the ship. I now had time to get a second glance at Pearson off our right wing. I saw two chutes go out and all four of his engines were on fire. Now our two wing planes were down, and we were next to concentrate on.

All this time, everyone was hollering on interphones and it was quite difficult to report all planes. Before I could look around, another 190 was coming right at me. I started to fire both guns and after about 20 rounds, my left gun stopped and right after this, my right gun stopped. Here was this 190 coming at me and I had both guns out.

I grabbed both charging cables. Charged my left gun and my right gun was not able to be charged. By this time, he was on me and I got off about 10 rounds before he peeled off. This ship was the one that caused us all the trouble. My right gun failed to fully chamber the round, and a shell was stuck half in and half out of the chamber, making it impossible to charge.

This 190 lodged a 20-millimeter in our No. 3 tank, blew off our right rudder, knocked out our No. 1 engine and made a 2 x 3 foot hole in our flap and wing. Another few inches and we would have caught fire. We began to leak gas at a rate of 25 to 50 gallons a minute, and radio man said our bomb bay looked like Niagara Falls.

We were crippled. We feathered No. 1 engine and our plane began to rock up and down. My tail turret was shaking back and forth (shaking hell out of me – all due to rudder condition) and I had to leave here. I was hysterical and screamed over the interphone to see what was wrong. I thought we were in a spin but co-pilot said we were all right and to take it easy.

I laid a piece of flak suit on floor behind turret, and I fell to my knees to stand by for other aircraft. My turret was out of control and only way I could operate her was under power, and this was still quite a job. I will to this day never understand why my tail turret never came off or why I wasn't killed. I will always be thankful for this moment.

My turret was shaking so badly that French said, "Feather No. 3" as the turret was affecting motion and control of the ship. We now had two feathered engines, but since we were flying at 20,000 losing a little altitude at this point was not too much of a major problem. We did not have nearly as much speed now.

Looked up, another FW-190 coming in. I had one gun going – left one. I began to fire – he was at close range and I was at a disadvantage. He probably thought tail was unmanned as it was shaking so badly and I could not be seen. I jumped up and stood up inside firing at him.

He started his attack at 400 yards and came in to about 20 yards before I blew him up. His shells were hitting our ship but he burst into flames just off my tail. I got him and that Jerry, I knew, would never fly again. He burst into flames just as he began to peel off to our left so the left waist gunner verified the kill to S-2.

There were other attacks. I shot at every ship coming in and I got plenty of good hits. The FW-190 has an armor nose and front and it is quite hard to down one without pouring much lead into him. P-38s showed up and fighters disappeared and I began to breathe again. Gas now covered my turret, and much of it leaked in the back. I wore my oxygen mask even at low altitude as fumes were so bad.

About this time, our rudder snapped loose and turret quit shaking so we unfeathered No. 3 engine and continued on three. We were all by ourselves; one B-24 was lagging along about 2,500 yards off our left wing. (Later found out this was Lt. Heitz.) We were in sad shape and I can honestly say that I died a hundred deaths this day. My prayers to myself, I guess, were heard. I thought it was over when I saw four FWs getting ready to come in for the kill and above two P-38s started for them.

Things looked bad. French said to prepare to bail out over Germany. Cochran said that if we were attacked by one more ship, we would lower our landing gear and surrender. We would have been blown out of the sky with one hit as gas was all over the ship. I had only about 40 rounds in my left gun, and my right gun was jammed. Since all the raids were mostly at 6:00 level, we would have been sunk. These two P-38s pointed their nose at these FWs and they dived thru the clouds and we never saw them again. We were flying at 12,500 when we unfeathered No. 3, and we were holding altitude. Navigator said we were 20 minutes out of friendly territory and these 20 small minutes seemed like 20 hours.

The P-38s were the most beautiful sight possible. We had no radio to contact our fields. No VHF to contact other ships and we could shoot no flares because of all the leakage of gas. We were lucky I guess to still have our oxygen and interphone. I went to the waist and together with the two waist gunners, we threw out everything we got our hands on from flak suits to ammo, to radio equipment. Pilot called to Timms, navigator, and asked our position. Timms hollered back that we had been in friendly territory for two minutes.

Jack French

Pilot Jack French managed to crash-land his crippled bomber in Allied occupied France.

The boys in the back said "We've got a lot of fighters up here!" Because they came from the back, and that's the first alert we had, this swarm of German fighters. They came zipping through us. And we were so far out of the bomber stream that we had no fighter escort.

The first time the fighters came through the formation we lost about a foot of one of the prop blades on the No. 1 engine, so we had to feather that before it tore the engine off. And they also shot my right rudder apart, so that was no good. And eventually we feathered the No. 3 engine because that cut down on the vibration from that rudder. The prop stream was dropping that rudder back there. We figured it was gonna tear the airplane apart, so we immediately dropped back. There were no airplanes so that a formation was left.

The airplane that was in back of us to our upper right, he went by us from the cockpit on back and he started to turn toward us, so I had to turn away from him. We could see the other airplanes being blown apart, and I was pretty busy trying to keep control of our airplane. Both Doc and myself – Doc Cochran, the co-pilot – were having about all we could handle just to keep our airplane flying.

You'd see an airplane there one moment and gone the next, pieces flying everywhere. So you're looking around, waiting for the next one to see if you're gonna blow up. Fortunately we didn't get hit in the bomb bay again because if we had, we probably would have blown up like the rest of them. We had big holes in the wing, and in back of the No. 2 engine there was a huge hole, the skin torn up and flapping. We just kept the darn airplane flying, and there wasn't anybody else around. Everybody had either gone down or had dropped out.

Once the fighters had gone and we were on our own, we were just flying dead reckoning, because we didn't have much of our instruments left. The compasses were out, so we knew which direction France was in, so that's what we headed for. And we started up the No. 3 engine again because we needed it to keep in the air, even though the guys in the back threw out everything they didn't need.

Somewhere the gunner on our left side spotted a Focke-Wulf 190 lining up from a distance, and we figured we just about had it because with all the holes that we had in the wings and the gas tanks, gasoline was pouring into the bomb bay. We opened the bomb bay some so that it could get out, but if we'd have had a tracer hit that it would have blown sky high. But all of a sudden, out of the blue, a P-38 showed up, and as soon as the P-38 showed up the 190 went down to the deck, and I don't know what happened to the P-38, whether he went down after him, I have no idea. But shortly thereafter the P-38 came back up and flew the wing for a while, and we waved. Thanks, God! Then Timms got his maps out, what he had left of them because a lot of them blew out when we opened the bomb bay to get rid of some of the gas, but he had enough left so that as we looked down through the clouds he finally spotted a couple of places that we knew, and we realized we were over France.

Bill Bruce

Lieutenant William S. Bruce was the pilot of the Bonnie Vee, which was named after his wife, Verlyn. He sent this written account to George Collar.

3:00 a.m., Sept. 27 – We were up at this hour for breakfast and then to the briefing area. We had a full load of gas so we knew it was going to be a long, long flight. The ship had a full load of 1,000-pound bombs and all the .50-caliber machine gun ammunition we could squeeze in.

We waited on the runway for some time for better weather and finally all 37 ships were airborne. We flew across the North Sea into enemy territory within a short time. Then the long run deep into Germany. As I recall, we had heavy cloud cover, and would drop our bombs by radar or pathfinder ships (these were radar-equipped planes that led us to the target in case of bad weather).

There was some confusion as to the proper target – finally we were on the bomb run and dropped our bombs, dove down 500 feet and headed for England. At this point we had only flak to contend with. After a short while we saw what appeared to be our own P-51 escorts, which we had not seen all morning. However, there were so many of them that too late we knew they had to be German ME-109s. They sure were. It was just unbelievable how many enemy fighters came at us in large groups – sat back and below us and shot the living hell out of us. They had their wheels down – stayed in formation and raked us steadily with machine gun fire and 20-mm cannon.

We had to have our tail and waist gunners fire at the ME-109s who were shooting at our wingmen simply because we could not get the ones on our tail.

It was just a hopeless situation – there were just too many of the enemy fighters. I saw at least seven ships go down in flames; four of our group and several German ships. Our fighters were nowhere in sight. I could not understand where the hell they could be.

Our ship, the "Bonnie Vee," had been hit several times – two engines were on fire and the interior of the plane was in shambles. The gunners kept firing, but finally they were all wounded or dead. At this time I knew we were in serious trouble with no hope of flying any longer. I finally gave the bailout order because at this moment only one engine was running and not too well at that.

I asked my co-pilot to unbuckle my seat belts before he bailed out. Just as he stood up to do so a 20-mm cannon shell cut him in half.

At this point I really knew it was the end of our flight. The right wing was rammed by a German fighter, tearing it off. Next, the left wing blew up and only the fuselage remained. We were then at 19,000 feet. It must have just exploded because the next thing I knew I was clear of the plane and hurting very, very much.

I did not open my parachute for a number of reasons. One, I was on fire or so I thought. Two, I figured the fighters would shoot at me. And third, I was kind of groggy and covered with blood.

After what seemed an eternity I saw a farmer plowing his fields. I pulled the ripcord. The chute opened and I hit a very large tree within four or five seconds. My right leg was hung up over a branch and wrapped around my neck. It took me some time to untangle myself and climb down this fifty foot tree.

By this time what was left of my ship crashed into the forest not too far from me along with several others, causing a massive forest fire. No one evidently saw my chute – however, I heard a lot of yelling and screaming about something. It was probably about the fire. Several dogs growled at me but were finally called by their owners.

It took me about ten hours crawling through the trees and along the stone walls to find a house. At this time I knew I was badly hurt – could not stand up – covered with blood and really, really hurting.

I crawled along a fence to a farmhouse. A man and two women came out and carried me into the house. They tried to wash my face and give me some milk but I could not even swallow. I think they thought I was dying and I wasn't so sure I wasn't.

After a few minutes their grandson (I guess) who was about 10 or 12 years old came in and pointed a small rifle at me. His grandfather knocked it out of his hands. With that, the little bastard ran out of the house and returned with seven soldiers all carrying sub-machine guns, or what I know now as burp guns.

Their fear of me was incredible. They pointed their guns at me and started yelling. Not being able to move, and lying flat on my back, I certainly did not pose a threat to them. Finally one officer, after trying to communicate with me, spoke in French. This I understood. He questioned me as to whether I was carrying a pistol – I said "No." Then he searched me and was satisfied that I wasn't going to shoot them all.

Next he wanted to know the Bomber Group I was in and what type of plane I was flying. I gave only my name, rank and serial number as we had been instructed in situations such as this. Thirty minutes went by – same questions, same answers.

Soon several other German officers arrived and put me in a horse-drawn open farm wagon. We proceeded to drive to a village where it seemed like half the German population had gathered. I certainly was the center of attention. They cursed me – spit on me – hit me with rocks – sticks – fists and anything else they happened to have handy. Finally after the officer had had the glory of capturing me, they put me in a small barn. I really thought I was dying at this time. The crowd did not let up on me and continued to throw stones through the windows and pound on the walls.

After about three hours everybody left. I spent the rest of the night awake and hurting. About daylight the officers returned and asked me the same questions over and over – same response from me. Finally one of them hit me in the jaw with a pistol butt – fracturing it. I was carried out by four soldiers and we spent three days on the train, arriving at Frankfurt for two more days of intensive interrogation. By this time I had become almost totally paralyzed and was black and blue all over.

The Germans finally gave up and once again, under guard and on a stretcher, we spent the next week on a train, arriving at Obermasfeld, where a doctor finally examined me. I was told that my right pelvis was broken, my right shoulder was badly damaged and that I would not ever walk again or use my right arm. (Later, back in the States, I was told that my neck was also broken.) The next week they shipped me to Mennigod Hospital because the Germans had to make room for all the German soldiers wounded at Arnhem.

George Collar

In my opinion, Bill Bruce and his first co-pilot are the bravest guys I ever heard of. Maybe a month or so before the Kassel Mission, Bruce was a second lieutenant and he was flying a ship called the Bonnie Vee. He lived in Guilford, Connecticut and married a girl named Verlyn, and that's who he named the ship after.

His co-pilot was a guy named William Brown. He was from North Carolina. And they went on a mission, it wasn't a bad mission, but they got hit by flak and it damn near knocked the tail off the plane. At the same time, a piece came up and almost severed Brown's leg. There was blood gushing out. He's still conscious. Bruce is fighting the stick because of the rudder damage to the tail, and Brown's trying to help him but he can't because the blood's squirting from his leg. So he reaches down and pinches off the blood supply with one arm and then the engineer comes down and he put a tourniquet on and he fought that baby clear back to Tibenham, and they brought the plane in. And when they carried him off the plane they thought he was dead, but they cut his leg off and he was sent back to the States.

Bill Bruce, they fixed his plane up and gave him a new co-pilot the day before the Kassel raid, a guy by the name of Willet. He was higher-ranked and had been in the Air Force longer. He'd been in the Air Transport Command, but he wanted to get into battle, so he pulled a few strings. They told him if you want to get rank, you've got to get in combat. So they assigned him as co-pilot to Bruce on the Kassel mission. And they got hit, and not only got hit, but one of the German pilots pancaked down on top of him.

Bruce is hurt, and he saw his co-pilot, Willett, shot in two right in front of his eyes. Well, he bailed out and he smacked into this tree and he's badly wounded and burned, and he got down out of the tree and crawled about a half mile to a farm house, and a lady got him in there and was doctoring him up a little and her husband came in and the grandson came in with a gun, he was gonna shoot Bruce. And the grandfather took the gun away from the kid.

Finally some soldiers came, and one of them pistol-whipped old Bruce. And he finally ended up in the hospital. He recovered, and was up at Stalag Luft 3 and they had to march, and he ended up being at Moosburg when Patton came in. And he shook hands with Patton. But Bruce, and this guy Brown that got his leg shot off and fought it all the way back, the sonofagun should have got at least the DFC, if nothing else. I don't think they gave him that. They gave him a Purple Heart.

Chapter 8: Lessons Learned

Ralph Pearson
This excerpt is also from Rolland Kidder's oral history of veterans from Jamestown, New York, "A Hometown Goes to War."

Kassel was my 29th mission. After 30 missions you get to go home. But this day I wouldn't be going home. We got shot down over Germany. The raid was really botched up from the start. Somehow we split off from the main formation and got too far south. We couldn't find the primary target and finally dropped our bombs on a secondary target and headed back for England.

Because we had gotten off track from the main attacking force, we had lost our fighter cover. By this point in the war, the Luftwaffe had been weakened and our biggest worry was antiaircraft flak over Germany, but today it was different. I was the pilot in the No. 2 plane and all of a sudden my earphones crackled, "Fighters attacking from rear!" Our gunners opened fire with their .50-caliber machine guns but they were no match for the FW-190 German fighters. The Germans had equipped these fighters with something new – a 20-millimeter cannon that would explode on impact. They stayed back, out of range, and lobbed the shells.

The skipper's plane was ahead of me one second – and gone the next. It had been hit and the tail had broken off. Then a round hit us, right under me in the nose of the plane. The instrument panel came up at me, the glass on the gauges came off, somebody yelled "Fire!" and I knew we were going down. I ordered the crew to jump as I held the plane straight and level. For a while it was quiet. The plane was flying fine, all engines were running, it was just me and this B-24 cruising along through this beautiful sky at 25,000 feet. Then, snap! The control wheel went limp in my hands. The elevator cables had burned through. As I turned and started toward the fire behind me and the bomb bay doors through which I could jump, I figured I was a dead man.

On our plane, we suspect that Lieutenant Hendrickson and Lieutenant Stearns, our bombardier and navigator, died when the cannon shell exploded in the nose. The rest of the crew made it out okay, but we're not sure if Johnson, our flight engineer, jumped or went down with the plane. Reports say that two chutes were seen coming from the bomb bay just before the plane rolled and exploded. I'll lean on that for comfort.

After I had ordered the crew to jump, I felt terribly alone. I had no communications and, for all I knew, the whole squadron had been shot down. It had probably been only five minutes since we had been hit, but it seemed like an eternity. I knew that the battle was over. I flung off my oxygen mask and helmet and headed for the fire and bomb bay.

As I turned, I suddenly saw Sergeant Johnson behind the pilot's seat. He was bent over, buckling on his last strap. When he straightened up, I gave him a visual inspection. We only had split seconds as the plane was out of control. I stepped back to my left and waved for him to jump out. He, in turn, waved for me to go. I felt like grabbing the bastard and throwing him out, but there wasn't time. The plane was going down. There wasn't time to argue. It hurt my pride, but I waved for him to follow, and I jumped.

The plane was burning and in a turn as I went out. I tumbled as I fell. We were still at 25,000 feet, without oxygen, and it must have affected my memory because I never remember pulling the ripcord. What I do remember is that when the chute opened, it jerked me so hard that my beautiful fleece-lined flight boots came off. As I floated down in my stocking feet I thought, "Nuts, some German kid is going to be wearing those comfortable boots."

On the way down, the fighters who had shot us down made a couple of turns around my parachute. I tried to play dead because we had heard that sometimes pilots had been machine-gunned after parachuting out. But these guys just circled and I imagine called in my position because when I landed, there were three or four soldiers waiting for me. As a matter of fact, the soldiers looked friendlier than the farmers with their pitchforks who were standing around. My face had been burned pretty badly and one of the soldiers said something and it sounded a little like the Swedish word I had learned as a kid which meant "smarting" or "burning." I said "Ya," because my face felt like it was burning up. My face was badly burned and all of my hair had burned off after going through the fire to get to the bomb bay doors.

Considering the bombing, the war, the hatred, the misery of the German people, I can't really complain about my treatment. The Wehrmacht soldiers put me in a motorcycle sidecar and drove me to a Luftwaffe hospital nearby. It was obvious that their pilots got first-class treatment. The hospital was clean and well-equipped. They put me into some kind of holding area and early the next morning took me in for treatment. I had second and third degree burns all over my face. The German doctors were careful, though, and disinfected and cauterized my whole face, covering me with bandages like a mummy. I couldn't talk but there was a small breathing hole for my mouth and nose and slits for my eyes. The most I could eat were bread crumbs that I could push through the mouth hole. But I have to hand it to the German doctors, they did a good job. I have no scars today. It was also lucky that I had flung off my oxygen mask and helmet; otherwise they would have probably fused to my skin in the fire.

Doye O'Keefe

Mission 29 – Two to go, then home. This day started like most every day. Our name came on the board to fly the evening before. It's true, we had been flying quite often. We were beginning not to laugh much anymore. We were combat tired. I read Psalm 91 this morning, as Mom had suggested so long and so far ago. We ate at 3:30 a.m. and then went to briefing. I was such an old veteran now at this flying game, hundreds of hours of combat flying, I hardly paid any attention at the briefings. The target was some factory area. We went down for our equipment, dressed into flying gear, and rode the trucks out to the plane as it began to get light. English bombers were returning from their night raids on Germany. The sky droned with the noise of returning planes. Soon to begin again the American daylight bombing, as weather permits. It would be English bombers at night and American by day. Only weather caused any letup. Failure or losses slowed nothing down.

We flew on course with most of the Wing. Our plane was flying in the slot position of the lower echelon, the last position in the last lower flight. Not a good defensive position. (Note: Later research showed we flew in the top echelon, lead squadron.) We flew to our IP or turning point for our bomb run and started in. We opened the bomb bays. Clouds below so we would bomb by radar. Finally, bombs aweigh. Down they went from all planes. Amazing! No anti-aircraft fire. No flak. We hadn't even been shot at. We closed up the bays and continued to fly.

I heard Lieutenant Pearson, the pilot, talking to the navigator, Lieutenant Sterns, and he was telling him that we had surely dropped our bombs on the wrong target. We were not over Kassel. "Where is our fighter cover?" the pilot asked. I stood up between the backs of the pilot and co-pilot, watching. I turned from my radio channel to the intercom and suddenly above my head Johnson in the top turret began shooting his machine guns. Over the intercom Pearson said, "Bandits in the rear of us!" Hendrickson said, "Close my nose turret doors." Suddenly machine gun and 20-millimeter cannon fire hit the top turret area. Terrible noise as the shells ripped through the plane and exploded as they hit the metal.

It's true. We had passed our IP point of turning, missed Kassel, sighted in on what was thought to be Kassel and dropped all the group's bombs on a town called Goettingen. It put us out on our own, away from the rest of the Wing and away from our fighter cover. We were about thirty miles northeast of Kassel from where we were supposed to be.

Out from our fighter protection, just one group, the Germans had sent up approximately 100 FW fighter planes. They would come straight in at 6 o'clock level and all open up. We were the lowest and last plane in our group formation. We were first on the Germans' list I'm sure. Our plane had received a heavy group of hits now, above my head – inches above. Again (3 seconds) through the bomb bay and lower nose section. Hundreds of exploding shells hit us.

At my very feet shells burst between both feet on the edge of the flight deck. Smoke from exploding shells began to fill the flight deck. Johnson released his seat and tumbled out of the top turret, alive, but crumbled to the floor. Was he dead? Amazing I wasn't hit (5 seconds). Fire. Fire in the crawl space in the lower flight deck. High octane airplane fuel spurting from the right wing lines into the bomb bay area (3 more seconds). Fuel fire. Extinguisher useless! Only one way out for us all in front. Have to open the bomb bays (5 seconds), took a big breath, held it, jumped down into the fire. Closed my eyes. Reached for the door opening handle. Pushed. Thanks God! It works electrically. I could have never cranked them open in time. I held the handle back. They were opening all the way

(5 seconds). I could feel my face blister. Keep eyes closed. Hold breath. They were open! Damn, I was hot. My clothes were beginning to burn. They were open. No way to get back. Jump for your life. Head first out into the twenty degree below zero, 22,000 foot altitude. Don't open the chute. Remember, don't open the chute. I tumbled over and over, rolled around and continued to fall.

I spread out my arms and legs to slow me down. I had lost my cap and goggles. Lost one of my flying boots. I rolled over on my back and looked up. There was our plane above me and a little forward. Don't open the chute. I watched the plane. It was now burning badly in the wing area on the right side and flames were coming out of the bomb bay area. I saw two chutes open. I don't know who. It leaned to the right a little. Turned away from the formation. The right wing collapsed. The whole thing fell with a roar and torch of flame.

Good God! The whole thing took less than a couple of minutes. Who was it that got out? I had no way of knowing. Johnson was dead surely, by machine gun fire. Probably Sterns and Hendrickson too in the nose area. How about the rest? Maybe I'd never know.

I kept on my back watching the biggest air battle in history as I fell. A steady roar of gunfire in the air. Planes kept falling down on fire. Chutes seemed to fill the air. Planes and parts of planes just seemed to fill the air with a long column of smoke trailing each down. Damn, what destruction. What a fight. Whoa! The clouds are now above me. The sun isn't shining now. I'm below the clouds. I have to turn over and see the ground. I must have been falling for a good two minutes to fall from four miles. At least no one will be waiting for me when I land. Yes, falling face down. I can see fields. Good, in the country. Now trees. Must be pine trees. There are railroad tracks. A small building. White chickens on the ground. Now, pull the ripcord! Lord, what a hell of a jerk. It opens up and I look around dangling there. I threw the ripcord down and just said, "Damn." Well, the fellows could have gotten out anyway. I opened up the way for them from the flight deck or they could have never made it out.

I was going to land in a plowed field, about ten acres. Get ready to hit and roll! It worked. No one around. I gathered my chute in my arms and ran about 75 yards to the trees. Looked around as I unbuckled my harness and hid the chute under brush.

Unsnapped the good ol' shoes off my harness and ran uphill as fast as I could. All the way over the top. Found a low brush tree to the ground and crawled all the way under and hid. First you get your breath. I took out the camera I carried on missions, dug a hole with my hands and buried it. Took off my Mae West. Checked myself over for possible wounds. My face was blistered was all. Then changed into my shoes. Boy, so far everything had worked. Delayed chute opening. Wasn't caught yet. No one waiting for me. Then put on shoes for walking. I had a package of K-rations in my pocket for food. It had worked. Man, I'm sure a long way from ol' Centralia now. I've never been so all alone ever. Now, stop, think, plan. By golly, this ol' boy is going to get home. It's all worked so far. I can do it!

Chapter 9: "Come on back, you bastards!"

Peter Belitsos

Peter Belitsos was the co-pilot on the Bruland crew. This is an account he wrote for the Kassel Mission Historical Society.

I was originally the co-pilot on Lt. Edmund Speers' crew in the 701st Squadron. This crew was formed in the States and had flown together on twenty or twenty-one missions prior to Sept. 27. We went overseas on the Queen Elizabeth, landing in Scotland on D-Day, before joining the 445th at Tibenham.

About my experiences on Sept. 27 – when the guy that came around to wake up the people scheduled to fly passed by Speers' bunk without calling him out, I rolled over and started to go back to sleep. I was tapped on the shoulder and told I was flying with Lt. Bruland's crew. After the briefing, I was taken to the hardstand where I met Palmer Bruland for the first time. I introduced myself and was introduced to Lt. Norman Cuddy, the navigator. We then got on board. This took place before dawn and I did not meet the rest of the crew or see them face to face except for the engineer.

I was at the controls when the German fighters came in and on the internal intercom system. There was no warning from our crew and, according to Bruland, none from the other planes. Apparently it happened that fast. The first sign for me was a thud that shook the plane and then the inboard engine on my side caught fire. Simultaneously I saw that almost all of the planes in my line of vision were on fire. I thought we had run into a monstrous machine that put engines on fire. At this time Bruland took over the controls and I started the engine feathering procedure with the engineer. I was so engrossed that I did not look out and I did not see the full extent of the devastation taking place. The engine was feathered and there was a gaping hole in one of the prop blades extending out to the edge. The fire did not go out.

No one on the crew was hurt. I heard the gunners firing and remember one of them shouting, "Come on back, you bastards –

sons of bitches" and whatever else came into his mind. He wanted another shot at them.

In the meantime, the engineer and I went through the fuel transfer procedure to stop the flow of fuel to the damaged engine. The fire would not go out. We stayed with the plane for what seemed to be a considerable time, hoping to get back to France. We lost altitude down to about 10,000 feet (from 20,000 feet). The pilot gave the order to bail out since we could not extinguish the fire.

Everyone cleared the plane. Bruland was the last man out. He later told me that he had problems getting out. When he let go of the controls and headed towards the bomb bay, the plane lurched and he had to go back and regain control. He then trimmed the controls and tried again. After a couple of attempts, he was able to bail out.

Carroll Snidow

Carroll Snidow was the co-pilot on the Hautman crew. He sent this account to George Collar.

They woke us up very early on the morning of Sept. 27, 1944. The briefing was to be held at 3:30, which was about an hour earlier than usual. Jonesy – Lt. Maynard Jones, the navigator – and myself, walking to the mess hall in the darkness of night, figured it must be Big B.

It was a cool morning and you could tell fall was fast approaching. We had a very good breakfast although we had powdered eggs. They tasted very good. All the crews in my barracks were scheduled for this mission.

Johnny Friese, my bombardier, was not on the mission that day. The Runt, navigator on the commander's crew, was not sure whether he was scheduled or not, so he went with us to the briefing. We ate our breakfast slowly as we had plenty of time. We arrived at briefing on time. The Runt found he was not scheduled so back to bed he went. Before going back, he came to me and told me to "Give them hell, Snidow," an expression both of us gave to the other if he wasn't flying that day. It was a joke between the two of us.

Briefing was interesting as usual. Jonesy and myself were greatly relieved to find our target was to be Kassel, Germany, instead of Big B, Berlin. We were also in good spirits because we were to be back at the base by 12:30, which is very early to return from a mission.

We had a normal takeoff and climbed to assembly altitude. We were flying No. 2 ship in the slot of the lead squadron, assembling at a low altitude crossing the channel and part of France. Flying was hard because we were flying directly into the sun. There were about four aborts with a 10/10 cloud cover at about 8,000 feet.

We dropped our bombs okay that day but our whole group missed the target. We did not get any flak when we should be getting plenty of it. After dropping our bombs we thought we had made a milk run. Everything was coming off according to plan. Then all of a sudden all hell broke loose.

I was listening to the VHF radio channel so I didn't get the warning. I looked out of my co-pilot window and saw what I at first thought was small flak. It was very heavy and close. Then I found the truth. Looking at the ship ahead of us, I saw their waist guns firing. Fighters! I don't know how many there were but it was beaucoup. I saw the ship in front of us go down with its rudder on fire. I imagine it blew up. Just then an FW-190 came alongside of us and seemed to be flying in formation with our lead ship. I believe if I'd had a gun I could have blown him to bits.

The shells were bursting around us everywhere. I saw a FW-190 low at 2 o'clock with its landing gear, the left one, down in a sharp bank. It evidently had been hit. I looked to the right and saw a FW-190 about 20 feet above the ship on our right wing. It dropped about 20 or 30 small firebombs right on top of that poor B-24. I saw a waist gunner bail out of that ship before it went down in flames. About that time something hit my window and put a hole in it. A piece scratched my knuckle in two places. The enemy fighters knocked out our tail gun on their first pass. Waldron, our tail gunner, was injured in the leg. My oxygen system was also damaged. Just before the fighters left, our No. 4 propeller ran away. We started to feather it but it was too late as our oil pressure was gone. Land, our top turret man, was really firing that gun. A FW-190 was coming in on top of us, evidently to drop firebombs on us, but Land blew him out of the sky. He did a good job that day.

Then I looked at our No. 4 engine. The whole prop and engine was coming out of the wing. What a sight. The propeller whirling in its full velocity made a 90-degree turn and came toward me. I thought that I had bought the farm then. The prop, No. 4, came over into the No. 3 prop and engine and knocked it out of the wing. Prop and pieces of prop were going everywhere. Luckily, none hit the ship.

There we were in the middle of Germany in a B-24 with two holes in the right wing where the engines had been. No tail turret. Radio almost out and one of our tail rudders mostly shot off. The bandits had left us. We saw four fighters way out in the distance at 12 o'clock. We didn't know whether they were friendly or enemy. They turned in to us, so I thought again that we had bought the farm. It was an anxious few minutes until they came close enough to find they were P-51s. A few minutes later, two P-38s came and flew on our wing. We were out of formation now. Only three out of 36 made up the formation and we saw them gradually leave us, homeward bound.

We started losing altitude so we threw everything out that we could, including our flak suits, guns, auxiliary power units, etc. At that time we were flying at 27,000 feet altitude. We got in contact with the P-38s on our wing to give us a radio fix to our nearest friendly airport. They gave us a heading to a field in France and told us it was about 30 miles away, or about 15 minutes away. We kept losing altitude at the rate of 300 feet per minute. It was going to be close, but we thought we had a chance.

Evidently the P-38s gave us the wrong information. We kept losing altitude for about 40 minutes until we were down to approximately 7,000 feet, coming out from over the cloud overcast. We were flying at 120 miles per hour, which is almost stalling speed for a B-24. Our P-38s were still with us. We still figured we had a good chance of getting home.

Then more big trouble. They opened up on us with flak. We were so low and going so slow that we were a perfect target. None of us had flak suits for protection as we had thrown them overboard to lighten the load. The flak was so close that it was rocking the ship and the concussion had blown out our waist gun windows. There wasn't anything to do but leave the ship. We gave the order to bail out. Land went first from the flight deck, followed by Giesler, Jones, myself and then Hautman. Before jumping, I went back to my seat to get my handkerchief and hat. I don't know why I did, but all I can say is I did. I couldn't reach them so I went without them. I did get my shoes, which were tied together under my seat.

I remember my jump. I can honestly say I wasn't afraid because I trusted my chute. I just took a step out of the bomb bay and then I started floating. You have complete presence of mind when you are sailing through space. Just as soon as I left the ship, I started falling head over heels. I tried to fall straight but I couldn't until I remembered something S-2 had told us once: Stiffen up. That I did and sure enough it worked. My next thought was to pull the ripcord. I started to pull it, but again I remembered the S-2. Delay your jump. I did this for a couple seconds and then I pulled her. She really opened nicely without scarcely a jerk. When I opened my chute I dropped my shoes but caught them with my feet. While floating down I was trying to get my shoes but when I reached down for them they slipped away.

I then looked around me. I saw our ship now without anyone on board in a steep bank to the right and very low. It hit the ground and I am glad I wasn't in it. It looked as if the B-24 was spread out on all of Germany. Black smoke came up from the few remains of the airplane.

I then looked below me. I saw that I was going to land in an open field near some woods, and right beside a railroad. There were approximately 20 people working in the field, so I knew that I wouldn't have a chance of escaping. I then looked above me and I could see Hautman's chute. About that time I hit the ground. I was finally on the ground without a scratch. Ed Hautman hollered at me before he hit in the woods over a hill. I haven't seen him since.

I got out of my chute and awaited my captors. They soon came upon me, and thus the war was over for me. I was surprised to have one of the women in the group speak to me in good English. She wanted to know if I was hurt. If I was American or British. And then she told me she had a husband in West Virginia and that he liked it over there. I assume he was a prisoner in America. She told me everything would be okay with me and I would be treated fine.

They took me to a nearby road and there we waited for about an hour. In the meantime, they brought Land and Giesler up. We waited about three hours where they searched us. Then they brought in another crew that had been captured. We then had a short ride in a charcoal burning truck to a railroad station. It took us the entire night. After changing trains many times we got to Oberursel near Frankfurt.

After interrogating me they left me in solitary confinement until October 3rd, at which time I was sent to my permanent camp, Stalag Luft 1, Barth, Germany, on the Baltic sea. The above account of my last mission was written about one week after I arrived at Stalag Luft 1. It was written in a notebook given to me by the Red Cross and written while the facts were still clear in my mind. My companion in this camp was Bill Smithdeal, a B-17 pilot shot down about the same time as I. He was from Roanoke, Virginia, and I had known him before the war.

When we were taken from solitary confinement to the train to Oberursel, they placed us on the train in alphabetical order. Smithdeal and Snidow placed together. It was a good feeling to see someone from Roanoke during that period. We remained prisoners until the Russians liberated us in May 1945, approximately eight and a half months. I was with the 445th Bomb Group, 703rd Bomb Squadron of the 8th Air Force located at Tibenham, England. This was my 18th mission, exactly at the halfway mark, as at that time we flew 35 missions before you would be rotated home.

Glen McCormick

On the 27th of September it was a routine mission through the point of dropping the bombs. We were heading to the rallying point when we were attacked by fighters. The fighters were both FW-190s and ME-109s and there were a lot of them. They started hitting the planes at the rear of the formation and rushed right on to the lead airplanes. Our plane was one of the later ones hit. We were hit from above and I personally never saw the plane that hit us.

Our top turret gunner, Robert Shay, was hit and we were on fire. The hydraulic reservoir in the bomb bay was on fire and that is right beneath the fuel pumps. It was obvious we weren't going to get the fire out. Those crew members in the nose bailed out through the nose wheel door, and those in the aft section bailed out from the tunnel door. The crew members on the flight deck were in the airplane when it exploded. One crew member, the radar operator on the flight deck, came to after the explosion and had time to deploy his chute. He, at the time of exploding, was down attempting to open the bomb bay doors so that those on the flight deck could bail out.

The radar operator was badly burned because of the flash fire. I was the first to bail out from the rear of the airplane. I delayed opening my chute to avoid detection if I could. I landed in a tree and my chute caught in the top of the tree. It was about 10 feet from the ground. I swung on my chute to the trunk of the tree and slid down to the ground.

An interesting footnote: As I was freefalling, my oxygen mask was flipping me in the face and I decided enough was enough and pulled it off and dropped it. To my surprise, it went up and not down. I realized then that I was falling. I opened my chute when I dropped into a cloud undercover. I didn't know where the ground was and I wasn't going to take a chance. After passing through the clouds, I saw two airplanes heading toward me and said, "Uh-oh, I'm going to get shot for sure." It turned out that they were 51s and not ME-109s. One of them went right on by and another circled me and waved. I thought, "You sonofagun, you're going back to a nice warm bed and I don't know where I'm going."

Chapter 10: A Long Way Down

Frank Bertram

When the group flew in toward the target – the tactics of the Air Force were I won't say to zigzag but you'd go from one place to another to avoid areas of known flak guns, because if the Germans could see you, they could hit you. They were that good. Even at 22,000 feet they could come damn close if they could see you clearly, with the great optics they had.

So we did our usual deal till we came to what they called the initial point. The initial point in a bomb run is where the bomber is turned over to the bombardier, and he takes control. And from the initial point to the point of impact, which could be anywhere from ten to thirty miles, the bombardier has control of the ship. The pilot has no control whatsoever. You're on a straight heading, no matter what comes through the formation, what kind of flak you get, you've just got to rough it out, straight ahead. As all the planes in back of you do.

This day when we got to the initial point, we had to make a little left turn. We went further left than we were supposed to. I immediately called the pilot, Reg Miner, and said, "Hey, we're going the wong way! We're going too far left." I said, "Call them up and find out what's going on."

He came back and said, "They said, 'Hold it in. Hold it in.' We kept turning left and I thought, 'We're gonna miss the target completely.'"

The target was not visible too much from the air, but with the radar scope we had the target picked up, and with the little that we did see from the air to the ground, and the paperwork I was doing, we knew where we were exactly.

But for some reason, the main pilot called back and said "Keep it in. Keep it in."

We were not the only one that caught the mistake. You could look out the pilot's window and you could see the flak off to the right which we were supposed to be going through. Why we kept going to the left we'll never know. We never did find out.

We came to this point and released the bombs, about seven or eight miles past where we were supposed to release them. It was near the town of Goettingen. As it happened it was in an open field, probably killed maybe a couple of cows. Then we proceeded on our way to follow our regular method to come out. That was a left turn off the target, a right turn, which took us on a southeast heading, then another turn to the right which took us on a northwest heading, which was the angle to head for our base in Britain.

Usually after each turn you assemble, but these were quick turns. They weren't turn and go fifty miles, then turn and go another hundred. We were going ten miles, and then five or ten more miles, and another five or ten miles. So the turns scattered us; the planes move away from each other to avoid collisions, then they come back together when we're headed straight home.

While we were just getting back together, someone in our plane called out, "There's a dogfight!" And all the time in the back of my mind I'm thinking, "Oh boy, are we gonna catch it from headquarters when we get home" because we dropped the bombs uselessly. Someone claimed it was a secondary target, but we had no secondary target that day. It was just drop them over Kassel; if you don't see the target, just drop them anywhere.

Then our radio operator, Joe Gilfoil – who was mortally wounded that day – said, or someone said, "There's a fire!," or "We smell smoke in the bomb bay."

Boy, that hits a nerve.

So Gilfoil said, "I'll go check it out." He was a very eager young man. And as he went into the bomb bay, all hell busts loose. I'm looking out my little window – I sat in back of the pilot and had a window about one foot square – and here's this flak. But maybe three feet around when it explodes, a sort of a grayish black. And I'm thinking, "What the hell is this? We're at 22,000 feet and these guys are shooting through the clouds and hitting us like this?" I couldn't belive the accuracy. Usually flak is more about the size of a Chevrolet Blazer when it explodes. It would blow up a plane if it hit direct.

Then someone called out, "Here comes out fighter escort!" And I said "Good." I look outside my little window, and there's a hell of a lot of commotion, noise going on, and I saw these radial engine planes. I thought, "Oh, good, those are our P-47s." Until all of a sudden they peel off and there was the swastika. And about that instant, boy, they start flying through the ships. There were shells, explosions, and guns clattering. You puckered up immediately and the lead hit the stomach. Words cannot describe your feeling. Only those that were there can know the feeling. It's absolute sheer terror for a while, panic for a while, and then anger for a while.

At that point all I saw was four planes. Apparently they were ten abreast, but I just saw the right side of our plane, and these planes shooting at us. And all of a sudden a big explosion hit the ship and the top turret gunner who was right opposite me came crashing to the ground. The turret got a direct hit from one of these planes, and it blew the Plexiglas out and smashed it right in this guy's face and he fell down right at my feet. His name was Mac Thornton. I looked down and I knew he was dead. His face was just frozen. The blood was solid. At that point in time in September it was very cold. I think it was 20 or 30 below zero at that altitude, so everything freezes instantly.

I panicked at that point. I could see explosions going through the ship into the bomb bay. I thought, "Oh, man, how are we gonna get out of this?" The interphone was out. We knew we were gonna have to bail out. So I went to the bomb bay door and I almost fell over poor Thornton, got my foot caught in his arm and almost panicked to get out of his way. So I went and I could not open the bomb bay, it was stuck. There were holes, and there was gasoline pouring in the bomb bay. To this day I swear the fact that the Germans blew that turret off really saved us from exploding, because I think that sucked all the gasoline fumes from the bomb bay right out through the top. Otherwise I'm sure we'd have blown up, as many of our ships did that day.

I was wearing what they call a chest pack chute. I put it on, and I crawled up to the nose wheel to check that and see how the guys up there were doing. The nose turret gunner was firing at the planes as they went by, because the attacks were from the rear. As they'd go by, the gunners up front would shoot at them. And the bombardier, I don't know what he was doing, because after he dropped the bombs, he probably was back in the waist.

I got up to the nose wheel, and I tried to open the nose wheel door and it was frozen shut. I thought, "Now we're doomed. We're trapped." So I thought, "I'll see if I can kick it open."

And all this time I'm nervous. I'm scared. Anyone says he isn't is lying. Because I expect the ship to go down and explode at any moment.

I kicked and kicked, and I got the nose wheel doors to come open. I damn near fell out because I kicked so hard. I pull myself back up and one leg is dangling, so I pull myself in. Now I'm sitting on the edge of the nose wheel looking down at nothing but clouds and once in a while they would clear a little bit but the clouds were pretty dense. I'm looking down, dangling in space, and the plane is starting to yaw – that is, going from side to side, and up and down a little bit. As I learned later the engine was on fire, and there were all kinds of things I didn't see because I'm inside the plane. So I back up to get back in the plane, and Jeez, I look behind me – all the guys are lined up with their parachutes ready and they're pointing to me. "Go out! Go out!"

I said, "I don't want to go out! That's a long way down!"

And they said, "Go out!" So I went out, feet first. And I don't know how long – I didn't free fall, like you're supposed to do. I probably counted to ten or fifteen and pulled the chute. The chest pack has a little pilot parachute which comes out first and grabs the air, and then that pulls the main chute out. There's always the possibility that doesn't work and you have to claw your way through, so the more time you've got the better it is. As it happened, mine took off and popped, and boy, it was a jolt. I thought my legs would fly off. We were lucky – we had brand new parachutes, brand new harnesses, brand new electric flying suits that day – it was the first time we wore them. Brand new beautiful gabardine flying suit. And I went out with just my electric boots. I didn't have my shoes with me. Other fellows jumped out with shoes, they were luckier.

I had grabbed my little good luck charm, which was a little baseball mitt that my wife had given me as a good luck toy, and I put that in my pocket. I had my prayer book, which I kept in my shirt pocket all the time. And we had an escape kit which I grabbed, and shoved that in one of my pockets before I went out. And I had a gun, too. We had .45s and we weren't supposed to take them, but some guys took them. And I know that I had taken the clip out, but

I had the gun with me for some reason, which I got rid of on the ground. It had no firepower at all with no clip in it.

By the time I pulled my chute and it popped open I looked out. Our plane was gone. I didn't see anybody else. I couldn't spot any other chutes in the area, but they all went out right after me. As a matter of fact, those in the waist probably went out first.

Reg Miner

The Kassel mission was my twentieth mission. For most of the crew it was the 19th mission. That one we were just talking about gave me more night disturbances, let's say, in retrospect than the Kassel mission, because on the Kassel mission there was nothing I did then, or didn't do, that was a problem. I didn't have any real alternative. I might as well tell you what happened.

I was leading the high right squadron, and radar-equipped, and the lead ship in the lead squadron and the deputy lead were both radar equipped also, so there were three of us with radar aboard. And I came to the initial point, and we turned much sharper than we should have turned and we headed in a different direction.

So I can see the target up ahead. Flak over it, and B-24s. And my navigators call me and say "Hey, we're not headed for the target." I already knew that from my own observation. But I called the lead and told him, "Hey, we're not headed for the target." He said, "Hold it in formation. We're going to bomb as a group." Now the plan was to bomb in trail, which means every squadron will fall into position behind one another and bomb on the lead bombardier. So that plan was changed, and we're going to bomb in trail.

I don't know if there was a secondary target or not, but my feeling is that the commander, McCoy, made a decision, he said we can't pick up the target, we'll go to a secondary target. He's got to make a decision, what are we gonna do? And what the hell, he's dead, we never had a chance to ask him how come. Because we had radar and his deputy lead had radar, why he didn't call the deputy lead and say, "Hey, we can't pick up the target, you pick it up." I don't know why he didn't do that. No way of knowing. I know damn well if we'd have been leading we wouldn't have done what we did. So that's one of the mysterious things.

But we make our turn, and we start heading back for home, and I see white puffs out front. Holy Jesus, that's something new. I never saw them before. Bertram called them black in his dissertation, but it was white. Small white puffs. And I looked down on the lead plane, I mean the lead group, which I'm flying off, and holy Cripes, there's a bunch of FW-190s coming in, like ten of them, nine abreast, eight, something like that, shooting at them. Holy Christ. And by that time, we're getting hit.

My autopilot went out. The plane started up in the air, so I overcame that, and flew it manually from there on. And I had a couple of engines out. We had a fire on each wing. A small fire at the gas cap. And there's nothing I could do. I mean there's no fire extinguisher to handle that problem. There is for a fire in the engine, but not in the wing. So we fly on, and the last thing I remember seeing – I rang a bailout button, whether it rang or not I don't even know, but the guys in the waist, we had no communication by that time, so I didn't know what had gone on back there.

Finally the co-pilot said, "Hey, is it okay if I go?" And I said "Yeah, it's okay." Then I figured Jesus, I'm getting down to about 10,000 feet, I'd better get out myself. And I look back, and oh, Jesus, the bomb bay doors are still closed. You normally go out the bomb bay doors. So I was annoyed that the guys didn't tell me that. It wouldn't have made any difference because I found out fast enough anyway, but it was one of those things that I had a brief annoyance.

I had oxygen and a flak vest and earphones, and a microphone. I had to rip it all off and head down the flight deck, to drop underneath, and crawled up through the tunnel to the nose wheel doors and they were open. I was hoping they were open because I assumed the guys went out that way.

By the time I got to the nose turret I grabbed hold of the opening, and the plane started to spin. So I dropped down, head first, and rolled over on my back, and now, Jeez, the plane's spinning above me. So I said, I'll wait a while and see if I can get out from under this thing, the chute might foul on it. So we rode down like that for a while and I lost a boot, my left boot came off. Oversized flying boot, I wore oversized ones for warmth. So that came off. And finally I thought, "Jesus, this is quite a while, I'd better look at the ground," and I roll over, holy Jesus! I pulled the ripcord and the next thing I knew I was on the ground. I mean, I never had a ride in the chute that I can remember, it was instantaneous, zip, bang, and I'm on my back on the ground.

I look in back of me and there's the plane sitting there burning, about 100 feet away. And I wasn't hurt at all. It was a green meadow. It was like I'd fallen out of bed. So I whip off my chute and Mae West, start getting ready to head for the woods that I could see across the way on the railroad tracks, and about that time a couple of guys came running from the town, and cut me off, and took me to the police chief's house.

Chapter 11: The Sweetest Rose

Paul Swofford

When I got over to England, we thought that the brand new airplane we took over would be ours, we'll put our nose art on it, and we'll fly it on every mission. The first thing they said was, "Get your gear off this airplane," and we never saw it again. What they did was they sent it to a depot and removed the ball turret, because they didn't need it. They said, "Who's gonna be shooting down? Fighters are gonna be up there coming down on you. They're not gonna come up from underneath, they lose speed that way.

We had the Sweetest Rose of Texas on the Kassel Mission. That was my seventh mission, and my crew's seventh mission. We had one substitute. My bombardier, Mandino, did not accompany us. He was indisposed for some reason, so we picked up an airman, I don't even remember his name. My co-pilot was Ward Smith, or Smitty as we called him. He was a fine formation flyer himself. He was three or four years younger than I was. I was only 23, but he was just 19 or 20, but he had a remarkable head on him, and he would help me make decisions.

My navigator did not notify me that we were off course. So as far as I knew we dropped our bombs on the assigned target of Kassel. I did not know we were out of the bomber stream, because when you're on the bomb run the pilot is 100 percent concentrated on one thing: flying in the right formation.

The first thing I knew something was wrong I could see the empanage on several planes start shredding, just chunks of the empanage folding up. You can shoot part of the wing off. You can shoot part of the belly off of the airplane, but if you get shot in the empanage, the tail section, your elevator and your rudders, your horizontal stabilizer and your vertical stabilizer, any part of those, you're in deep serious trouble. And I knew, seeing those chunks come off there like that, that something was wrong.

Then disaster struck my plane. We lost all communication, interphone and external radio communication. The only one that I could talk to was the co-pilot. I've got to take my mask off to talk to him. Or the engineer. I couldn't call to the back. I had to send my engineer back through the bomb bay to see how they are.

Then I lost my Number 2 engine, and our windshield was shattered. When the windshield was hit, some fragment, I don't know if it was a shell or what kind of fragment, hit my radio operator, Thum, in the leg. The engineer had to get back to him to apply a tourniquet. But he is the only one who sustained any major damage. The flying glass in the cockpit got both myself and the co-pilot. We always wore these leather helmets and goggles. Whenever we were ready for the bomb run, or getting over enemy territory really, we'd put on a flak suit, and put on the goggles, and a big metal helmet that didn't fit. It was just a big metal thing that you could shake your head and it would just roll around on you. It had earflaps on it that would protect you.

Both my co-pilot and myself got a face full of flying glass. I felt the blood running down my face, and I looked over at the co-pilot, blood is running down his face. I didn't know if he was fatally wounded and he didn't know if I was fatally wounded. There was blood everywhere. But it turned out that it was just flying glass that got us around the foreheads, and the blood was just pouring down us. The engineer looked up and saw us, and he thought we both had had it, because all he could see what blood. But it wasn't serious. It didn't rate a Purple Heart for either one of us, but my radio operator, Thum, did get the Purple Heart, and of course he was off my crew for a few weeks with that injury.

The airplane was hard for me to fly. I could hardly control it. At a time like that, when you're flying formation, the pilot who is not flying formation is observing all of the instruments. The first time I could glance down to take a look at my instruments I could see that the No. 2 engine was dead, and immediately – no, I didn't immediately – I had a thought. My thought was, if I feather that engine, they would get me. And I've thought since that that was probably the reason that my aircraft was spared any further attacks, because the fighters couldn't see that I was damaged. I could see that there was hardly anybody left to fly formation with, because all of these planes had gone down.

I didn't feel it was safe to feather the No. 2 engine until we got some fighters back. So I said to the engineer – on the deck of the airplane we had a Very pistol – I said, "Get every red flare you've got and fire it, because we've got to get the attention of the fighters," because we knew there were no fighters around.

So we fired the Very pistol and apparently some of the fighters came back. Of course we could always tell our own fighters, we called them "little friends." Then I feathered the No. 2 engine because you can't fly it with an unfeathered engine, you won't have enough power to sustain flight. And that's when I observed that the one prop blade had a big chunk missing, about one foot from the tip of the blade. It was a chunk as big as my fist. Apparently one of the 20-millimeter shells from one of the fighters had hit the prop. And by then I could see that my whole nacelle was just peppered with shots. The nacelle is the casing for the engine. So it wasn't just the propeller, it was the engine itself that got shot up. So we lost the engine. We lost all hydraulics. If you don't have hydraulics, you can't operate your gear. You can't operate your flaps unless you do it manually. And you've got no brakes when you land.

Lieutenant Donald Smith being our squadron lead became the lead for the few remaining airplanes we had. He set his speed at cruising speed. I can't talk to him. It was impossible for me to keep up. My only alternative at the time – normally you'd cruise at say 90 percent of your attainable speed. I have to throw my throttles to the firewalls – all the way – I have to put my mixtures in full rich, which means I'm using about twice the fuel that anybody else would use. I didn't know if I'd have enough fuel to get back. And I have to put my propellers in a high RPM that we only use for takeoff and landing. And when you run the engines continuously in the same manner that you use for takeoff and landings, your engines are not gonna last long. So my fear was that I'm gonna lose another engine, because when you run those engines full throttle, the full rich kind of keeps it somewhere cooler but the critical thing about an airplane engine is the cylinder head temperature. You've got to redline that.

If you get your cylinder head temperature too hot, you're going to ruin your engine right then and there, just like an automobile that you run without water in the circulating system.

It was at least an hour or more, or two hours, before we got out of enemy territory. And I just knew that somebody's gonna come and pick me off.

Since I could talk to my navigator, I said, "Keep me advised as to when we get out of enemy territory." At that time, after D-Day, our front lines were somewhere in France. So when we got out of enemy territory you could heave a big sigh of relief. The first thing I did when that happened, I pulled my throttles back, I set my throttles, my trim, and so forth. I couldn't maintain altitude, so we just started a gradual descent because here we are at say 23,000 feet. And I told the navigator, "Give us a direct course to our home base, and keep advising me how many miles we've got to go."

So we were just about alone then for the rest of the mission, coming back to home base. But we knew we had problems.

Henry Dobek
Henry Dobek was the navigator on Lieutenant Paul Swofford's crew.

When we got to the initial point there was nothing unusual. We were flying along following all these guys. They started on the bomb run, usually a bomb run is around ten minutes. And we're waiting, waiting, waiting for the bombs to drop. Nothing happened. We just kept right on going. So according to my charts, we had already passed Kassel. Finally the bombs went, and I figured out hell, we're 40, 50 miles past Kassel. I figured we were at a town called Goettingen. And then we dropped our bombs, turned around, started heading back, and that's when we got hit by fighters.

I didn't know what the hell was happening. All of a sudden fighters came, and I don't have a gun as a navigator. All I did was look out the window. Airplanes going down. Parachutes all over the place. Fighter planes flying back and forth. I just sat there. Then we got hit in the No. 3 engine, and so we had to shut that one off. And I think it was a 20-millimeter shell hit the Plexiglas of the pilot's windshield, and I didn't know that until I crawled up and looked up front. They had little tiny pieces of Plexiglas in their face, and just little droplets of blood. It scared the hell out of me. I didn't know if they were hurt or not. But all it was was superficial wounds. It only happened in a couple or three minutes and it was all gone. Some American fighters came back, and they engaged the German fighters, and we just took off. I think there were maybe three of us flying in very loose formation going back home.

Chapter 12: God's Will

Eugene George
Eugene George was the co-pilot on the Brent crew.

We went in for breakfast. We had a flying officers' mess and a ground officers' mess and an enlisted men's mess, and the flying officers' mess was considered the worst of the three and the ground officers' mess was the best. We would take our wings off and go in there at times, because the food was better. On the Kassel mission, the food was so bad that morning. They did have some canned peaches, and that's all I ate for breakfast. I had not started drinking coffee yet. I learned to drink ersatz coffee when I was imprisoned in Germany because that was the hot beverage during the cold winter.

I was not aware of any mishap in navigation until I heard a discussion over the intercom among the navigators. What upset me was that they were discussing over the radio that we were off course, and of course the Germans could hear this. I felt that this was distinctly a navigational error and we were pulled out of the bomber stream, and of course it's dangerous to try to re-enter that.

Now, I say the navigators, I think this was two navigators that were discussing over the lead navigator, and as part of this discussion I heard the lead pilot say "Stay in close and follow me."

We also knew we were without fighter protection, and there was some communication to try to get our fighters. Of course we were telling the Germans at the same time we were without the fighters.

I also remember our tail gunner saying "There are fighters coming in from the rear."

And I said, "That's great."

And he said, "They're not ours."

So I knew they were approaching from the rear.

I was very much aware that we were under fire. What made me aware of it was our own guns started firing, but my concentration was right on the wing, I was totally locked in to keeping the aircraft in formation. I was watching the engine instruments, and I thought the engine was burning, which it was, and I could see the engine right next to me was burning. I didn't know if I should pull the fire extinguisher or not. Brent was still just sitting there. We were losing power, and I pushed the emergency button to give the crew enough time where I thought they would bail out and go through the procedures that we had learned when leaving the aircraft.

I tried to raise the rear of the airplane and the front of the plane on the intercom, and I couldn't get anything from either direction. I knew we'd been hit, but I didn't know whether something had happened to them. I could see flak coming on the nose of the airplane because it was in front of me, and the Germans were approaching from the rear, coming up, rolling over and split-S-ing down, coming out. I saw one of them do this when I was getting the top turret gunner out.

After I gave him enough time to get out, I could see in the cockpit area, the radio operator and the engineer, the top turret gunner, were supposed to leave on the sound of the alarm, open the bomb bays, and we would keep on flying the airplane until they got clear, then we would go out. I went out and the top turret gunner, whose name incidentally was Constantine S. Galuszewski, he was from East Tonawanda, New York, and the radio operator was Sam Weiner, who was from the Los Angeles area. But he was still in his turret, and I had to crawl up there and jerk him by the seat of the pants.

Weiner didn't even have his parachute harness on. So I jerked Galuszewski out of the turret, but in doing that I saw the German plane turning and splitting S after having made his run, a beautiful airplane, very, very close, as close as three-quarters of the way to the other end of the room.

I got Weiner's harness and shoved it at him, and opened the door into the bomb bay, and it was just a mass of flame. The fuel gauges which were on the left were spitting like blowtorches, and the bomb bay doors were closed and we would have been trapped if they had remained closed. And they operated hydraulically. There were fires all over the place in the bomb bay. It's amazing. I'd see areas of flame chasing up pipes and pipework, things like that. And the switch to open the bomb bay doors was right between those two blowtorches which were the fuel gauges. I thought I could hit that switch if we had hydraulic power, I could open the bomb bay doors. If we didn't, I'd have to wind it and I didn't think I could survive the flames. But I could jump through all of this flame on the catwalk to get there, and I hit the switch on the way over to it, and I jumped through and got there. And the bomb bay doors opened.

But I still had the responsibility of these two enlisted men. So I went back through those blowtorches, and Galuszewski was just sort of standing there in a daze. I started snapping Weiner's harness on him. Everybody had chest packs; I had a back pack. I'd been off oxygen for a while to do all of this, and I didn't know but what my parachute was burned when I walked through the fire. So I walked through the fire and I walked back through the fire.

While I was standing over Weiner and getting him put back together, Brent came by and told Weiner to hurry up, and he went through the door into the flaming area. I never knew whether he went back to check on people in the waist or whether he went on out or what happened. Or whether he was injured in going out because the fire obstructed his vision; I was concerned about that. I got Weiner put together, ready to go, and Galuszewski, and they were behind me, so I went on out. And they went on out too, as the aircraft broke up. The three of us were the only ones who survived of the crew.

Brent didn't survive. I never knew what happened to him.

Sammy Weiner

Sammy Weiner was the radio operator on the Brent crew. This is his written account of the battle.

What does a man think of during the momentous seconds his life is hanging by a thread? "I've got to make it." These words of self-preservation I shall never forget. A man is powerless to combat the workings of fate and I believe it was God's will to wipe my number off death's list that fateful day of September 27, 1944. I was one of three survivors of our B-24 Liberator bomber crew.

Having flown over the Channel two days in succession, we briefed at 3:30 in the morning of the third day and sat down to the usual breakfast of cold pancakes. I had no stomach for the pancakes but gulped a cup of coffee. A week later I would have given a year of my life for a stack of those soggy cold cakes.

Our group had already bombed the identical target several times without encountering difficulty, so this time, too, we expected another grand "milk run." Our objective was Kassel, Germany, with its important marshaling yards. This time we were not to return by the usual course, but sideswipe Frankfurt, pick up our fighter escort there and return by way of France. My squadron was in the lower left position of the huge armada that again roared across the Channel that early dawn.

Standing by with my liaison radio, I kept in constant contact with our division leader. Watches were synchronized every half-hour. Today the usual chatter on the interphones about blondes or poker was absent. Perhaps this was due to the physical fatigue and mental strain of the stepped up bombing. An hour before we reached the I.P. (initial point) I helped the pilot and co-pilot don their heavy flak suits. Soon after, my orders came from the navigator.

"Objective ahead; be prepared to open bomb bay doors."

"Righto," and I lowered myself into the wells, waiting for the bombardier's final words. Then it came.

"Bomb bay doors open."

The doors flung down. Seconds passed as our ship kept its steadied course. Amid the shattering noise of the motors I could hear the words "Bombs away."

I returned to my position on the flight deck to receive the bomb strike message. The bomb run had lasted five minutes. Over the target there had existed an undercast at 13,000 feet, which necessitated instrument bombing. I continuously asked the nose turret gunner about flak and always, to my surprise, his answer was negative. There was still no sign of our fighter escort nor of Jerry fighters.

I could see the black smoke over the city that once was Kassel. The pilot's voice was joyous when he spoke to the crew. We were heading home. This was his thirty-third mission, and with only two more to go I certainly didn't blame him for being buoyantly happy.

It wasn't more than a few minutes after we heard the pilot's voice that all hell broke loose. Our engineer began blasting away with his two "fifties" in the top turret. From the side window I could see the fire of twenty millimeter shells bursting too close for comfort and the skies were suddenly filled with Focke-Wulf 190s that had risen out of nowhere for the kill. In a very few seconds, we, as the saying goes in England, "had it." There were three simultaneous attacks, one up through the bomb bay, and the others, front and port sides.

One burst of a twenty millimeter shell came through the side into the liaison transmitter only two feet in front of me. Splinters from the shell pierced my right leg. The stinging sensation made me mad as a hatter. "Those damn Jerrys," I kept repeating. Turning swiftly, I saw the bomb bay aflame with a portion of the doors blown off. Almost with the strength of a demon, I tore the rest of the flaming door off, burning my hands and the left side of my face, and was just about to reach for the extinguisher when the pilot sped swiftly past and jumped out the open space. "My God," I thought, "what had happened to him!" In passing, his hand somehow had released the door leading to the top turret, for, as if perfectly timed and previously practiced, the engineer, too, dropped out the bomb bays.

It all happened so quickly there was no time left to think of anything except donning my harness which luckily was still within reach. Only yesterday there had been issued to me new equipment which was so tight and uncomfortable that I had removed it hours before. Instantly I was on my knees, trying to fasten the buckles. Nervously I pulled with all my strength, holding my breath, sucking in my ribs. My life was hanging by a thread. Vaguely, I could see the co-pilot standing by, shouting at the top of his voice.

"Abandon ship!" And then to me, "Hurry up, Sammy boy, there's not a second to lose."

At last, after what seemed hours, instead of only a few seconds, my harness was fastened and my chute snugly attached. I was halfway to the bomb bays when all pandemonium broke loose. There was a sudden, thunderous blast and the plane broke completely in two. Had I run the gauntlet of my chances to get out alive? I was being crazily tossed all around the flight deck, while the tottering half of the plane was still running on the remaining engine.

Bruised and battered, but fully conscious, I tried to get myself into an upright position. The broken piece of ship was wobbling like a dangling teeter totter toward the earth. If it went into a nose dive, all was lost. "I've got to make it," I was muttering crazily. And then, suddenly, the section shot straight into the sky, throwing me out into the welcome blue space, before plummeting to earth.

Doubling into a ball to protect my chute from fire, I fell about six thousand feet before pulling the cord. Drifting slowly down, I hit the ground with a thump, rolling over and over. It was wonderful to feel old terra firma sliding under me once more. Silently I gave thanks unto God for having spared me. The odds had been heavily against me, and I knew it. My escape from the broken, burning plane was little short of a miracle.

Chapter 13: "Like a Garden Hose"

Web Uebelhoer

Do you know the phrase "initial point"? That was where you made a final turn and straightened the plane out and you turned it over to the bombardier, and he was actually flying the airplane through the bomb sight. Almost immediately – all of us were connected on the crew by interphone – I can hear the navigator, the radar navigator, all of them, "Hey, we're drifting away from the main stream!" I had a command pilot, Jim Graham, on board. He sat on the right seat. And when I had a command pilot on board, I did not ever try to communicate outside of our aircraft. I was flying the aircraft, and I was talking to my crew, and the crew was saying "Hey, we're off course!"

We assumed, because there are not any of them living now, that McCoy and Chilton misidentified the target. I think they thought that they were bombing Kassel, and they were actually going toward Goettingen.

The mistake, in my opinion, was made in navigation.

Before the bombs were dropped, I happened to glance down at the cloud cover, and do you know what chaff is? Various ships in the formation had thrown that out. And we were someplace around 20,000 or 22,000 feet, and I looked down, and this chaff had completely fooled their radar. The explosions from antiaircraft guns were at least 5,000 feet below me and just blowing the hell out of this chaff.

After we dropped the bombs, we looked out, and we were thirty-some airplanes all alone. And the fighter planes did not see us go. We had a conference the evening of the mission, and the fighter pilots, their leaders, were questioned, "What in the hell were you guys doing?" Well, I don't know what they were doing, but they were not aware that we were drifting away from the bomber stream, so we were out there all by ourselves.

And then my tail gunner, John Hubitz – he's dead now – called me on the interphone. "Captain, there's a hell of a lot of aircraft behind us!" And I thought they were our planes just playing around, because normally, in that stage of the war, there were no Germans around. So I said, "John, keep your eye on them and keep me informed."

"Okay."

Then the next thing, the bursts from their cannon began to spot, and I was aware that those were not friendly fighters, those were bogeys.

I was almost in the lead of the formation because of the assigned position in the flight. I didn't see a whole hell of a lot. An FW-190 came across our right wing and kind of just positioned himself, and the nose turret – a .50-caliber machine gun is a large weapon – two .50-caliber machine guns, and the nose turret gunner in my aircraft was spraying them like a garden hose, and that's just about as far, closer than that ship [a cargo ship passing in the Savannah River just outside the hotel], he just shot and shot and shot, and we found out later, the German aircraft were heavily armored. Normally a .50-caliber gun just tears an airplane apart. But nothing happened. The left landing gear came down, and I don't know what the hell happened to him. Another one came across our left wing, and of course a fighter aircraft can fire just straight ahead. And he just sat there and looked at us, and we looked at him. Then he peeled off. But it's training. Fear, training. Training overcoming fear.

Chilton's plane was about as far as that light post, maybe 50 feet, I was flying that close to him. And McCoy was sitting in the right seat, so I was looking at McCoy. And I was also looking at the waist window. An FW-190 – all these attacks came from below – and hell, he was within 50 feet, this German. Kind of standing on his tail and almost stalling out. Just shot the hell out of that, I could see the gunners moving around in the ship, and the ship was full of – it had an orange appearance – and McCoy was doing something, signaling me but I didn't know what, and very shortly after that he lost control. He rolled to the left, and went down. I saw some guys get out of the plane. Four or five people.

Now the lead ship's shot down, so I'm the leader. The guy who was flying on me, he was on fire. I don't know what happened to him. But pretty soon we became aware that four or five or six airplanes were all that was left, and boy, four P-38s – that's our fighter aircraft – came right over the top of us and we realized the cavalry had arrived, and we were relatively safe.

I don't know what happened to my crew, but when all this was going on, our crew wasn't in the fight. And I got on the interphone and I chewed those guys out, "Hey, let's get in this fight!" And my god, I think every weapon on that ship was firing. And that's when the P-38s came across.

The gas tanks and the oil reservoir were rubber lined, and some sort of a weapon fired through the No. 2 engine – I didn't realize this happened until I got back down on the ground – some sort of a projectile, not explosive, went through that oil reservoir and that sealed itself. That engine was working. So that was all the damage that I had. And of three other airplanes that returned to Tibenham, I think just one airplane got back with no damage.

After the mission I had the feeling – entirely unsubstantiated – that I ran away from the fight. Because that really happened. God protected me and three others, and this was my 18th mission. And Martha Miner, Reg Miner's wife who has since passed away, we were talking about this mission, and I expressed my feeling that I chickened out and ran, and she said, "Hell. The guys who parachuted, the war was over for them, and you had 12 more missions to go." I didn't look at it like that until Martha made that remark, that I still had 12 missions to go.

I flew again in about five days. We went back to Kassel. And boy, those fighter pilots made damn sure that they protected us this time. I'm sure the flak came up, but we all came back.

I can't say I was more scared after the Kassel mission than I was before, because I was always afraid, and to put a degree of fear, I don't know if I could do that. I did a lot of praying. And I can remember, sitting here with the controls, there was aluminum sheeting, that's all that protected me from whatever, and prayed to God that if I got it, Bam! Just wipe me out, don't tear my eye out or something like that.

Ray Carrow

Pilot Ray Carrow's co-pilot, Newell Brainard, was one of five fliers who survived the initial battle only to be murdered on the ground.

The Kassel mission was my 21st mission. Our group was the lead group. Our squadron was the lead squadron. And as we approached the target, the lead plane veered off to the left. We were supposed to keep radio silence, but some of us didn't. I was one of those who didn't. I said, "We're going the wrong way."

And they said, "Just stay in line," or words to that effect. And we could do nothing but to take the order. We dropped our bombs on this other town and we were making a turn to the right to get back to where we came from, and that was when we got hit.

If we had stayed with the main group of planes, they were being protected by our fighters, but we were off all alone, sitting ducks. Eventually our fighters did come and they shot down some of the Germans, but by that time the damage had been done.

The plane next to me, to my right, was on fire. And then I felt my plane being hit. Then I saw parachutes all around the place, and I knew that something serious was happening.

After a while we lost one engine, and then we lost another engine, and then it reached the point where I couldn't control it anymore. I looked back to the flight deck, and I saw that the bomb bay was a raging inferno. Apparently some gas had leaked in, the fumes were there, it was hit by a shell of some kind, and it exploded and caught on fire.

In some of the stories that you read it says that my co-pilot touched me on the arm to tell me there was a fire. How could anybody know that? He was killed when he went down, so he couldn't have told the story. I was the one who touched him on his arm, and I pointed to the fire. He immediately got up and left, and I never saw him again. And I assumed that he didn't make it. It was a pretty scary situation. I had on a flak vest. I had on a Mae West. I had on a parachute. The pilots had to use a seat parachute, which fit into the bucket of the seat. The other guys had chest parachutes. But this was a seat parachute, so I had only the straps. I had a pair of shoes tied on to one strap because I was wearing these heated flight boots. As it is, I lost one of them on the way down, so it's a good thing I had my shoes.

With all of this bulky stuff, and the tenseness of the moment, I couldn't open the seat belt, and that's what saved me. Because by the time I finally opened the seat belt, the plane had split in half, with the fire in the other half, and when I got out of my seat, when we were going down, I started climbing up toward the hole, and got to the edge and jumped.

The plane had split right in front of the bomb bay. That part was already weakened because of the fire, so that's where it would naturally split. I didn't know where I was, how high up or low down. I counted one, two, three, fourfivesixseveneightnineten, and I pulled the ripcord. I had luck with me that day in a sense. When I pulled the cord I was in a cloud layer, and when I came out under the cloud layer there was the ground just a couple of hundred yards below me. That meant I had fallen nearly all the damn way, and it's a good thing the chute came open at that time because I would have been squashed.

I landed inside a fenced-in labor camp. There was an old Wehrmacht soldier with his rifle pointed at me, and the one word that came out of his mouth was "Jude?"

Of course, I wasn't going to tell him I was a Jew. I never wore my dogtags when I went on a combat mission, because that's a giveaway. And with my name, they could take me for anything as far as my looks are concerned. I got away with murder. Unfortunately, Newell didn't, but not because he was a Jew or not a Jew. If you are a recipient of a bomb from the air on your house and some of your family were killed, and you captured one of the guys who did it, you're gonna kill him. That's what happened to him. I didn't know that, though, until many years later when I met Kay, and she told me.

When I landed in the camp, the first thing I did was, I was sitting on the ground and I took off the boot, and I put on the shoes. And finally the soldier told me to get up, and I started walking to one of the buildings there. On the way I saw a body. The body was face down. And I wanted to go over to see who it was, if I knew him. I started walking over and the soldier told me to go away. But what I did see was that the back of this guy's head was blown away. Completely blown away. I never did find out who it was. For a while I thought it was my engineer but I couldn't prove it.

As a result of this incident, the back of my head was burned. It burned off the hair, burned off the eyelashes, and burned off the eyebrows. I didn't go through the fire, but that damn thing was hot enough to singe my hair and my skin.

James Engleman

James Engleman was the flight engineer/top turret gunner on the Reynolds crew. This account was included in Missing Air Crew Report #9761, and is reprinted from the 8th Air Force News.

Moments after the tail gunner, Harry G. Twigg, shouted into the interphone, "Fighters, 6 o'clock!" exploding shells were hitting the plane while others exploded in close proximity. We were badly damaged. The left inboard engine spewed flames reaching back to the left runner. There was a fire inside the plane on the command deck, over the bomb bays. The oxygen and hydraulic systems were shot out, as were our radio and intercom. The right rudder was flapping wildly as it clung to the stabilizer by the middle hinge. The upper surface of the wings and fuselage were riddled with bullet and shell holes. The top of the tail turret was open like a tin can. Two feet of wing and flap were missing off of engine No. 2.

The attack was over in about five minutes. From the top of "Little Audrey," I could see no other aircraft, friend or foe. We were now alone. The pilots were working to shut down engine No. 2. It would not feather. The fuel valve was closed off and the fire died out. Inside, Twigg, wounded in several places, put out a small fire. The waist gunners were severely wounded. There was a strong odor of gasoline on the flight deck. The bomb bay doors were opened to reduce the hazard.

After losing some altitude (we had no oxygen), with diminishing power, we flew westward, hoping we might reach an area held by advancing Allied forces. About 15 minutes after the attack ended, I saw a single engine fighter coming up on our rear. As it was in a position to attack, I prepared to shoot. The pilot changed course, showing his AAF [Army Air Force] insignia. It was a P-51 Mustang. He came abreast of our left side and motioned to his earphone. I shook my head no. Just then we received flak from a ground battery. As there was nothing he could do for us, our little friend departed.

We crossed the Rhine River at about 800 feet. The pilot, Donald N. Reynolds, dropped lower to escape the fire – to no avail. To prepare for the crash the crew took their ditching positions. Shells were hitting almost until we crash landed. Our pilots did a great job. The point of landing was near the railroad station in

Polich, twelve miles southwest of Koblenz, at about noon, local time.

Within a few minutes armed soldiers arrived by truck. They sought to make an opening to the flight deck to permit the radio operator, Bob Sheehan, the navigator, Jim Withey, and me to get free from the wreck. In the rear, the waist gunner, Lars Larsen, was dead. The nose gunner, Bob Long, was mortally wounded. The waist gunner, Maynard Danner, was seriously wounded. Twigg was less seriously wounded. All four men had been hit two or three times in the last hour.

Shortly after getting free of the plane, the six of us who were able to walk were led under guard to what I believe was Niedermendig air base. I saw a man I recognized from the 445th Bomb Group, but I don't know his name.

Jim Withey

Jim Withey was the navigator on the Reynolds crew.

I had never flown with this crew before. I knew we were off course, but that's about all, because I was really just along for the ride, to get my last mission in. I didn't give a damn about anything. We were following the group.

All of a sudden, there were fighters all over the place. We'd taken our ball turrets out so we had no protection underneath, and the Germans were kind of hanging below us where we couldn't reach them, and there were no fighter pilots there for a while. But it only lasted two or three minutes or something like that.

We lost an engine, but we escaped, and we started heading back. Then we ran over a 20-millimeter gun range, and they got another engine. We had too many seriously injured people to try to bail out, so I told the pilot to crash land. There was just a little bit of a hill, and we bellied in. It was a beautiful landing. But our problem was, just before we landed, the fuselage cracked around the pilot's shoulder and slid over, and one of the tail rudders fell off, and I got crushed in between the two seats because I was up there navigating. I was knocked out, but I was okay.

Another thing is, I'd gone back to check the injured, and then I went forward to navigate and I sent the nose turret gunner to take care of them, and he got killed within a couple of seconds. They were still firing on us, over the 20-millimeter range.

There were nine men on the crew, and two of them got killed.

Jack Erickson

Jack Erickson was the radio operator on the Golden crew. This is from a "Wartime Log" that he kept.

Upon leaving the briefing I picked up my flight gear, parachute, Mae West, and donned my heated flying suit. I climbed aboard a 6 x 6 and was delivered to the hardstand where our assigned aircraft was parked. The plane was a B-24H still in olive drab paint. The name painted on the nose was Tahellenbak and it was decorated with a devil holding a Neptune's fork. I believe it was probably one of the oldest Liberators that was still operational in our group. The bulk of the planes were newer J models and were unpainted in the natural shining aluminum finish.

At the hardstand I joined the rest of our crew which included the following officers and NCOs: Pilot – Lt. William F. Golden, Lockhaven, Pa.; co-pilot – Lt. Robert C. Christie, Palm Beach, Fla.; Navigator – Lt. Edmund Boomhower, Catskill, N.Y.; Bombardier – Lt. Theodore C. Boecher, Chicago, Ill.; Engineer – T/Sgt. Earl C. Romine, Reynoldsville, W.Va.; Radio Operator – S/Sgt. Jack M. Erickson, Oceanside, Cal.; Armorer-Gunner – Sgt. Robert R. Bagley, Audubon, Iowa.; Waist Gunner – Sgt. Edward H. Feltus, Englewood, N.J.; Tail Gunner – Sgt. Norman J. Stewart, Altadena, Cal.

Lt. Golden told the crew that the 445th would be leading the 2nd Combat Wing until the group turned for the target. We were assigned to fly the slot in the lead element of the group. This is not the most desirable spot to fly tight formation in.

Our crew had been reduced from 10 men to 9 men inasmuch as the Sperry Ball Turrets had been removed from our aircraft to reduce weight and allow the craft to fly at a higher ceiling. We had been assured that the Luftwaffe was kaput and therefore the belly gunner was not needed. How wrong that decision turned out to be.

Once at the aircraft, each crewman began the pre-flight inspection of those items falling into his area of responsibility. I pre-flighted all of the radio gear and pre-tuned the SCR-287 transmitter to the assigned frequency. I made sure that a flak suit and a flak helmet had been delivered to my station. I then tested my A-10-A oxygen mask and plugged my F2 Electrical Heated flying suit in to make sure it heated properly. It gets mighty cold at 23,000 feet. Next I checked out my Mae West to be sure it contained live CO_2 cartridges. Once I was satisfied that it was in good working order I put it on. Next I strapped on my parachute harness and sat down at my radio position all set for another mission.

The crew chief had completed the pull through of the engines and Lt. Golden now started the No. 3, then the rest of the engines in proper sequence. They coughed and sputtered and emitted lots of smoke, but those big Pratt & Whitneys soon roared to life. The engines were warmed up running at 1,000 RPMs until the oil temperature reached 40 to 60 degrees Centigrade.

The wheel chocks were pulled by the ground crew and we taxied away from the hard stand and got in line for take-off. Finally, we reached the end of the runway and Lt. Golden gave the engines their final run-up. The magnetos were checked, the flaps extended, and the cowl flaps closed. All hatches and the bomb bay doors were secured. The brakes were released and the throttles pushed wide open and our big-assed bird plodded down the runway to reach the 130 MPH take off speed. Soon we were leaving the ground and were airborne. The landing gear was retracted and locked.

Once airborne, I entered the takeoff time on my radio log. I then zero-beat the SCR 287 transmitter to the assigned frequency and loaded the fixed antenna. I tested the intercom system by calling each position individually and then the all station call. Everything tested OK.

For the next hour or so we continued our climb to the assembly area and once above the overcast we spotted our buncher ship and soon joined the formation for our flight to Germany.

The weather over Germany was 10/10ths overcast and the group's navigator had to rely on navigational aids to locate the target. Upon reaching what was thought to be the initial point of the bombing run, the group turned and headed for the target. Later, I was to learn that the group had missed the IP and were headed for Goettingen, which was approximately 30 miles northeast of Kassel. Bomb bay doors were opened and on the signal from the lead bombardier, the bombs were dropped, falling about a half-mile short of Goettingen. Bomb strike observations could not be made due to the dense cloud cover.

The group now turned and circled, setting a course that would join up with the main stream of the 2nd Combat Wing for our return flight back to our base at Tibenham. Due to the navigational error on the IP, the group was well out of the main bomber stream and we were on our own without fighter escort. After about 10 minutes of routine flying we were suddenly attacked by Focke-Wulf 190 fighters of the Luftwaffe's Gruppe II of Jagdeschweder 4, one of Germany's elite fighter groups. More than 100 FW-190s attacked the group from below, making a head-on assault in waves 10 planes wide. They had come up from beneath our formation without being observed and made their frontal attack on our vulnerable underbelly.

I first saw the FW-190s from the window at my radio position. They flashed by from the front to rear so fast I could hardly identify them. Everywhere I looked I saw the swastika marked aircraft. The sky seemed to be full of them. In horror I saw our right wingman's Liberator take many hits. Debris was showering from the B-24. As it started to peel off it suddenly broke in two just aft of the wing and the two pieces plummeted toward the earth some 20,000 feet below. I did not see any parachutes emerge from the flaming pieces and I assume all aboard went to their deaths.

Pivoting my stool around, I looked out through the windshield between Lt. Golden and Lt. Christie just as the lead ship of our element disintegrated. Debris from the stricken bomber was streaming back straight toward our aircraft. Instinctively I put my arms up to shield my face. I don't believe that any of the debris hit our ship as the slipstream apparently carried it above us.

The voices of our gunners were screaming fighter locations over the intercom – "Bandit at 3 o'clock low – enemy fighter at 10 o'clock high" , etc. All eight .50-caliber machine guns on our plane were firing bursts of API ammunition in an attempt to stave off the enemy fighters. Our Liberator began to shake and vibrate from the recoil of the machine gun fire.

From what I learned later, the group's gunners did a great job and inflicted heavy losses on the Luftwaffe attackers. The 445th gunners were officially credited with the destruction of 23 FW-190s and an additional five probables. These kills, however, only represented the toll credited to the returning and surviving crews. It was known for certain that other losses were inflicted by the crews that did not make it back to base to report their hits.

Suddenly, our plane shuddered as it took hits in the No. 3 engine. From my vantage point directly below the engine I saw a cloud of black smoke pour out into the slipstream and metal parts flying through the air as the engine came to a stop. Lt. Golden immediately feathered the prop. A few seconds later the plane shook badly as the tail turret took a direct hit by a 20-mm cannon shell. Sgt. Norman Stewart, the tail gunner, was gravely wounded and was removed from the shattered turret by Sgts. Bagley and Feltus.

As I looked out through my window, I saw many B-24s falling in flames. I saw several parachutes blossom out, but not nearly enough for the number of crewmen that had manned the planes going down.

In a subsequent attack, our right wing was hit in the flap area by cannon shells and a large hole was opened up near the trailing edge of the wing. I could see wires and hoses dangling into the slipstream. Lts. Golden and Christie fought the controls to keep our aircraft from going out of control.

I turned on the Liaison transmitter and quickly keyed an SOS to our home base relaying the destruction of the 445th from the Luftwaffe's onslaught.

As the intercom system was knocked out, I arose from my stool and stood next to Lt. Golden. He told me to tell the crew to bail out. I nodded to him in affirmation of his order and turned to where Sgt. Romine was operating the Martin upper turret, which was located directly above my radio position. I grabbed him by the leg and gave it a quick tug. When he looked down at me, I motioned for him to jump. I then opened the door on the flight deck that led to the bomb bay and saw Bagley and Feltus looking toward me from the waist position. I signaled to them to abandon the aircraft. They quickly hooked Stewart's parachute ripcord to a static line and dropped him out through the camera hatch. They both immediately followed him out.

Lowering myself to the catwalk below the flight deck, I grabbed the bomb bay opener handle and tried to open the doors. Apparently, the hydraulic system had been knocked out for the doors didn't budge. I remembered that in case of a hydraulic failure, there was a hand crank located on the catwalk at the center of the bomb bay. I edged my way to the emergency crank and began to turn it. The doors started up but soon I couldn't move them any more. As I recall, the opening on each side of the bomb bay was only about two feet wide. No sooner had I opened the doors when Sgt. Romine dove through the opening. He was followed a few seconds later by Lt. Christie.

I then crawled along the catwalk to the nose of the plane. I opened the doors to the nose turret and helped Lt. Boecher climb out. I told both he and Lt. Boomhower to bail out through the nose wheel hatch. I then quickly crawled back to the flight deck and observed Lt. Golden still at the controls. I climbed up beside him and told him that everyone else had jumped. He told me to go and I gave him a salute and I turned toward the half opened bomb bay. That was the last time I ever saw him.

In the brief seconds it took me to reach the open bomb bay, the fact that I had not had my parachute inspected or repacked since my first mission flashed through my mind. Would it open and function properly? All bomber crewmen were issued detachable chest type chutes with the exception of the pilot and co-pilot who used back packs. Since my first mission to Strasbourg when I was nearly knocked out of the open bomb bay by a piece of flak while releasing a hung up bomb, with my chest chute lying on the flight deck, I had worn a seat type chute that I had scrounged and had kept in my locker. Luckily I had been wearing my flak vest and was not injured by the spent flak hit, although it knocked the wind out of me.

I had not turned in my chute for repacking for fear of losing it. As I prepared to jump, I said a little prayer that the chute would function properly. I then dove through the opening head first. As soon as I hit the slipstream, my helmet and oxygen mask were ripped from my head. I had neglected to buckle the chin strap.

I resisted the urge to pull the ripcord at this altitude without a portable oxygen mask and bailout bottle and took a free fall which seemed like an eternity to me. As I fell, I saw a chute far below me. I was rapidly catching up to it. The ground now seemed to rush up and I could distinguish farmhouses, fields and trees below. At approximately 2,000 feet, I pulled the ripcord. About two seconds later I felt a sharp, strong jolt as the canopy blossomed and bit the air. It was very reassuring to look up and see the large white expanse above me. The sudden deceleration caused my right foot flying boot to keep on going and I ended up with only the heated boot liner on my right foot.

I had often heard that parachutists never remember what they do with the ripcord after the chute opens. Mine was still in my hand and by god, I was going to remember what I did with mine. I stuffed it into the rear pocket of my flight suit.

As I drifted earthward, I watched the chute below me descend and land in an open area between two wooded areas. Approaching the ground, my chute drifted me right over the heads of a group of farm workers. I was barely 100 feet above them but not one of them looked up or saw me.

Jack Laswell

Jack Laswell was a gunner on the Smith crew, one of the four that returned to Tibenham. He sent this account to Bill Dewey.

I was flying in the left waist position of the D.W. Smith crew, away from all the action. I looked out the other side and saw what appeared to be P-51s barrel rolling up from our rear. On looking closer, I could see that they were Me-109s with enlarged scoops underneath. At the same time, we saw red balls exploding in front of the attacking fighters. Then all hell broke loose. Following the Me-109s were a large number of FW-190s. They were coming in from our rear and below.

It just happened that the ball turrets had recently been removed from our planes. The fighters would come in, fire, roll over, and then head for another target. One FW-190 came up on the left, between our tail and our wing, so close I could see his face. I fired until he dropped from view. I'm sure that I didn't miss – his windshield was completely shattered. At the time we were too busy to follow any particular fighter.

The rear guns were firing and Lonnie Davis, in the upper turret, kept asking where his fighters were. I don't believe that any got high enough for him to see. About that time, planes were going down everywhere and the only thing that we could do was to protect our plane and watch. Our wing ship, which eventually landed in Southern England with, as I recall, about twenty 20-mm holes in their plane, stuck close to us during the fight and this probably is why we got back in one piece.

During the fight, I saw a flight of four P-51s dive into about 25 FW-190s. It looked like one P-51 took on about 15 FW-190s.

But, as I stated before, we were too busy to watch any particular area during the whole encounter.

When we landed, we were told, during the interrogation, that we were the only plane (of the 701st Bomb Squadron) to land at the field. Also, when we went to get our shot of whiskey, which was standard practice, they let us have more than one because no one else was coming back to the base.

Although we had lost others in combat, this was quite a shock to a 20-year-old, just recently out of high school.

They gave us a week off and the radio operator and myself went to Scotland.

Would you believe that the second mission after we got back, on 7 October, was again to Kassel? It turned out to be a "milk run."

Photo by Cpl. Isadore E. Kamens

Chapter 14: The King Kong Krew

John Knox

I didn't want to enlist because I was in love with her, so I just figured I'd wait. I knew I was A1. I kind of thought I'd go in the Air Corps because I was so small, and I worked for Curtiss-Wright. I just assumed that. Then I made the mistake. They said don't ever volunteer in the Army, you've heard that expression, and I volunteered to go to gunnery school.

Ray Lemons and I both went to gunnery school, and then we went to Sheppard Field, Texas, to become flight engineers on B-25 or B-26 medium bombers. We were in the same class but we didn't know each other. Then we thought we were gonna be on a B-25 or a B-26, be a flight engineer, and that puts you way up to tech sergeant, a pretty good rating. Then they put us on a B-24 and we didn't know anything about the mechanics, so Ray became a waist gunner and I became a tail gunner. And he helped me out when I was shot. I got a direct hit from a 20-millimeter cannon shell, knocked me for a loop and knocked my turret out of commission. The plane was on fire. He opened the door and got me out.

DeDe Knox

He was operated on his knee without anesthetic. Before he went overseas, he was out in Colorado, and the pilot said that's it, they were ready to go overseas but they had a delay, and he wanted me to come out, because some of them were getting married. My mother said you can't let them get married, because she wanted a church wedding, and she said, "You can go," but his mother chaperoned me. At that age, you never heard of that now. So I did go to Colorado and spend that week with him before he went overseas. And we were married after he got back. The Air Force flew him home every weekend so he could see me, and finally the doctor said "Jack, you go back home and get that girl and marry her and bring her back so you can stay put long enough for us to operate on your eye."

John Knox

I lost an eye. Shrapnel penetrated the optic nerve, and shrapnel put my knee out of commission. I've had a stiff knee all my life. This has been a terrible thing. You can't sit right. You can't do anything right. That's why I can't fly anymore, because when we went to Kansas City, the last 8th Air Force reunion we went to, my god, I got on the plane, I couldn't get my leg under the seat in front of me. I'm standing there, everybody's getting on the plane. I told the stewardess, "I just simply cannot sit down, what am I gonna do, get off?" So she arranged a bulkhead seat.

DeDe Knox

Because he was supposed to light one candle, he was supposed to be on the stage and honored in Kansas City and I said, "What are we gonna do?" And he said "I'll figure something out." That was four planes during that trip, and he said this is going to be our last trip by plane.

John Knox

After Ray and I left Sheppard Field, they assembled our crew in Salt Lake City. That's where we met Jim Baynham and the co-pilot, Charlie Bosquet, and the flight engineer was Howard Boldt, who just died recently, from Houston. We didn't have a navigator and a bombardier. After Salt Lake City we went to Colorado Springs to do our training on B-24s. When we finally got the navigator it was John Cowgill, he was from Kentucky. And Hector Scala was the bombardier.

Boldt was the flight engineer. He was shot up worse than I was. He was just getting in the bomb bay waiting to bail out, and he got shot in the legs. And Bosquet and John, the navigator, they were two that weren't shot, and the radio operator was Jim Fields from California, and he was wounded. And then the other waist gunner, opposite from Ray Lemons, was Olen Byrd. He was kind of a Texas farm boy, not very well polished, and the last Ray and I saw of him he was sitting down on the floor of the airplane under the waist gun kind of looking at us. And the plane was on fire. We don't know whether he was afraid, and we had the door open to bail out, that was right there too. And I remember looking at him and I remember Ray saying, "Come on, Byrd, come on," and he said "No, no, no."

We don't know whether he had a bullet in him or whether he froze, scared, all we know is we think he went down with the plane. And to this day, Ray and I were the only ones who saw him, and we don't know why. He had a funny look on his face. But he wasn't dead. But with all that stuff on him, he could have been bleeding internally, and the plane was raked with cannon shells and shrapnel. The plane was in bad shape, and on fire.

So we don't know about Byrd. He was just a real quiet guy and all he did, he'd just gone to gunnery school, he hadn't gone to any mechanic school or anything like that, he was strictly a gunner. And then we used to have a ball turret when we went over, and we had a ball turret gunner, his name was Jed Lord. I don't think we flew maybe one mission and then they took out the ball turrets because we had better escorts and the missions were getting easier, and that thing created a drag, so we could go a little faster. So we rotated. And Lord happened to be the one that day that didn't fly. When I didn't fly he flew the tail turret and when Ray didn't fly he flew the waist gun. So he was the one, and he went ahead and finished all his missions, and stayed over there a couple of years, I think, in ordnance.

125

The Kassel mission was my eighth mission, and I think it was Jim's tenth. We rotated, so I lost one there. And then one time the pilot and co-pilot and the flight engineer, I think they took Ray along on that one, a bunch of them flew gasoline over to France. They got credit for a mission for that. So even on that crew we had a different number of missions, but I think eight was the minimum. People ask me how many missions I went on and I always said "Seven and a half."

In the back of the plane, we didn't know that we pulled away from the group. And then all of a sudden I saw a plane on my tail, and I assumed it was an American plane. Then I got looking close and I said, "No, that's not a P-47. That's an FW-190." And boy, he was coming in on me. And I'm shooting at him.

There's nothing over the intercom about planes or bandits or enemy planes or anything. Nothing. And he's shooting at me and I'm shooting at him, of course he's got 20-millimeter cannons and maybe even a 30, and I've got a couple of little .50-caliber machine guns. And he, just, one of them hit my turret. I never saw all those 130 planes at all. And to this day I can't figure it out. It's weird. We were fairly in the back, and I think the attack started in the front. But I didn't see a lot of planes being shot down or a lot of German planes or engines. I didn't see anything. But the plane was already on fire when I got hit, so you know they made some passes at us. There was a fire in the bomb bay. I heard nothing. I heard nothing about a fire. I heard nothing about bailing out. I heard nothing about bandits in the area. Nothing. I'll never figure that one out.

The turret must have shattered, because I had shrapnel all over. I knew my eye was hit, and I knew my leg was hit, and I could see the tear in my pants and the blood coming out. And I just got out of the turret and clipped on my parachute. I was kind of half in and half out, and I bailed out and counted to ten. I wanted to clear the rudders. Then I pulled the cord right away, because I was kind of woozy. And that's what I shouldn't have done probably because I passed out. We were at 23 or 24,000 feet.

What had occurred to me was, if I wanted to live, I had to get out of that burning plane. My desire to live overcame any fear of bailing out.

I saw Boldt while I was putting my chute on, and Ray had the door open, just that second or two before I went through the hole. He was sitting to my left, right under the waist gun. Boldt was the flight engineer and he got out of the top turret, got his parachute on, tried to put out the fire I guess and couldn't. And the bomb bay doors were open. I don't know whether he opened them or whether they never closed, and he was on the catwalk. That's where he and the radio operator were supposed to bail out, just right where the bombs went through. And he was standing on that. And he was just ready to step off the catwalk and fall through the bomb bay doors, and I guess he got raked in both legs.

Boldt and I both landed in trees. I had one bad leg and he had two bad legs.

Some German enlisted men cut me down, and I don't know whether they took me to a field hospital or right to a hospital. They took me somewhere, and the doctor said he was going to operate on my knee, but he didn't have any anesthetic. He said that a nurse, it may have been a Catholic nurse or some of those nurses in Europe wear kind of habits, they're like a nun, so I don't know really which it was. He said, "She'll hold your hand. I've got to operate on your knee." He spoke pretty fair English. And I passed out. The next thing I knew I was in this boys' school which they'd turned into a POW hospital.

After Christmas, I came back from another place where they looked at my eye, as a prisoner of war, and that's a funny story. I was put in the bed right next to Boldt. That's the first time I saw him. We were side by side, and we both had a cast over our legs and all the way up our body. And we'd sit there and play cribbage. They had a little cribbage board. We couldn't sit up because of those casts. But he was in one of those electric scooters for the last 30 years, I think. He had a terrible time. And he was a big man, and having a stiff leg, the worst thing you can do, being big, is fall on your own legs. I think he had a terrible life. But he was very, very cheerful. He was the most upbeat guy. The last 25 years he called me every five or six weeks. The last time he called me was just about a month or two before he died. And he would just talk about how they're taking care of him, and real upbeat, laughed, and he had nothing to be happy about because he had everything in the world wrong with him. His arm, finally, he couldn't use his arms because he'd used them so much to pull himself up, they went bad. He would have loved to have gone to the reunions, but he said he just couldn't get around.

John Ray Lemons

Kassel was a mission as you well know, September 27, 1944, and we were told what it was to be, it's going to be the Henschel munitions factories where they make the tanks and engines and all kinds of things for the war effort. And we figured from what was said at the briefing that it would be a fairly easy mission. There shouldn't be any problem. We'd have fighter escort, and the flak wouldn't be anything terrible, that you couldn't survive from. So even on my own plane I remember one of the guys kept saying "This is supposed to be a milk run."

I said, "I don't like that word. I never have liked that word. I don't like the word milk run. No mission is ever a milk run. You might say that afterward but this is when we're on the mission." And that shut him up. I don't remember which one it was who said that. And they were just joking, but little did we know what was about to happen.

On that particular day our position was the high right. Not the high high right. We were the high right, and we were about Number 3 down the line on the high right.

And Baynham was a good pilot. All of a sudden from solid cloud cover, you couldn't see the ground. It was 100 percent solid cloud. And we were probably 23,500 feet, and I'm going to say the clouds were at ten or twelve thousand feet, so we were well above the clouds. But all of a sudden all we heard was something is happening here, coming from the rear. And before you could say two more words, we were already hit. They came up 6 o'clock low where the ball turret position would have been a good one to shoot. The only person who could see was the tail gunner, or the waist gunners could get 'em once they got closer. The top turret guy couldn't do anything because they were beneath him. And we were on fire I would say in less than a minute.

The first indication I had was that I heard all the noise on the plane, and then the flames rolling out of the bomb bay, and you could see what was going on to your left and to your right. I was on the left side, but I could see both ways and man, there's stuff going everywhere you looked.

It was so sudden I guess you might say that you really didn't have a chance to realize that you were in serious trouble. And you'd never experienced that much of a volley of firing at you. I knew later on that they were shooting a lot further back because they had cannons. They were shooting 20 or 30 millimeter cannons and we were sitting there with a thousand yards on a .50-caliber. So they had an advantage right off the bat. Of course from what we always had been told, they liked to go for the tail, and liked to go for the engines. First thing get the gas tanks, because that gives you some definite problems right quick.

I fired the waist gun but I have no idea if I hit anything. They were coming so fast and furious because all of a sudden they were just right into you and gone, and what they did, they went ahead, and by that time I was gone. I mean I was out of the plane by the time they started coming back. Now Baynham stayed with the plane apparently after I got out, put it on automatic pilot and getting everything set up so he could get out.

I'll explain why we had the problem in the back. The tail and the two waist guns, none of us that particular day thought about having the parachutes right there handy, or your escape shoes wired to your harness like you're supposed to. So I laid both the parachutes for the waist gunners against the bulkhead, and here we are back at the waist windows, and all of a sudden we need those parachutes. And it gets further complicated. That particular day, they'd issued me a brand new harness. And being secure that there wasn't nothing ever going to happen, I didn't worry about getting it fitted. The loose straps were probably about six or eight inches loose, and I had to get the chutes, put mine on, put Byrd's on, and Knox had already crawled up, he'd already been shot up pretty bad, he was crawling and bleeding.

I got the hatch open, got the two chutes on both of us, and this is less than a minute I would say. I got the hatch open, and Knox, I had to kind of just shove him, get him out. Then Byrd, the other waist gunner, kept pointing to me to go first. I was trying to point to him to go first. I'll go next, because I've got the chutes on him and mine too. He refused. He said for me to go, so I went. And he's gonna follow me, I assumed. Well, I don't know whatever happened to him because he was killed. Whether he got hit, whether his chute didn't open, I have no idea, but all I know is from what reports I found out that he was found dead near the little town of Gerstungen. That's where he was buried and I finally found this out many years later.

But anyway, I don't know what happened to him. Knox got out and he was badly wounded. He lost an eye and he'd been hit in the leg, and was bleeding pretty bad.

So I got out. I immediately pulled my ripcord, 23,500 feet. They were shooting. I was right in the middle of the battle. Guys behind me still getting shot at and guys in front of me were still getting shot at, and guys to the right, high right, were still getting shot at. An Me-109 went right by me, from me to that wall right there. I could almost touch his wingtip. I thought he was dumping my chute. He might have been dodging me, I don't know. I was already getting lack of oxygen, and all of a sudden I don't remember anything until I came to about 12, 13,000 feet, and I went through the clouds. And then I could see the ground. I see the ground coming up. I said, "Man, I've got to watch those trees. I don't want to land in those trees." So I guided my chute, and sure enough I landed okay, and dumped my chute, and folded it up. Before I could even get that folded up, two irate farmers had me, with pitchforks. They were screaming at me. I had no idea what they were saying.

"Amerikanisch! Amerikanisch!" I was trying to tell them I'm an American. But luckily for me, two young Wehrmacht soldiers, they come racing up, with bayonets attached to long tom rifles, probably 16 years old.

"Raus! Raus! Raus!" I knew that means "get out of here," somehow, run. And I had on flying boots, what do you think you can do running in flying boots? But anyway, I followed them. They were pushing me ahead. And those two farmers let 'em go. And luckily for me, they kept marching me towards some little town, and as we got further, I could still see parachutes coming out of the sky. Everywhere we'd go, another half a mile or quarter mile, we'd pick up two or three more guys, and so we had about a dozen. We started heading to some little town. By that time we probably had 15 or 16 guys. And some guy who was a German, well-dressed official, stopped, screaming and just cussin' us out and raising cain and hawking at the two German Wehrmacht guys. And finally he was just going down and screaming at everybody, and he had his pistol out and he started flailing it.

I was in the front row, and he hit me across the face three or four times. I felt like I was getting clobbered. And those two young soldiers woke up and said "Hey, Raus! Raus! Raus!" And that guy let us alone. We were convinced after it was all over he had to either be the burgomeister or some big shot, or some public official, because he had on fancy boots and a full dress uniform.

That was the last we saw of him. We went to this little town where they kept me, and Eberhard Haelbig has confirmed the town was Eisenach. The place that they held me I said was a city hall. He said it was a Wehrmacht barracks. In the basement, that's where they had me, and we had about 25 guys. And the next morning, we had these guys that were all in bad shape, burned, shot up, with broken arms, or all kinds of injuries, needing medical help. They brought in four litters, and each of us that could walk put some of these wounded guys on these litters and carried them to the train and put them on the train. We marched probably two blocks or a block and a half to get to the train station. And the local citizens were screaming at us, and these two soldiers still were guarding us, getting on the train. And the next thing I know I was on the train going to Wetzlar for interrogation.

I found out many years later that the bombardier, navigator and the radio operator all landed and wound up in the same little town of Nentershausen, and all three were killed the next day by locals. The guys that killed them, one was a soldier, and the other two were labor camp guards. The first one was killed by a soldier who was on leave that day and why he picked him out I have no idea. I think he killed Fields. And that's what Hassenpflug now has kind of qualified and clarified actually and matter of fact, two of those guys were actually in the Nuremburg trials and one of them committed suicide before he got sentenced. The other was hanged.

Jim Baynham

I don't remember hearing any warning before the first attack. And all of a sudden you guys started hollering that we were being hit.

We got the smoke out of the cockpit and then some more started coming in. Our generators were on fire, so we opened the windows and blew the smoke out. I remember we had one front pass, that's the only time I really saw all the planes, because they were coming at us and the light was blinking as they were shooting, but most of them came from the back.

We didn't have those ball turrets. They came underneath us with 30-millimeter cannons, or 20-millimeter, and just lobbed them into us. Broke up the formation with those. In the lead element, the right wing ship just erupted in flames. Every crack in it you could see burning, and it just tailed off. That was the first one I saw go down.

After the crew jumped, the flight deck looked real empty. It was lonesome. And I looked down and didn't have my leg things hooked up, so I had to hook my chute up, and then I thought, "Maybe I can get 'em to quit shooting at us. I'll lower the landing gear." I figured maybe they'll figure they don't need to do anything else. And a 109 came up on my left wing, right next to it like he was flying close formation, and I looked out and saw him right before I got out of the seat. I'd like to know who that guy was.

I bailed out at 12,000 feet. They always told us that if you were free falling, when the ground started getting larger it's time to open your chute and that's what I did. I figure I was about 2,000 feet.

I landed on my butt, and then my head. It kind of knocked me out for a few seconds, and when I got my senses back, I was getting dragged along with the wind.

Some potato farmers were sitting right there with pitchforks. There was another kid that got picked up, I don't remember who he was, I think he was a navigator. Two of us wound up in this village, and it was one of those scenes just like everybody ran into. It was violent, because of one guy that was really leading the cheering section. He had a red face and was shouting in German, and shaking his fists. But there was a woman who spoke English, somewhere or another I thought I knew that she was an English teacher, that may or may not be true, but she spoke English and she calmed everybody down.

Well, the press had cartoons of us diving, machine gunning children in the schoolyard, things like that, and add to the fact that, I think they told me that day that this guy had had his family killed in a bombing raid. I was there for a little bit and then they walked us for a mile or two to some little village where there was kind of a little city hall with a one-room jail. There wound up being several of us before the night came, and when night came they took us and walked us somewhere to a station where a train was stopped, and we got on it. And then we went into Eschwege, which was an air force base fairly close by, and we almost got lynched on the platform there. Our guards went inside the station to contact the base, and the crowd was a big crowd, and they all got violent. There were eight or ten of us, and I think we were not far from being lynched, and the guards finally came back out and they calmed everybody down.

We spent the night in that air base, and then we went to Oberursel, to an interrogation center outside of Frankfurt. I remember coming into that Frankfurt station, and a big old barrel like you see in Casablanca or somewhere with the trains steaming. Some guard must have spoken English because he told one of the guys in our group that the night before they had lynched some flyers from some of the steel girders. And then we walked the streets of Frankfurt probably for a mile or two going to a place, and it was just brick rubble everywhere, a lot of buildings standing. It was a spooky place.

The first guy I saw that I knew after I got to Wetzlar, the temporary camp, was Ray, and he was on the other side of the fence in another compound. We just happened to spot each other, and his face looked like he'd been beat up. It was swollen badly.

John Ray Lemons

These two young Wehrmacht soldiers had brought us to this town, and the burgomeister stopped us. He was vehement in his anger. He was just swinging at everybody in the front row, and I was in the front row. I bolted out of that line and that was a mistake. I should have stayed. And that's when he pulled that pistol. I thought he was gonna shoot me. And he started bopping me with that pistol, in the face. The two young soldiers finally realized that they had to get control of that group and they started yelling "Raus!" and he walked off and left us. Luckily for us, I think.

Howard Boldt

Howard Boldt was the engineer/waist gunner on Jim Baynham's crew. He wrote his account of the battle for George Collar.

Our mission this day started pretty ordinary. We had heavy cloud cover in the target area and I did not know until a few years back that a navigation error had us bombing the wrong target. We were about twenty or so minutes away after dropping our bombs when I noticed a very large number of fighters rising up behind us. I was flight engineer and top turret gunner and had one of the best (or worst) seats in the house.

I called our tail gunner, John W. Knox, and asked if he saw the same thing. He replied "Yes, and I hope they are ours."

I started looking around to see if any others were around and at that time we picked up a few bursts of flak. They were right on us at about eleven o'clock as they had to be using radar. Just then we caught a direct hit between the No. 1 and No. 2 engines in the center of the wing. It left a hole about eight or nine inches in diameter with the metal pulled up around the edges. It must have had only a time fuse which was lucky for us. We also lost the aileron from our left wing at about the same instant. This really distracted me and when I turned around the fighters were on us. Several came in on our tail and although we were shooting at them there was no evasive action. We were bound to have hit some as they were so close.

I had parallax in my optical sight and it was useless and I had to use the iron sight. I ran out well over a hundred rounds from each gun before they stopped. Smoke was getting thick and I looked at the glass in the door to the bomb bay. It was red as if you were looking into a furnace. I knew it had to be gas fumes as our overflow lines came down between the bomb bays. We should have blown up right there.

I dropped out of my turret and went up to the pilot, 1st Lt. James C. Baynham, and grabbed the side of his helmet and told him that we were on fire and let's get out. I motioned to the radio operator, James T. Fields, and we grabbed our emergency chutes. I opened the floor hatch and dropped into the nose wheel compartment. The fire was pushed back by the wind coming through and I hit the auxiliary bomb door lever. The left two doors opened all the way but the right doors only opened about six inches. We had lost all hydraulic pressure. As only fumes were burning, opening the doors blew all the flames out.

Fields was right next to me on the catwalk and the co-pilot, Lt. Charles M. Bosquet, was coming down from the flight deck. It was at this time that I was hit, breaking both legs, and out I went. I pulled my ripcord immediately as I had been off oxygen for a time and I was not sure how hard I had been hit.

Fearing I would pass out without pulling the ripcord, I opened my chute as soon as I cleared the plane. I looked down. My left boot was gone and I was bleeding very badly. I looked at my right foot. Blood had filled the boot and was dripping rapidly over the side. Everything turned white and I could not distinguish anything. A fighter circled me but I could not see if it was one of theirs or ours. So I hung real limp as if I was dead. Then I passed out.

Later I regained consciousness but I could not distinguish anything but colors. I saw green beneath me, and about the time I figured I was over a forest, I was in it. My chute draped over the top of a large evergreen. I was hanging possibly fifteen feet or more from the ground. I ended up right next to the trunk but between limbs. The branches were close together. I tried to get out of my harness but I could not use my legs to relieve the tension on my chute snaps. I gave up and figured that if the Germans wanted me, they would have to get me down. My legs had quit bleeding.

I must have hung there for about 45 minutes. No one came so I decided I would have to try again. I remembered that I had a pocket knife along with a few cigarettes and a lighter in my jacket pocket. I cut through my shroud lines, took off my harness, and lowered myself to a sitting position on the limb below. I was very fortunate that the limbs were close together. I lowered myself to a sitting position all the way down. The lowest limb was about five feet from the ground, and as I was six feet two inches, I was again lucky. As I hung from the lowest limb I realized that I was at a point of no return. I could not get down as I could not use my legs and I could not go up. I finally pulled myself up a bit and started swinging my body and legs back and forth. When my legs got in front of me, I let go and fell on my back.

The ground was covered with the needles from the tree but I still hit hard and this started my legs to bleed again. I realized then that I had left my emergency kit, which was on my harness, up in the tree. My wife had knitted me a wool scarf and I tried to use that for a tourniquet but it kept stretching and would not work. I passed out for several hours at a time. Coming down, I was scared about being captured but after a few hours in the woods I was ready. I knew that I would not make it too long without attention and the most they could do would be to shoot me.

I went through my pockets and buried my escape money, maps, etc., and covered the place carefully with needles. Night came and I decided to attract some attention so I gathered some of the needles from the tree and started a fire. I was careful not to set the whole woods on fire, as I did not want that much attention. Just as I got my fire going I heard an air raid siren in the distance. I figured the British bombers were coming and then I heard them. I knew that they flew very low so I put my fire out real quick, as I did not want them shooting at me.

I became very thirsty and I remembered seeing what I thought might be a pond about a hundred and fifty feet from me. The only way I could move was in a sitting position. I would raise my behind and go backward, dragging my legs. I made about a hundred feet in a little over three hours and where I had thought there was a pond did not turn out to be one. I did, however, go directly to a wagon rut in a trail that had some water in it. I did not worry about how clean it was.

Somewhere around 10 a.m. a small reconnaissance plane came over very close but I could not see it. It must have spotted my chute in the tree. More than four hours later, at approximately 2:30 p.m., I heard a twig snap. I raised up and about fifty feet in front of me was a German soldier with a machine gun. He hollered something that I did not understand but I put my hands up as that appeared to be a good idea. He then yelled "Pistol!"

I shook my head as I did not have one. At this time, five more soldiers came out of the bushes. They came up and checked to make sure that I did not have any weapon and then everybody seemed to relax. They took a look at my dog tags and my name, Boldt, which was German. My hair was very blond and my eyes blue. They looked at me with, "Why the hell are you fighting on that side?"

Then they searched me. The first thing they pulled from my pocket was the lace-trimmed garter that my wife had given me. They must have thought that a girlfriend had given it to me. That really got their attention. Then after they pulled out my daughter's booties (born about 12 days after I left the States, on July 10, 1944) that my wife had sent me, this seemed to make an impression on the one in charge. That put me down as a family man and from then on we got along very well.

The soldier in charge appeared to be well-educated and he said something that sounded like cigarettes. I thought he wanted mine but I had smoked them all up. I tossed the empty pack toward him.

He pulled a cigarette from his pack and put it in my mouth and lit it for me. This was a real surprise and I immediately became suspicious but he happened to be a nice guy. Again, I was very lucky.

The soldiers laid their guns down about eight feet from me and went to get my chute down from the tree. I guess they decided I was in no condition to try anything and they were right. They got my chute down. I had wished that I could have destroyed it but of course that was impossible. The soldier in charge came over with my emergency kit and wanted to give me a shot of morphine that was in it. I did not want it. I wanted to keep a clear head in case I would be interrogated. I finally convinced him that I did not need it.

Then they got two limbs and used the lines from my chutes to go across to make a stretcher. Then they went down the seams on my chute and completely dismantled it. They did exactly what I had wanted to do even if I could not understand why. Then they put me in the center of the stretcher. I was carried for quite some distance and then placed on a small hand drawn wagon. They pulled me the rest of the way into a small village.

As we entered, I noticed some men working on the rail line repairing some bomb damage. There did not seem to be many people on the street but I was wondering what their reaction might be. I had heard that the civilians were pretty rough, and especially with airmen. German newspapers published propaganda that we were all gangsters and were let out of prison to bomb women and children.

I rose up on one arm to see who was going to throw the first rock just as a young girl was walking across the street. They thought that I had risen up to look at her and this one pulled out the booties and he shook his finger at me with a grin. I could not help but grin also, as that was the last thing on my mind. This girl was wearing a blouse of parachute silk and that was the reason these guys cut up my chute. If they brought it in intact they probably would not have been able to keep it but if it was in pieces then it was theirs. That silk was very valuable, a real item with the German girls who used it for blouses, etc.

I was taken to a small clinic or doctor's office. The doctor was looking very much like one of my uncles – large head with a burr haircut, no neck, and looked pretty tough. Looks were deceiving as he was very nice. In fact I became suspicious but he did not ask questions although he knew a little English. He started picking fragments out of my left leg with his fingers as some were close to the surface.

After looking for a few minutes, he turned and said, "For you, der var ist over."

I replied, "I guess you are right."

John Knox

Charlie Bosquet wrote me a letter about 20 years after the war. We didn't know each other too well because I was an enlisted man and he was a pilot. But it was a weird letter, like he was having mental trouble, all mixed up. I wrote back and told him if there was anything I can do, let me know. But we weren't that close. He was closer to Jim (Baynham). And about six months later he was dead. His family wrote to us.

When I was a prisoner of war my mother got some information from the Army Air Force, of the addresses of all my crew members, and she wrote to all the wives, or mothers, to find out how many of them are alive and how many are dead, because I was the only one that was missing in action. All the others were accounted for, either they were dead or they were POWs, but I wasn't accounted for until one of my older letters from Germany which I still have, all those letters, arrived at the house the following March, after all the mail carriers kept telling her "You might as well quit writing, all of the letters are coming back."

DeDe Knox

He was probably dead.

John Knox

And then when they got that letter that morning the mailman got in the car and took it right to the house. And DeDe called up my mother, and that's the only way she knew that I wasn't dead. But I've got all the letters my mother wrote to Jim Baynham's wife and Hector Scala's mother. They wrote back, who was missing, who was a prisoner of war, and who was KIA.

Walter Hassenpflug, right, showing Frank Bertram where his B-24 crashed.
Kasselmission.org

The Kassel Mission Memorial in Friedlos, Germany. Photo by Walter Hassenpflug

An anniversary ceremony at the Memorial in Friedlos. Photo courtesy of KMHS.

American and German survivors of the battle. Photo courtesy of KMHS.

One of the plaques which tells the story of the battle. Photo from kasselmission.org

Jima Schaen Sparks and her mother, Sarah Schaen Naugher, whose husband, pilot Jim Schaen, was killed on the Kassel Mission while she was five months pregnant with Jima.

The three plaques of the Memorial. Photo from kasselmission.org

The Bruce crew. Photo from kasselmission.org

This on back of picture from his mother sent   Lt John P.Willett
to my Mother 1944-45 ?

Co-pilot John Willett was flying his first mission with the Bruce Crew. KMHS
photo

Pilot Bill Dewey at the controls of a B-24. Dewey became a lead pilot after the Kassel Mission, completed his 35 missions and stayed on as a briefing officer. He was a co-founder of the Kassel Mission Memorial Association. Photo courtesy of Linda Dewey.

Left: George Collar, navigator.   Right: George Collar, "terrorflieger" Photos courtesy of Doug Collar.

The 1990 Kassel Mission Memorial dedication drew 600 people.
Kasselmission.org

145

Ira Weinstein relating his experiences at the Thunder Over Michigan air show.

The Walther crew. Photo from kasselmission.org.

Erlyn Jensen, the sister of command pilot Don McCoy, who was killed on the mission Photo from kasselmission.org

The Pearson crew. Photo from kasselmission.org

The Sollien crew. Photo from kasselmission.org.

Of the 117 dead on the Kassel Mission, six were from this crew. Because the plane exploded, there was nothing left of the five onboard at the time of the explosion. Because the explosion occurred when the plane was at a very low level, the explosion was contained within a relatively smaller space. At the time, because everything was pulverized, it was thought that nothing of the bodies was recoverable. With today's DNA testing, that has changed. Because of the work of a dedicated few individuals who, with the assistance of the Kassel Mission Historical Society, worked ceaselessly to urge the U.S government to retrieve these remains, a dig commenced in the Summer of 2015 to recover what is left of the plane and the men. The dig team was aided in locating the "hot spot" by KMHS member and Kassel Mission Museum owner Eberhard Halbig, who lives in Eisenach. See more on the MIA project below.

The Hansen crew. For more on the search for MIAs visit kasselmission.org *Photo from kasselmission.org*

The Uebelhoer crew. Photo from kasselmission.org.

The Swofford crew. Bombardier Augustino Mandino was not on the Kassel Mission. *Kasselmission.org*

The officers on Paul Swofford's crew reacting to a mission that was scrubbed. From left, navigator Henry Dobek, bombardier Augustino Mandino, co-pilot Ward Smith, and pilot Swofford, who'd been looking forward to getting the mission in. *Photo from Paul Swofford.*

The Chilton crew . Photo from kasselmission.org.

The Bruland crew *(photo from kasselmission.org)*

Lt. Carrow's ship, "Patches," was mortally wounded in the initial fighter attack. Five airmen were killed, and the plane crashed at Iba, Germany. The remaining four crewmen were captured and held at Stalag Luft I at Barth, Germany and Stalag Luft IV at Gross Tychow, Poland.

The Carrow crew. Co-pilot Newell Brainard was murdered on the ground. *Photo from kasselmission.org*

Major Don McCoy, right *KMHS photo*

Back row, left to right: Edward Hautman--Pilot, Thomas Land--Top turret gunner, Stidman--Not a member of the crew in Germany, Orvel Howe--Waist Gunner, John Tarbert--Waist gunner, Dale Maugin--Nose gunner, Gordon Waldron--Tail gunner. Front row, left to right: Carroll Snidow--Co-pilot, Maynard Jones--Navigator, John Frasca--Bombardier. Not shown: Harold Giesler--Radio operator who appears to have replaced Stidman.

The Hautman crew *(photo from kasselmission.org)*

Pilot Ed Hautman, left, and co-pilot Carol Snidow. *Photo courtesy of Carol Snidow.*

Pilot Stanley Krivik, left, played football for Fordham before the war and was a place kicker for Notre Dame after the war. "He was the strongest person I knew," said radio operator John Cadden, right, whose life Krivik saved by carrying him unconscious from the plane after it crash-landed.

Percy, the plane Stanley Krivik flew on the Kassel Mission.

Radio operator John Cadden, center, and pilot Stanley Krivik, right. Photo
courtesy of Linda Cadden Gibson

The Krivik crew. Photo courtesy of Linda Cadden Gibson

The squadron formations (graphics from kasselmission.org)

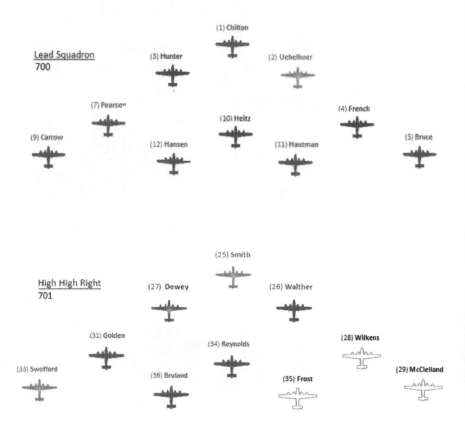

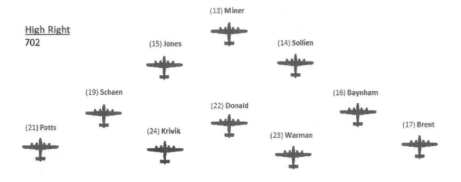

High Right
702

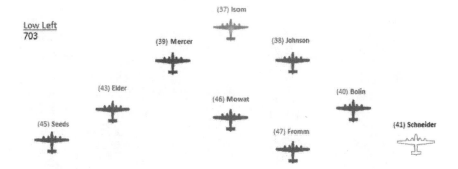

Low Left
703

John and DeDe Knox

Lt. Leo Lamb, the only American fighter pilot killed on the mission.

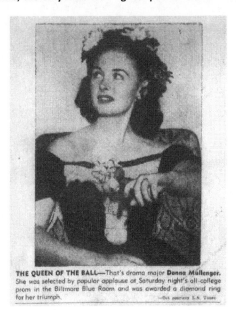

THE QUEEN OF THE BALL—That's drama major **Donna Mullenger.**
She was selected by popular applause at Saturday night's all-college
prom in the Biltmore Blue Room and was awarded a diamond ring
for her triumph.   —Cut courtesy L.A. Times

Donna Reed was a classmate of Leo Lamb at Los Angeles Community College, making a second connection between the Kassel Mission and "It's a Wonderful Life." *Photos courtesy of Catherine Lamb*

Kay Brainard Hutchins with a collection of all the units she encountered as a Red Cross girl during World War II.

Pilot Reg Miner.

160

Kay Brainard Hutchins as a Red Cross girl in WW2.

**Newell Brainard, Kay's brother, who was
murdered by civilians after bailing out.**

Feinde von einst, Freunde von heute: Der amerikanische Luftkriegs-Veteran Joseph A. Reus (links) und der 87-jährige deutsche Jagdflieger Heinz Federwisch aus Erfurt (rechts) fielen sich nach der Gedenkfeier in die Arme.   Fotos: Kurt Hornickel

Luftkampf 1944 eint heute zwei Nationen

Feier zum 66. Jahrestag der Luftschlacht über dem Kreisgebiet

VON KURT HORNICKEL

HERSFELD-ROTENBURG. Von Menschenmassen umringt war gestern Vormittag die Fliegergedenkstätte im Wald bei Friedlos. Trotz des schlechten Wetters kamen viele Ludwigsauer, aber auch Zuhörer aus dem Landkreis und benachbarten Bundesländern, um diese in ihrer Form bundesweit einzigartige Veranstaltung zu erleben. Seit 1990 kommen die Feinde von einst an diese Stelle im Seulingswald, um sich in Freundschaft gegenüber zu stehen, im Gedanken der Versöhnung, aber auch in

Walter Hassenpflug

der Freude darüber, überlebt zu haben.

Seit 20 Jahren erinnern dort Gedenksteine mit den Namen von 118 amerikanischen und 18 deutschen Fliegern an einen der verlustreichsten Luftkämpfe des Zweiten Weltkrieges. Das Desaster der „Kassel Mission" vom 27. September 1944 eint die Gegner von einst. Im Jahr der deutschen Einheit wurde die Gedenkstätte eingeweiht, und zum ersten Mal bildeten am 1. August 1990 amerikanische Bomberbesatzungen und deutsche Jagdflieger einen feierlichen Kreis der Verbundenheit.

Der Friedloser Walter Hassenpflug, der als Zwölfjähriger einen abgesprungenen Amerikaner an der Sol aufspürte, hatte ab dem Jahr 1986 Kontak-

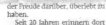

te zu den Fliegern in Deutschland und den USA geknüpft und sich zum Wegbereiter der Versöhnung gemacht. Ein Gedanke, der auch am 66. Jahrestag auf große Resonanz stieß.

Aus den USA reisten James C. Baynham und Joseph A. Reus an, zwei Flieger, die nach dem Abschuss ihrer Maschinen in deutsche Kriegsgefangenschaft geraten waren. Von deutscher Seite kamen die Jagdflieger Gerhard Kott und Heinz Federwisch vom damaligen Jagdgeschwader 4. Beide sind bereits 87 Jahre alt.

ZUM TAGE

James C. Baynham

HINTERGRUND

Die Erinnerung bleibt wach

Durch die Gedenkstätte ist Ludwigsau zum Treffpunkt der Veteranen geworden. Denn sowohl auf deutscher als auch auf amerikanischer Seite haben sich Verbände gegründet, die die Erinnerung an die Ereignisse des Zweiten Weltkrieges wach halten. So kam aus den USA eine Reisegruppe, die von Mona McGregor-English, der Tochter eines amerikanischen Kriegsgefangenen, angeführt wurde. Sie sprach für die „Kassel Mission Historical Society" Worte der Mahnung. Es kam aber auch Heinz Weuach, dessen Vater als deutscher Flieger an diesem Tag bei Neustadt an der Werra den Tod fand. Oberstleutnant a.D. Günter Fichte, Vizepräsident der Gemeinschaft der Flieger der deutschen Streitkräfte, mahnte eine Verjüngung des Gedenkens an. (kh)

An article about the 2010 ceremony at the Kassel Mission Memorial.

Umarmung nach 66 Jahren: Jim C. Baynham und Lina Eberhardt bei dem Treffen in Mönchhosbach, nahe der Stelle, wo der ehemalige US-Bomberpilot 1945 abgeschossen wurde. Im Hintergrund einer der sechs Söhne Baynhams. *Foto: Struthoff*

Jims langer Weg zurück

Nach 66 Jahren besucht ein US-Air-Force Pilot seine Absturzstelle in Nentershausen

Von Kai A. Struthoff

NENTERSHAUSEN. Einen waschechten Texaner kann so leicht nichts erschüttern. Doch vor dem Besuch in Nentershausen war dem 87-jährigen Jim C. Baynham aus der amerikanischen Erdölmetropole Dallas doch etwas mulmig zu Mute. Verständlich. Denn vor 66 Jahren wäre in der idyllischen Gemeinde sein junges Leben beinahe zu Ende gewesen.

Auch Lina Eberhardt aus Mönchhosbach wird den 27. September 1944 nie vergessen. Die damals 17-jährige war Lehrmädchen auf einem Bauernhof. „Plötzlich kamen Tieflieger", erzählt sie, „ein Flugzeug zog eine lange Rauchfahne hinter sich her, dann entdeckte ich den Fallschirmspringer – und es sah aus, als winkte er mir zu".

Jener Fallschirmspringer war wahrscheinlich Jim C. Baynham, ein 20-jähriger Air-Force Pilot, dessen Bomber einer von 49 Flugzeugen war, die an diesem Tag bei einer der verheerendsten Luftschlachten des 2. Weltkrieges über Nentershausen abgeschossen wurde. Jetzt ist Baynham wieder zurück. „Wenn Sie damals mit 17 Jahren schon so gut ausgesehen haben wie heute, dann habe ich Ihnen sicher zugewinkt", scherzt der hagere alte Mann mit dem schlohweißen Haar und nimmt Lina Eberhardt dankbar in den Arm.

Von Frauen gerettet

Fünf US-Piloten wurden an diesem Tag in Nentershausen ermordet. Jim Baynham aber verdankt vor allem den besonnenen Frauen des Ortes sein Leben. „Ein Mann war sehr aufgebracht und wollte mir etwas antun", erinnert sich Baynham. Später erfuhr er, dass dieser Mann seine Familie bei einem amerikanischen Luftangriff verloren hatte. Einer Lehrerin, die auch etwas Englisch sprach, gelang es schließlich, die Lage zu beruhigen. „Danach wurde ich gut behandelt", erinnert sich Baynham und erzählt, wie er zu Fuß nach Cornberg gebracht wurde und dort in einer Zelle landete.

Trotzdem dauerte es 66 Jahre bis Baynham sich überwand, nach Nentershausen zurückzukehren. Nach dem Tod seiner Ehefrau vor einem Jahr hatte er beschlossen, sich der Vergangenheit zu stellen. Das war nicht leicht für ihn. „Ich hatte noch viele Jahre nach dem Krieg Albträume und Schweißausbrüche."

Und ihn quälten auch Schuldgefühle, dass er damals an dem Krieg beteiligt war. „Wir schämen uns, dass wir einer Kultur angehören, die oftmals auf ein blutiges Ende zusteuert", hatte Baynham am Montag bei der zentralen Gedenkfeier im Seulingswald bei Ludwigsau gesagt (wir berichteten). „Aber wir freuen uns, dass wir unsere menschlichen Schwächen überwunden und das Gute in uns wieder aufgebaut haben."

Auch Jim C. Baynham kann auf ein gutes, erfülltes Leben zurückblicken. Lange Jahre war er in der Baubranche tätig, reiste um die Welt und zog mit seiner Frau sechs Söhne groß. Vier seiner Söhne haben ihn jetzt auf dem schweren Weg zurück nach Nentershausen begleitet.

Aus Fehlern gelernt

„Wir haben gelernt, uns gegenseitig zu respektieren, zu ehren und gegenseitig zu lieben", sagt Baynham über das Verhältnis zwischen Deutschen und Amerikanern. Beide Völker hätten ihre Lektion aus dem Krieg gelernt. Doch mit Blick auf die neuen Kriege, die inzwischen geführt werden, sagt der alte Mann: „Es wird leider immer Menschen geben, die einander hassen."   **UNTEN**

Another article in a German newspaper.

Sarah Schaen Naugher, pilot Jim Schaen's widow, at a Memorial Day parade.
Facebook photo

**David Aubrey Brumfield and Ashton Olivia Brumfield, Sarah Schaen Naugher's
grandson and great-granddaughter, at pilot Jim Schaen's grave in Arlington
National Cemetery.** Photo courtesy of Jima Schaen Sparks

Martin Brunotte and Jima Schaen Sparks at Martin's father's grave in Gerstungen, Germany. At left are Martin's mother and Walter Hassenpflug.
Photo courtesy of Jima Schaen Sparks

American, two Germans bound together by loss

By VINCE CRAWLEY
Staff writer

FRIEDLOS, Germany — Jima Schaen Sparks is a South Carolina schoolteacher whose father, Jim Schaen, died in a World War II air battle over Germany five months before he was born.

Martin Brunotte is an engineer from Jim whose father, Martin Brunotte, died in the same battle one month before he was born.

Gerhardt Mett is a furniture maker from former East Germany whose father, Gerhardt Mett, died in the same air battle Sept. 27, 1944, near Friedlos eight months before he was born.

Sharing a common bond, the three met at the joint American-German monument on a wooded hillside overlooking the village of Friedlos, near Bad Hersfeld.

"It's a very special place," Sparks said at a gathering Tuesday to commemorate the 50th anniversary of the air battle.

Like the others, Sparks is 49 and carries her father's name. She also said she feels a special connection among the group, even though their fathers fought on opposite sides.

"I never knew anyone who grew up under similar conditions, whose father was killed before they were born," Sparks said.

Then, four years ago, Sparks came to Germany to attend the dedication of the memorial at Friedlos. That day, she met Brunotte. And at Tuesday's 50th anniversary commemoration, she and Brunotte were introduced to Mett.

"The first time I ever talked to him it was like the Twilight Zone," Sparks said of Brunotte. And, Mett shared many of the similarities. All were named after their fathers. All had two half brothers from their mothers' remarriages. All understood the strange emotions surrounding their births,

S&S: Vince Crawl
Martin Brunotte (left), Jima Schaen Sparks and Gerhardt Mett were all born after the deaths of their fathers in the air battle over Friedlos, Germany, in 1944.

which they have trouble describing to outsiders.

"It's interesting, but it's not that sad, because I never met him," Sparks said. Her father was a bomber pilot, flying a B-24 Liberator the day he was killed.

"I didn't know him," Brunotte said of his German fighter pilot father, who flew a Focke-Wulf against the formation of Liberators. "Only from photographs and from his brothers, my uncles. And I have old diaries."

The three said that they do not ponder the possibility that their fathers killed one another.

"The first time we met here, it was in friendship," Brunotte said. "And we had not one other idea than that."

Tail gunner Sam Mastrogiacomo, who didn't fly the Kassel Mission but was on the Gotha Mission, on which the 445th Bomb Group lost 13 planes, and later was interned in Sweden after his plane was crippled on another mission.

Navigator Ray Ische and his wife, Reggie, flanked by his mother-in-law and younger brother with his Red Ryder BB gun. Ray is one of eight Kassel Mission fliers whose remains have not been found. His great-nephew, Chris Wahl, is a member of the board of the Kassel Mission Historical Society. *Photo courtesy of Chris Wahl.*

Guenther Lemke, a friend of Walter Hassenpflug who also served as his translator. *Kasselmission.org*

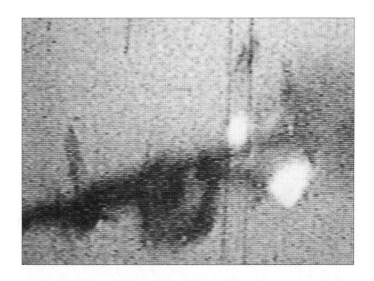

German gun camera footage of a hit on a B-24 on the Kassel Mission.

Paul Swofford receiving the Silver Star for heroism after a Congressman in his church heard the pastor relate Paul's story and expedited the award.

169

Eb Haelbig with one of the many artifacts he collected from planes that crashed on the Kassel Mission. *KMHS photo*

Chapter 15: Nightmares

The wife of pilot Jim Schaen, and the mother of command pilot Don McCoy each had a nightmare on September 27, 1944. Kay Brainard Hutchins' mother clipped a newspaper article on September 28 that described the previous day's air battles. It was the only article found in her possessions when she passed away.

Sarah Schaen Naugher

Even as the battle raged in the skies above Bad Hersfeld, halfway across the world its reverberations were being felt.

I still lacked three hours toward my degree. There's a college in Jackson, Belhaven College, where you could go for three weeks and get three hours. So Daddy came to Mississippi State and picked me up and took me to Belhaven and enrolled me to take United States History for three weeks, and I'd be through. I was thrilled to death that I was going to get through and by that time Jim is going to be through with his missions and be back, and our little girl was, well, we didn't know whether it was going to be a girl or a boy but I was very pregnant by then, and I had a roommate in the dormitory, and this is my story.

About three days before I was to finish up, we went to bed as usual about 10:30 at night, and I was sound asleep. I really wasn't worried about Jim. I didn't have him on my mind. I'd already written my letter for the day.

About 12:30 or 1, sometime in the night, I was awakened by my bed turning. I was about to fall out, so I reached my hands under the side of the mattress to hold on, and the whole room was just going around and around, and I had never had a dizzy spell in my life. I had never been sick a day the whole summer when I was in school and pregnant.

I called to my roommate and said "Please get up and turn the light on." She turned the light on and everything stopped. We both got up and sat a little while, and I said, "I'll get back in bed and you cut the light back off and we'll see what happens."

As soon as she turned that light off the bed started turning again and the whole room started turning and I screamed and I asked her to turn it back on. This happened three times. And she said, "Sarah, there's a bed down the hall in somebody else's room. I'll go down there and sleep and you leave this light on."

So I left the light on that night. The night of September the 26th, 1944. And I stayed up the rest of the night. And the next morning she said, "Now you go and see the nurse because you don't need to go to school today."

I went down and told the nurse that I had been up all night and she said "Don't go to school." She was scared to death something was going to happen to me and me being pregnant and not supposed to be, so I went back to my room and stayed all day and she sent an excuse to my teacher and told her she had excused me for the day.

Late that afternoon my roommate came back in and said "Sarah, you know that place down on Capitol Street that has real good ice cold orange juice? Let's get on the bus and go down there and get you some orange juice and I think you'll feel a lot better."

I said, "That sounds good to me." So she and I went out to where we had to get the bus and went downtown to Capitol Street, and oh, that was such wonderful orange juice, and after we had it we walked out, and I bought a paper. The paper was dated September the 28th. The headline on the paper was "40 B-24s Shot Down on Mission Over Germany."

When I got that paper it was just like a knife sticking in me. I thought if I ever hear from Jim after this I'm not going to worry anymore.

I never did. His letters stopped coming. The last one was dated September the 26th, which was the night that the room was spinning. I did not relate the two, because I did not hear from the government until about two weeks later and they said he was missing in action.

Erlyn Jensen

My mom had a terrible, terrible, nightmare. I remember it so well. I heard her just hysterical. And I got up and my dad was walking her. I said, "Dad, what's wrong with Mom?"

He said, "She just had a bad dream, she'll be okay. Go back to bed."

Well, it turned out that dream was on September 27th. And we didn't find out that Bill had been killed that night until December 10th. Now to me, that gives you the creeps, doesn't it? And I remember coming home, I had gone to school, I mean we knew he was missing in action and we just knew he was going to be found. Information certainly didn't pass as quickly as it does now, but it was December 10th. I was to go and be in a school Christmas program, and I had gone to my piano lesson after school and then was to hurry home so that Mom and Dad could take me to the school program. And I got off the bus from my piano lesson and I heard screaming, all the way up, the two blocks, and found my Mom on the couch at home, she had just gotten the phone call.

I ran across the street to her very dearest friend, who was a German lady that we just all loved, and I said, "Mrs. Lutz, you need to come quick. My Mom needs you." And she came down and helped, and then my Dad got home from work. And all I remember was thinking, I'm supposed to be at that program tonight to sing in the chorus in the Christmas program. My Mom was settled down by then and my Dad said, "Erlyn, we're not going to miss the program, Mom doesn't want you to miss the program, but she won't go with us. And we left her at home with Gertrude Lutz, and he and I went up to the school.

In retrospect, we found out that that was the night that my mom had that terrible nightmare. It was after that, when Dad looked back on the calendar. I don't know for what reason he would have particularly made note of the date, but he did. And when we got the word that he was no longer missing in action, that he had been killed in action, Dad realized that that was the night that Mom had had the terrible nightmare.

Kay Brainard Hutchins

Kay Hutchins was the sister of Newell Brainard, the co-pilot on the Carrow crew.

This is a strange thing. This is a 1944 article, and as you see, September 28, it was the day after the Kassel mission. The note says "Clipping found with papers in Mother's desk after she died in

1956. Why? Did she sense correctly that Newell was killed that day?"

She never knew he was killed. She did say to Daddy one time, "I have a feeling Newell…" well, we'd hear stories on the radio about some of the atrocities, dragging the prisoners along, and Mother said she had a feeling Newell was being maltreated. She had also predicted when her sister died of pneumonia. We didn't even know she was in the hospital, because she got sick on a Friday and I think died on Monday, and before we got the telegram she had said, "I dreamed about Ruth last night." She said, "We haven't seen her in so long."

"Raids cost Allies 49 bombers in Day. London, Sept. 28, Associated Press – Savage sky battles were fought over Germany again Thursday as the Luftwaffe sought to stem the mass Allied aerial assault which carried through its fourth consecutive day and cost the U.S. 8th Air Force 49 bombers and 12 fighters. Allied planes of every sort swept across the Continent in widespread attacks against Nazi industrial and supply targets, but the day's principal blows were struck by more than 1,000 Fortresses and Liberators and 700 escorting fighters of the 8th Air Force against Magdeburg, Kassel and Merseberg in central Germany.

She didn't have any other clippings like that about the war, but she had saved that.

Chapter 16: Daniel Boone and Simon Kenton

George Collar

Two farmers came across the fence with pitchforks, and they made me pick up that huge big chute, big bulky thing. I'm in my stocking feet, and they prodded me along and we headed towards the village. As we came in, the people came out of the houses and they lined the streets like a gauntlet, and all I could think of was old Daniel Boone and Simon Kenton running the gauntlet in the old days. And they were hostile. They were hurling epithets at me in German. And all of a sudden a kid about 15 years old came out and he kicked me right in the rear end.

The burgomeister had a courtyard in front of his house, or in the back of his house I guess because the barn was back there. It had a wall around it and a big gate. I trooped on in there with the rest of them, and they started to search me for a pistol. They made me take my pants down and they were hanging around my ankles, and I was standing in my stocking feet.

About that time I heard a commotion in the crowd and a guy came through and he was really angry. And he let me have one right between the eyes with his big old horny fist. I almost went down but I didn't. And I ducked. He swung two or three times more. I ducked. I was trying to get my pants up with one hand and fend him off with the other. Finally I got my pants buckled up and then I had two hands to work with, and he cut off the fight and went over and picked up a long-handled spade. Normally a spade has got a short handle. This one had a long handle and had a square nose on it. And he came at me with that spade.

I saw him swing and I ducked and I felt it whistle over the top of my head. And I thought, "I've got to get in close on this guy." So I closed right in on him and got hold of the spade and he got ahold of it and we were wrestling for the spade, and about that time there was an old man in the crowd with a big white walrus mustache and he had a green felt hat, and he came out and he started to help me. He realized that they shouldn't be killing this guy, even if he is the enemy. And about that time, the burgomeister and the village cop with that old scuttle helmet, they came to my aid and disarmed this guy.

Then I pointed at my feet, and they had a bunch of stuff that they'd collected, that fell out of planes and whatnot. And there was a pair of big felt boots, they used to put them on top of your GI shoes. The burgomeister gave them to me and I put them on, but they were about two sizes too big and my feet sloshed around in them. Later on at Oberursel I took some of the excelsior (wood shavings) out of the mattress and filled them up so they wouldn't be so sloppy. But the excelsior happened to be full of fleas and they bit all around my ankles.

Then they marched me up the street to the church, and they put me in this little jailhouse underneath the church at Lauschreden. I was the first one captured, and I was alone. They locked the door. And all there was was a little shaft of light coming through a small window.

I hadn't been there very long when I heard a commotion outside and they pulled the door and flung another guy in there. He happened to be Sergeant Eppley, who was the top turret gunner on our plane. I didn't know him from Adam. It was the first time I ever talked to him because I didn't know any of the crew members. If he hadn't told me who he was, I wouldn't have known who he was.

We're sitting there, and I said, "Isn't this a hell of a place to spend the rest of the war?"

And he started saying "I never should have done it. I never should have done it."

"What are you talking about?"

I find out the night before he'd been monkeying around with an English girl, and he wrote his wife a Dear John letter.

In the next few minutes, every time you turned around they're opening the door and throwing another guy in.

Pretty soon they opened the door and said "Raus!" We all stood up in a line, and they came down the line and picked three of us out. They picked me and Eppley and this guy, I thought his name was Summers, I know he was a lieutenant, and he said he was a navigator. And they took us three guys and marched us down the street, and up the street came two hay wagons. Each wagon was drawn by a team of horses. And there were a bunch of men and boys, they were either older men or younger boys, and they all were armed to some extent. There was one older guy, his name was Hans, he had black hair, and he had an old Mauser pistol with a wooden holster. It was a World War I Mauser with a big broom handle. Then there was an aristocratic looking guy on a horse, and he had a fine shotgun, and he was riding around through the hills and fields and he'd come back and report where there were bodies or where there were wrecks. None of these people were military. They were all civilians.

So we marched up the street. I still had no idea what they were gonna do with us. We're marching alongside the wagon and when we got up to what looked like a little orchard, with a fence around it, we went through the fence, and lying there on the ground, face down, was one of our fliers with no chute. He came down without a chute. And oh boy, then I found out what they wanted us for. We had to pick the bodies up. So when we picked him up, he was still warm, and every bone in his body was broken. He was limp. One German guy there had an envelope, and we took one dog tag off and that guy put it in this envelope, which they sent to the Red Cross obviously. And I remember reading that guy's dog tag. His name was Bateman, and he turned out to be a navigator on Johnson's crew which Dowling was the bombardier on. So we picked him up and put him in the hay wagon.

Then we marched around up and down hill and fields all day long, till almost dark, and we picked up a dozen or more bodies. Parts of bodies. We went in one little cow pasture and we found two legs, sheared right off, and this guy must have been big because his thigh was big and heavy, and he still had his flying boots on. And it was an officer because he had forest green pants on. We picked those legs up and brought them in.

We went up a hill one time and we found this plane crashed up there, and there was a turret. It looked like a turret had sheared right off and there was a guy in there and the top of his head was sheared right off. You could see his brains. And we found another guy that came down in his chute and he must have been killed in the fall. His feet were in a little creek. He was dead.

We came across a meadow and there was a guy laying in a pool of blood, and it turned out to be Joe Gilfoil. He was tossed out over the static line by those guys in Miner's crew after he got hit in the leg by a 20-millimeter. And it happened that Gilfoil had been on Schaen's plane before, and Eppley was a good friend of his. When we rolled him over and he saw who it was, he almost passed out. And Gilfoil was drained of blood, he was kind of a bluish pale color. There was blood all over the meadow.

That morning in the mess hall I'd seen a guy, I'd seen him before, I never knew who he was, he was in a different squadron, but kind of a big, rough-faced looking guy, and I thought who is that guy? I don't know why I noticed him. So we came across this plane that's crashed, and in the co-pilot's seat, here's a guy sheared in two. From his waist down is in the co-pilot's seat. The rest of him is missing. We look up ahead and about a hundred yards ahead, here's the upper part of his torso butted into a tree. He must have been in the plane when it hit and it just sheared him in two. When I rolled him over, my god, it was the guy I'd seen in the mess hall that morning.

I paid particular attention to his name, Geiszler. Martin Geiszler Jr. He was on Walther's crew. And everybody on that plane was killed with the exception of the pilot. And the pilot's now dead but I had a little article he wrote, and he said that after they got hit, he must have been blown out of the plane because he doesn't remember a thing until he came to in the hospital.

When I was in Stalag Luft 1, there was a fellow from Los Angeles by the name of Oscar McMahon in the same room I was. This Geiszler was from Bell, California, which is in the Los Angeles area, and after the war I got a phone call one day. It must have been the summer of '45, and I got a long-distance call from Bell, California, and it was Mr. Geiszler, this guy's dad. He wanted to know who I was and if I was the same guy that was on the Kassel Mission. I said, "Yeah."

He said, "We were at a Red Cross meeting and we met a fellow named Lieutenant McMahon, and we asked if anybody knew of anybody that was on the Kassel Mission and he said, "Yeah, I know a fellow who was a prisoner with me," and he gave him my name and address, so they called me. And he said, "My son, Martin Geiszler Jr., is missing and we don't know what happened to him. All we know is he went down on the Kassel Mission."

So Jesus, I hated to tell him, but I said, "Look, I've got to tell you right now. Your son is dead." Jesus, you could have heard a pin drop. I hated to tell him, but what the hell are you gonna tell him, you ain't gonna tell him he's alive. I could have said, "Oh, I don't know anything about it," or something like that but I didn't want to do that. So they said, "Can we come to Michigan and see you?"

I said, "Sure."

By god, if they didn't come to Michigan. During war it's hard to travel. They came clear to Michigan, he and the Mrs. And I didn't tell them the details of it, they never did know that he was torn in two, but I said, "I can definitely tell you that your son is dead because I was one of the guys that picked his body up." I said, "I hate to tell you that," but they thanked me for telling them because they didn't know. Well, it was only a couple of weeks after that the Red Cross notified them that he was dead. But those people, they used to send our kids presents, books and clothes, they'd go to Guatemala, they'd send us presents. He offered me a job. He owned a factory in Bell. He wanted me to come to work for him. They had one more son that was still alive. That's all I can tell you about Geiszler. But there was something about that guy's face that stuck in my mind, and when I turned him over that was him.

One other guy on this plane that I picked up was Bergquist, he was their radio man. We picked him up, dead. And like I say, there was nobody on that plane that lived, period, except the pilot. And the Mrs., when she found out the pilot was alive, she was bitter. But I don't think it was his fault, they're all hit. She thought, well, he shouldn't be alive if my son's dead.

Chapter 17: Gilfoil

Frank Bertram

Now let me tell you what happened to the men that were in the plane. The pilot came through okay. He took the plane as far as he could, then bailed out. The bombardier went out and broke his leg when he landed. Our radar operator, Branch Henard, went out and landed okay. I thought Mac Thornton was dead. As it turns out, he was right in back of me going out, which I couldn't see. You had goggles on, you had an oxygen mask. I couldn't tell who was in back of me.

There were three navigators. One of them was a fellow named Jackson. He was the pilot's navigator. He went out okay. He landed okay and he walked around for a couple of days before he got captured. Our engineer got out okay, and he didn't get injured. He was actually free for ten days, and he was probably the most nervous man on the ship. His name is Bob Ault, from Texas, a nice guy but very nervous.

The radio operator, Joe Gilfoil, lost his leg – a shell just about ripped it off when it hit the ship. The two waist gunners threw him out, hoping that the blood would coagulate, but I understand that his leg just about snapped off, and when they found him on the ground he was gone.

Of the men in the waist, Alvis Kitchens – Cotton was his nickname – he had a good section of his rear end taken off with some flak, not flak but the 35-millimeter [20-millimeter]. He got hit in the butt, and so did Bowers, although not as bad as Kitchens.

The tail gunner broke his ankle when he bailed out.

It was a good 40 years before I learned what happened to our co-pilot, Virgil Chima, and he was my best friend at the time. His body was not found until November 15th. Walter Hassenpflug dug this up, and what he found was that some women were looking for beech nuts up in the forest and ran across him, so he must have been laying there for six weeks, and yet, the mystery is, his parachute was missing. The shroud lines were cut. He was laying in the fetal position. But his body had decomposed so much by the time they got to him, I don't imagine that they ever figured out just what happened to him. But obviously, someone got the parachute, which was silk and was very valuable over there at the time.

All you can do is surmise. I know what it was like coming through the trees. He could have made a worse landing than me and maybe broke his back and couldn't move and just died there. It's very doubtful that someone had beaten him because it was so far up in the hills where nobody would go for any reason, and no one had gone up there prior to these ladies going hunting for beech nuts for food. So I'm inclined to think he badly injured himself, although why would he be in the fetal position? Of course he could have just drawn into that, knowing he was dying, trying to keep warm. Poor little guy. Nineteen years old. And the most meticulous guy on the crew, man, he checked everything to make sure his parachute and harness and instruments were perfect.

He had two brothers. One of them was a major in the 91st, which was the one with the Triangle A, the group that was in "12 o'Clock High." And then he had another brother who was a bombardier. There were four boys and three of them were in the Air Corps and Virgil was the only one who didn't make it. And his mother never did get over it. He was the baby of the family.

The same thing happened with Joe Gilfoil. He was the only child of an Irish family right outside of Boston. I guess his mother and father were at that time in their late forties or early fifties when he got shot down. Joe was 19. He and I had gone to communion that morning, as we did before each mission. He was a good Catholic boy. I was a Catholic boy. And we had one other man in our crew, Alvis Kitchens -- a very quiet kid, never said boo. Did his job. He'd go with the guys but he never smoked, he never drank, he was very religious. Very soft-spoken, just a good Christian lad, and do you know, 54 years later, he's still the same. All these other guys, including me, would go out and just raise all kinds of ruckus, drink and chase women, do all kinds of crazy things. Not him. Never.

Alvis Kitchens

Alvis Kitchens was a waist gunner in Reg Miner's crew. I interviewed him briefly at the 2004 2nd Air Division reunion.

We looked and saw all those fighters coming in, and we knew we were in trouble. You'd see one plane drop, another one going down on fire. I was injured by a 20-millimeter shell coming up from the bottom. It exploded in between me and the radio operator, Joe Gilfoil. I got part of it, and he got most of it. Me and Larry Bowers, we did what we could for him. He was bleeding real bad. We put a tourniquet on his leg, and just pushed him out. He was dead by the time he got to the ground. At least that's what they tell me.

I landed in a plowed field with German soldiers all around. They were watching as I came down. Of course I was lucky.

Larry Bowers

Larry Bowers was the radio operator on Reg Miner's crew. He replaced Weddle, who lost part of his foot when Miner crash-landed on an earlier mission. I interviewed him at the 2004 2nd Air Division reunion.

We were flying a regular mission, and suddenly there was a call from our navigator. He called Skip and he said we were off course. And Skip – Reg – called the commander and said we were off course, and he just said "Follow me." So we didn't have any choice. We followed him. And by that time we were completely off course. We dropped our bombs in an oat field, didn't hit anything, and when we turned off the target we weren't where we were supposed to be. About that time the Germans came up, and we didn't know it then but we learned later that the Germans had made these FW [Focke-Wulf], they'd put armor plating on them so that our .50-calibers wouldn't even penetrate them. They came through us and I guess it was five or ten minutes and they'd shot us all down. It was really a terrible loss.

We were basically shooting our guns. We didn't even know until we got through shooting the guns, and then we realized that we were hit. And this is back when the radio operator was back in the tail. We were the lead crew, and we had a mickey (radar machine) operator so we had to move the radio operator back to the back. He's the one that took Weddle's place, and he's the one that was killed. He had his leg almost shot off. And we had to decide what to do with him. We really didn't have time to do much with him, so we put a chute on him and tied a rope to it and dropped him out and then pulled the chute for him, and the chute opened and he hit the ground all right, but Collar found him. George Collar used to be on our crew. He found him, and he was dead when he found him. Which was really tough, but ... I don't know what else we could have done.

Anyway, then we all bailed out, and it's an interesting thing to bail out. I've always wanted to do it again, but my wife never would let me. But it's so interesting because you can do just anything you want to, you can turn over and over and you go round and round and you stop yourself if you want to, it's really interesting. And you don't really think about hitting the ground until you get close to the ground. When I started getting close to the ground there were some clouds below, and when I saw these clouds I said, "Gosh, suppose there's a mountain sticking up in these clouds." So I reached over and pulled my ripcord and I broke through the clouds, and there were civilians down there.

We were always briefed not to let the civilians catch you, because they don't like us very well and I don't blame them, really. So I started trying to guide my chute, and there were two things wrong. The Mae West, when you put the chute on, the harness, you don't have it as tight as you should. So when it's not tight it really and truly hurts, so you hold it apart, the chute opens, and then I decided I'd better try to guide the chute on one side so I could go in the woods.

The wind took me into the woods. I went in far enough where I could get away from the civilians, and I must have been free for about two and a half or three hours. Then I heard some people coming through the woods, so I crawled under a log. They stopped up there on the road, and one of them came out to take a leak. He was standing there taking a leak and he saw me under the log. He pulled his pistol out and I came out and said "Kamerad! Kamerad!" That's all the German I knew. That's when I was captured. He was a soldier. And they had picked up our tail gunner, Lamberson. When he hit the ground he broke his leg, so he was on the cart. He's dead now. He's the only one of the crew that I saw for, oh, gosh, until we went to dedicate the memorial. That was the first time I'd seen any of the crew.

George Collar

This is a letter that I sent to Bob Paul. "I know that you were a waist gunner on Stanley Krivik's crew. I know that your crew was the only one to get back to England from the 702nd Bomb Squadron after we all got shot up on the Kassel raid. I was flying as bombardier with Lt. Jim Schaen that day and we were one of the planes that were shot down. Of the 236 men aboard the 25 planes that went down in Germany that day, 117 were killed in action with the rest being taken POW. Some of them were pretty badly wounded. I would like to hear from you to get your story of what happened that day. I saw our old squadron commander Colonel Martin down in Dayton a couple of years ago and he said he heard that Krivik stayed in and flew in Korea. Nobody seems to know where he is now. Hoping to hear from you."

Here's the letter I got back. He said, "Dear George. I was happy to receive your letter. It was good to hear from someone who was on that mission. To answer your question about what happened to our crew, here are some of the facts.

"As you remember, the mission to Kassel was a relatively easy one up to the point where we were attacked after leaving the target. My first inkling of trouble was that one of our forward element ships, Steady Hedy, was suddenly on fire and going down. At that time I saw no enemy fighters. An instant later, however, I was hit in the right leg by a .30-caliber machine gun bullet and a second later a 20-millimeter shell shattered my heel. At the same time, Henry Puto, our tail gunner, was blown completely out of the turret, and the right waist gunner, Bill Rand, was struck in the face by a shell fragment just missing his eye and bleeding profusely. I put a compress on his eye and with the help of the cold temperature the blood froze and the bleeding stopped.

"The sky was immediately full of FW-190s no matter where we looked. Henry was out cold and Rand and I were busy for the next few minutes shooting at FWs. Rand got one and I got two before we picked up some help. This was in the form of a squadron of P-38s, which chased off the Germans and kept us from being the last ship to go down. We lost an engine on the first FW pass. He shot the prop off our right inboard engine. In a few minutes we picked up an escort of P-51s and headed for home.

"We in the back were pretty well banged up but the rest of the crew apparently were okay. Stanley Krivik decided against landing in France despite another engine losing power. He said that with the hydraulic system gone and the wounded aboard he needed a long runway and a nearby hospital. He did make it back to England and approached our air base, but the runway was blocked by some construction equipment, so they told us to go around again. We then lost a third engine and crashed in a field just outside of Diss.

The plane broke in half and was burning pretty badly. The heroism of Stanley Krivik and Bill Rand, who pulled everyone out except Dan Dale, our navigator, who was killed in the crash. We all wound up in the general hospital of Diss. Cliff Stromberg, our nose gunner, had a sprained ankle. John Cadden, our radio operator, had a broken back. Don Bugalecki, our engineer, had minor cuts on his leg when he was pulled from the plane. Stan Krivik had been knocked unconscious in the crash, so he was under observation but seemed okay. Len Trotta, the co-pilot, was okay when he revived. Henry Puto, our tail gunner, had some head wounds that cleared up. His flak helmet saved him from more severe injuries.

Bill Rand as I said before was wounded in the face. It's a miracle that he still has his eye. Thank God. As for me, my right leg was pretty well mangled and I was kept in the hospital for two months. All of us recovered. God was sure watching over us. Cadden's back was the most serious but they sent him back to the States where he recovered completely. Stromberg, Bugalecki and myself finished our missions, the Kassel mission being our 18th, so we flew 12 more before they let us go home. As for their status today, Stanley Krivik stayed in and flew in Korea but was later killed in some accident. Cliff Stromberg died in 1988 of a stroke. John Cadden, Len Trotta and I get together now and then.

"Don Bugalecki and Bill Rand are among the missing. We just heard from Henry Puto, who is retired and living in Florida. I'm semi-retired and working in the precast concrete business. So there you have it. Quite an ordeal, but I'm afraid nothing compared to what you fellows went through as POWs. I'd be very interested in hearing more about what happened to you. Enclosed is a picture of a model of the plane we were flying at Kassel. You might remember seeing it flying along with you or taxiing on the ground. Well, George, it was nice hearing from you and if you have any more questions don't hesitate to ask. I'd love to hear from you.

Sincerely, James R. 'Bob' Paul. P.S. A couple of afterthoughts. We were credited with four FW-190s that day. Bugalecki in the top turret shot one down. Stan Krivik and Bill Rand received the Soldier's Medal for heroism."

And he sent me another letter. It says, "Dear George. I'm sorry I have taken so long in answering your letter. I was away most of August and part of September on vacation and I know that you were in Germany before that. I think I might have some news that would be of interest to you. The clippings you sent me about your ordeal in prison camp had a picture of your crew. Immediately I recognized Joe Gilfoil and Richard Parsons, and I probably knew the rest of the crew of enlisted men. You see, your enlisted crew were in the same nissen hut as our crew up to the Kassel Mission. As you remember, there were two crews to a hut.

"We became very friendly with Gilfoil and Parsons. I wasn't really with that crew, but I was in the same hut, with the officers. I knew your plane at that time because you were usually in the same element with us on several missions. Joe Gilfoil and I used to wave and thumb our noses at each other while we were forming, before we went on oxygen. It so happens that your ship drifted in beside us on the Kassel mission after being hit.

"One of your port engines was on fire" – I say it was. I saw that. – "I saw men bailing out" – probably me – "in the front of the ship, but not in the back at first. Parsons was still in the turret and alive. They probably did not report to you because the same as we, they didn't see the Focke-Wulfs until they were on top of us. As you remember, they came out of the clouds. An FW flew up behind your ship, throttled back and dropped his wheels and flaps. He probably thought the plane was abandoned" – and was about to shoot it up. – "I was trying to fire at him but he was too close to our vertical stabilizer. You know what a pain that was for waist gunners to shoot around. As I said, Parsons was still in the turret and he blew that FW right out of the sky. I thought I saw him bail out after that. In fact, when intelligence interviewed me in the hospital I told them about that incident, hoping that Parsons would get credit for the FW-190. Apparently the information was lost."

Reg Miner

My co-pilot [Virgil Chima] had two brothers in B-17s. One of them was a pilot and the other was a navigator, and I've talked to the pilot in recent years. He said he'd had three co-pilots killed on him. One guy with his head shot off. And he was flying back when it was, in my opinion, a lot rougher. Things were really nasty. They didn't have fighter protection. The rate of attrition was such that theoretically you couldn't finish your missions. You wouldn't live that long. But he said, "Ah, it was no worse," I mean he inferred that we had it just as rough, but I disagree. We basically had it much better, except for aberrations like the Kassel mission.

Chapter 18: The German Pilots

Frank Bertram

Incidentally, last night on TV they had a guy named Dowling who'd been shot down with us that day. In this interview, all of a sudden they're showing this memorial, and I look, and that's me, and right alongside of me is Ossie Romm, an FW-190 pilot, and this was at that reunion about ten years ago. [Oskar Romm shot down three B-24s in the Kassel Mission battle.] As far as that memorial goes, if you look into it I think you'll find it's probably the only memorial of its kind in the world that has the names of the combatants on both sides, and they probably told you that in addition to all the Luftwaffe that were killed and the Americans that were killed there were also seven German soldiers in a hospital that got killed when one of the German fighter pilots crashed into this hospital, and I think that was very smart of them to put those men on the monument because they were killed as a direct result of this action.

When I went over and met Walter Hassenpflug in 1986, he introduced me to Ernst Schroeder, a German FW-190 pilot. The guy shot down two of our planes that day, and I don't know how many he shot down during the war. He was the father of seven boys. He didn't speak a word of English, but he's very well-known in German circles as an expert on military fighters at that time. He was an expert on the FW-190 and the Messerschmitts.

He had nothing but the greatest admiration for the Mustang. He said if it wasn't for the Mustang we'd still be fighting over there. He said that airplane changed the war, after they developed the drop tanks and they could protect the bombers going in. That changed the complete air battle situation. Actually the German production of aircraft was greater in September 1944 than at any point up to that time. The big problem was the lack of manpower and the shortage of petrol. But as far as planes, they had them. And they were good. The Germans were very, very brave people. And what I noticed, they just could not believe how friendly I was, and others were, towards them. They acted like we should hate them because of what happened 40 years ago, which I didn't even think about. I mean, you were just people; they just did their job and we did our job.

Malcolm MacGregor

When they put the monuments up in 1990, that's the first time I had ever heard about Schroeder. And Schroeder was talking to Gunther Lemke, who was translating for, who was the leader of our squadron, the 702nd, Reg Miner. He was talking to Miner, and he pointed out which planes he shot down, and he pointed right in the formation, because Reg was describing the formation to him, and he said, "Oh yah, these are the planes" he shot down. And ours was one of them. I asked him how he could be sure. That's when he said he saw the blood running out of the back of the airplane. So he was aware of it. When you shoot people all to pieces, I guess it must have been really bad back there.

The mother of the tail gunner, Bobby, I can't remember the name right now, Bobby's mother wrote my mother after she knew her son was dead, and she knew I was a prisoner, and she said, "I hope he didn't suffer." And I'm sure he didn't suffer very long, as it was all over in a matter of a minute or two. There was nothing left of those guys. That was probably pretty hard on Carl, too, picking up those guys and getting them out of there. I think Carl had a very traumatic situation, he never wanted to visit it again, he never wanted to get involved in the Kassel Mission, he said he didn't want to relive it. And I can see why. I would think he had a much harder time than I did.

Werner Vorburg

The storm group of the JG 4 was drawn up in August 1944 in Salzwedel. Its establishment arose in the framework of a concept of the German Luftwaffe command, which envisioned the breaking up of the weapon-filled bomber groups with a new tactic of tightly formed attack groups in order to attack them better after the loss of their tight formation. The fighters set themselves up exclusively out of volunteers who accordingly had pledged themselves with a handshake before their commander, Lieutenant Colonel von

Kornatzki: a) to only look for a fight with four-engine bombers, and whenever possible to avoid engagement with a fighter, b) to not open fire on the bombers until at a position of 150 to 200 meters, when the four-engines appeared in the target circle of the reflex gun sight, and c) to ram the bomber if weapons failed or the gunfire was ineffective.

In retrospect, the chance of surviving a ramming and jumping out with a parachute sounds very much like heroic suicide. It actually had, however, an ulterior motive: The closed rank of the attacking fighters was designed to disperse and waste the defensive fire of the bomber formation. Out of fear of the dangerous ramming, everyone would open fire at the closest distance possible, and through this, success would naturally be achieved. So the conditions and the will had to be created and motivated to fight the enemy bombers in a close squadron unit at the closest possible distance.

The storm group units in 1943/44 were considered elite units of the fighter corps and had no lack of volunteers.

One must keep in mind that the German airman knew about the escalation of the brutal, unrelenting bombing with parachute mines, incendiary bombs and high explosive bombs of residential districts of the central cities, the militarily nonsensical shooting by the host of superior escort fighters at everything that showed itself below, at farmers behind the plow, at bicycle riders, pedestrians and Red Cross ambulances, and that if a peace treaty were sought, not the slightest mercy was to be expected (that also caused hatred), and that the entire German people (not just the government) had to expect the complete and final annihilation of the German empire, as indeed it happened.

This knowledge motivated the storm fighter for his tasks.

The storm fighter was supposed to break through the attacking formations of robust and heavily armed bombers with no consideration of the hail of fire and destroy the bomber unit. The choice of the appropriate fighter plane fell on the heavy fighter plane, the FW-190, series A 8/R2.

Armored oil cooler, bulletproof windshield, 6mm fireproof plates and cabin sides, 9mm armor plate behind the pilot's seat and the complement of standard weaponry – gun type 151/20, 2MK 108 caliber 3cm – led to double the fuel consumption. To guarantee three hours of flight time, the fuel load was raised to 960 liters with the help of a 300 liter ejectable auxiliary tank and a 110 liter auxiliary tank behind the pilot's seat. A tanked up and fully armed FW-190 A8/R2 reached a flight weight of seven to eight tons. A 14-cylinder double star engine of the BMW 801 type with a 2,400 hp maximum tried to make up for this additional weight which was not so favorable for a fighter plane. The FW-190 was clearly inferior in dogfights with the escort fighters. Therefore, the storm units were sent against the bomber squadrons under the protective cover of lighter fighter planes, the Me-109.

The first missions were flown in August 1944 with four squadrons of 11 machines each. In spite of noteworthy success against B-17 units, the newly established storm groups already had eight wounded and 30 killed (among them the group commander and a squadron captain) on 11 and 12 September 1944.

Rarely reinforced, the II/JG4 flew on 27 September 1944, the first mission against about thirty B-24 bomber airplanes. After taking off from Welzow (south of Berlin) under the protection of two groups of Me-109 escort fighters and after repeated course changes and coming undisturbed by enemy fighters, the unit reached the Liberators and flew from behind into the stream of bombers that were numerically superior to us.

We divided up and flew toward individual ships. Whoever was not shot down by the bombers had success or had to ram. After passage from the back of the formation to the front, shot down ships were observed. Crews from four engine-planes, flying further ahead, were bailing out in rows before they were even attacked [author's note: This statement drew a flurry of angry letters to the 8th Air Force News, and was debunked by the other German fighter pilots, who pointed out that Vorberg was overzealous in his views. Of the planes that were shot down or crash-landed, every single plane had at least one casualty, and there is no evidence that anyone bailed out before their plane was hit].

Ten or twelve bombers exploded in the air, although they had already dropped their bombs. That also led to collision losses on our side due to the closeness when opening fire. After the march through the entire stream of bombers, we distanced ourselves quickly by swinging down from the place where the battle took place, in order not to be caught by enemy fighters.

Our losses included ten machines, one squadron captain and six other pilots. Three pilots were wounded, one of whom had rammed and lives today in Mannheim. I do not know how many of our storm group were lost on that day, since I have lost all records. We cannot today confirm our kills as the gun camera films were confiscated by the victorious powers and are reported to be presently in the hands of England's Imperial War Museum in London.

The storm groups continued attacks on four engine units until the end of 1944. After that they were called to action in defense of the Fatherland.

Ossi Romm

Oskar Romm, a German ace, was a pilot in Sturmgruppe/JG 3. This is reprinted from The Kassel Mission Reports.

The combat formation was led towards the enemy formation by the ground radio stations. After visual contact was established in the air, the leader of the combat formation was given clearance to attack.

As the squadron leader of the 15th Squadron, I had a good tactical position within the combat formation and attacked a flight of three bombers.

Just like during my first downing of a four-engine bomber over Oschersleben, 7 July 1944, my approach for the attack was divided into three actions, going off real quick. First to fire into the fuselage to hit the machine gun positions, then hit the pilot's compartment, and finally to hit and set fire to two engines on one side of the aircraft. If two engines on one side were on fire, aeronautical control over the plane was almost immediately put out of action.

I first attacked (in the manner described above) the bomber on the left position of the flight, then the one on the right and lastly the leading B-24 of the flight. I then pulled up in a steep turn and, while flying over them, observed them going down, spinning, burning, and the breaking off of wings in the area of the burning engines.

The film from my gun cameras showed the downing, demonstrating in an appalling way the location of the hits and the effect of the shots on the three aircraft. The most devastating damage was done by the two MK 108 39mm guns. I opened up aerial combat by first firing the two 13mm machine guns, then the two 20mm guns, and between less than 400 meters and ramming distance, with all six guns firing off short bursts.

On 28 September 1944, I again took off against penetrating US bombers in their mission to Kassel. I downed, in the usual manner, two Boeing B-17 Fortress bombers. Subsequent aerial combat with Lockheed Lightning P-38 fighters was without results.

Werner Vorberg

This account is reprinted from the 8th Air Force News of January 1989. It was translated by Donald Mathie of Boardman High School in Boardman, Ohio. The translation was arranged by Tom Reto of the 466th Bomb Group

At a meeting of the Fighter Pilots' association on 7 September 1988 in Geisenheim, Germany, I met a number of comrades who had participated in the air battle of 27 September 1944. In long conversations we attempted to call back to memory the events of 44 years ago.

The storm group of the 4th fighter squadron had suffered devastating losses during their first engagements on the 11th and 13th of September 1944 with the more than 30-fold superiority of the Americans. We had already lost 38 of the original 44 pilots, including the commander. The 6th as well as the 8th squadrons were out of commission for the engagement because only two pilots were available. The 5th squadron was again filled to full strength through replacements; the 7th squadron had the remaining pilots of the 6th and the 8th squadron added to their wretched number of five pilots.

Thus with great effort, we had finally scratched together twenty fighters that took off in two squadrons from Welzow. The 1st and 3rd groups of the squadron, equipped with ME-109 G10s under the command of Major Michalski, took over the duty of protecting the clumsy Rammbock 190 A8R2s from above. They also led the group through the cloud cover, with repeated course changes, to combat altitude of 23,000 to 26,000 feet.

It is without a doubt to the merit of the fighter officers of the 1st fighter division that they knew how to set our course, so that we did not run into Mustangs and Thunderbolts accompanying the stream of bombers. We reached our targets unscratched, because we were well prepared by the uninterrupted information sent by radio.

The two units formed spearheads with the flight captain in the middle. This way, all members of the unit got a bomber in his sights. For us in the fight, there was no "half life insurance" of being covered by the unit leaders or by a watchdog, as we had learned and practiced at fighter pilot school. Every individual carried the same risk but also had the same chance for success. There was only the spearhead – a storm attack according to the model of the infantry.

The defensive fire of the four-engine bomber, a seemingly impenetrable barrage, was broken through recklessly, and, as ordered, only from the attack distance of 650 to 1,000 feet and only after the four motors of the bomber filled the target circle of the reflex sight, did we open fire with our six weapons, in which the 3cm ammunition of the machine guns had the most effective results.

A miss of the giant monster was almost impossible at this short distance, from which one could recognize clearly the faces of the gunners in their firing positions above, below and on all sides and in the tail. Whoever was not shot down had success. Within minutes the terrifying, weapon-filled bombers stood in bright flame, ablaze, burning, bursting apart, losing wings, debris and entire engines, with which some attackers collided.

In hordes, crew abandoned their bombers. In a few minutes, the two units had swept the massive stream of bombers from the sky and by diving away cleared themselves from the area of the battle. Then the American P-51 escort fighters appeared. Our unit failed in the attempt to re-form.

On my return to Welzow, a wheel along with its shot-up support fell off when I let down my landing gear. I had to land on my belly.

More than half of those who had started out were missing. The 7th squadron, with its borrowed crews, was wiped out. The 5th squadron came away much better off. They must have broken off before the Mustangs and Thunderbolts appeared.

As far as one can draw conclusions from the crash sites of the downed planes, the greater part of the storm fighters' losses were probably due to the defensive fire of the bombers, which also the numerous engine hits on the returning machines proved. Only individual pilots were wiped out by the American escort fighters on the flight home. In an air battle with them, the awkward FW-190 A8R2 was unequivocally inferior.

Now the American reader of this report may ask himself, *Why German pilots at so late a time in the war were still ready for such deadly engagements with such high losses?* He who has ever experienced how, literally, everything from mouse to man was eradicated in the residential section of the inner cities of Germany from the Rhine to Dresden, he who has seen from above the terrifying saturation bombing and firestorms, only he will understand the reason for our rush into deadly engagements.

Chapter 19: Ace in a Day

Bob Volkman

We rarely got under a bomber, or even in close, because the gunners were flak happy, shooter happy, and if you have to get close to a bomber, don't go in with your nose pointing at one, come in alongside, slide in slow, because if you get too close, you're gonna get shot down by an American bomber.

On this particular day, we had joined the bombers. Vic Bocquin was leading the squadron. Bob Bain was No. 3 and I don't remember who No. 2 was. I was No. 4.

All of a sudden, Vic Bocquin says over the radio, "The bombers are being hit. Drop tanks." I had a little trouble getting rid of my tanks. By the time I got rid of them, they had all disappeared. There was a cloud layer below us at about 12,000 feet, and it wasn't very thick. So everybody went through those clouds.

What was happening, these Focke-Wulfs and Messerschmitts were hitting the bombers and then heading for home, and they were all headed east. And the bombers that were hit had gone off course in a northerly area, and they were behind us.

When I got under the clouds I saw two airplanes, a Focke-Wulf 190 and a P-51 chasing it. So the rule is, if you're by yourself, you've lost your group, join up with somebody as his wing man, protect him, keep him from being shot down. And that almost happened a little later on. So I joined the P-51 that was chasing the Focke-Wulf 190 and the Focke-Wulf 190, the first thing he does, he sees some high tension wires, and he flies under them. He hopes that Beyer and I will fly into them, which we didn't. A few seconds later, he turns his flaps. Full flaps down, in hopes that we would overshoot him. He must have been pretty smart. If we both overshoot him, then he's on our ass. But we dumped our flaps and we stayed right on his tail. And then he decided he was gonna belly in. And Beyer and I still feel sick about this. He started to skid across the ground. There was a house out there with a tree. He went right in between them. Big ball of flames. There were people in the house, and the people got killed. I knew the pilot was killed. And Beyer, the first time it came up, he said, "Don't give anybody my address." This is 19 years ago [around 1990]. We both had it on our mind. I might have killed a lot of civilians. I really should have taken half-credit, but he claimed he got five that day.

And then another Focke-Wulf 190 comes down out of the clouds. They all seemed to be heading east after they attacked the bombers. Beyer gets on his tail. He bails out. The plane crashes. And then it happens another time. So I was with him to see one, two, three, and later on he said he got two more.

After the third one, another drops down and he's between Beyer and me. And he starts to make a sharp turn, like he's gonna come around on our tail. I rack my airplane. And my combat film shows 140 hits on him. They gave me credit for it. But at the same time, I went into a high speed stall. I'm not more than 1,500 or 2,000 feet off the ground. I didn't realize it at the time, all I remember is I've got to recover from this stall. When you do a high speed stall, you lose lift. Not only that, you have the recoil from six machine guns going off. I was able to recover, and by that time this plane, I don't know if he bailed out or what happened, but then I see another Focke-Wulf 190 and he's got two Mustangs chasing him. I was able to see the numbers on both airplanes. The first one was Bocquin, and the second was Bob Bain, and this guy was heading east, too.

You know, they talk about engines and how fast you can go, that Focke-Wulf 190 outran the two P-51s. So I joined them as the third fighter. That was my original flight. I joined them, and the Focke-Wulf 190 went out of sight. Now maybe we didn't have enough gas, we were were pretty low. So the three of us broke off the chase and we headed due west and we landed. All three of us were almost out of gasoline. Full throttle for 20 or 45 minutes. So we land in a field near Amiens, in France, it's almost due west of Kassel, and we got gasoline, then we came back to England. But two things I remember about that. When I landed, I looked, and I really racked that airplane around, it's a wonder I didn't die. I didn't have a lot of altitude to recover from the high-speed stall. So I really racked the airplane around, and I got out, and I look at the airplane and there's drop, drop, drop coming out from the radiator.

By that time Vic had gotten out of his airplane, and I said, "I don't know what that is."

He said, "Take your finger and taste it. If it's ethylene glycol it's sweet." That's the liquid they used to cool the engine. It wasn't a lot, but if I'm losing coolant, I don't want to leave the airplane there. When we got our gas, the three of us took off.

And I remember there was a wrecked school bus there. I walked over to look at it, and it had a sign, "Rauchen verboten." Smoking forbidden. So I learned two things there: I learned what ethylene glycol was and what it tasted like, and I learned a couple words of German.

David P. Overholt
This account is reprinted from the 8th Air Force News

On 27 September 1944 I was flying Titus Blue, No. 3 position, with Leo H. Lamb on my wing, flying No. 4 position. I looked at the bombers and saw about six FW-190s go through the bombers and head for the deck. I saw one bomber explode and two others catch fire and fall out of the formation.

I called in the bandits and broke (at 18,000 feet) to the right and down. Lamb broke with me and Blue 1 and 2 followed me down as cover with Red Flight behind us. We went through the overcast with tops at 7,000 feet. I made no turn in the overcast. Lamb was with me before going through the overcast. When I broke out in the clear, I could see only one of the bandits and nothing of Lamb.

Over the R/T I heard someone calling for help. I believe it was Lamb. He said he had more than he could handle. While he was calling, I could hear his guns firing over the R/T.

I couldn't gain on that FW-190 so I broke off. I heard no more from that man that called for help.

The above statement is contained in Missing Air Crew Report #9243. German records also in that MACR file indicate that Lamb was killed in a crash at 1145 hours (German time) 300 meters north of Siebleben, near Gotha, in Thuringia. The crash was brought about, according to the report, by the ramming of a FW-190. Lamb was buried on 28 September in Gotha Community Cemetery V, III, Division, Field IIb, No. 50, left. The German report also included the comment that "a film container was saved and is being forwarded to the Evaluation Point West at Oberursel."

Chapter 20: A Wing and a Prayer

John Cadden

At our briefing that morning they announced that they had captured Brussels, and they captured it with the runways intact, so if anybody had mechanical problems or battle damage, instead of heading for Switzerland or Sweden, which was the practice up until then, we should try to make it to Brussels. It's never been brought out but it's influential in the story of our crew because after the battle damage we were all set to bail out. We didn't think we could get back to England, so we headed for Brussels.

My first indication of the battle – as a radio operator I was not in the top turret at that time – over the target and for a while afterwards the engineer took over the top turret and the radio operator operated the bomb bay doors. After the all-clear we would close the bomb bay doors and come back and monitor the radio for any messages that might come in. I had done all that after we dropped our bombs. The first indication we were being hit by fighters was from the waist gunners on the intercom, and you could feel the bullets whizzing through the fuselage. They both reported the Focke-Wulf 190s as I recall attacking, and our tail gunner, Henry Puto, was hit. Apparently he was hit right from the very start and knocked out of his turret. He had wounds to his face and to his legs. We didn't know where; we just knew he was wounded at that time.

We had lost one engine, and Stanley Krivik, the pilot, managed to get it feathered, but we had no oil pressure in another engine. So he alerted me to go down and open the bomb bay doors. He didn't say we're going to bail out but I knew that's the reason he wanted to open the bomb bay doors. I went down, and I was about halfway through opening the bomb bay doors when bullets started to whiz around the bomb bay. And that's the last I remember. I got knocked out. I don't know how long I was out, because I woke up by the nose wheel, which is farther away from where I should have been.

When I woke up, I was off my oxygen tank. I had the portable oxygen tank with me. I was off that, and I'd lost my helmet, and my head was buzzing. I didn't know what was going on. I gathered my senses. The first thing I went for was the bottle of oxygen, and I got back on the oxygen. Then I started to look around for my helmet. I picked up my helmet, and it had been hit. It's a steel helmet with the hinges on either side for the earflaps because of the earphones we wore, and it apparently hit just about where the hinge was and took the hinge off and made a big crease right through the helmet, by my right ear. That explained why my head was buzzing. But I wasn't bleeding.

The bomb bay doors were half open, so I went back to them. The firing had ended by that time. I went back to open them up again, and they're halfway open but there was no power. We'd lost all our hydraulic fluid. So I cranked them open manually, which takes a little bit longer. But I got them open. I went back up to the pilot and told him I had the bomb bay doors open. He was in conference with the navigator at that time, his name was Dale. And they were deciding where to go and what to do. They thought they couldn't maintain altitude but at the rate we were losing altitude we thought we could make Brussels, so he told me to go back down and close the bomb bay doors and get the wounded up on the flight deck where they'd be warm. By that time the tail gunner and both waist gunners were wounded.

When I first came up on the flight deck to report to Krivik that I had the bomb bay doors open, he looked like saw a ghost. His eyes opened wide and his jaw dropped. I don't remember much about the reaction from Dale. About a week later in the hospital Krivik came over to see me; he was in the same hospital. I said, "You had the funniest look on your face."

He said, "You were covered with hydraulic fluid, and I thought it was blood. I couldn't imagine somebody losing that much blood."

After I closed the bomb bay doors again, I'd say maybe we flew almost an hour, but gradually losing altitude. We were still heading towards Brussels. And when we thought we were close enough, we thought we'd drop down below the ceiling and look on the ground; you could pick up rivers and things like that. And when we came through the overcast, there was nothing below us but water. We were about 2,000 feet, no higher, and nothing below us but water. Everybody was surprised at that point.

In the meantime, as the radio operator I was the medical fellow on board. I had the first aid kit and I was supposed to administer whatever first aid I could.

All the time we were flying towards Brussels we had the wounded up on the flight deck and I had broken out the first aid kit. Bob Paul, one waist gunner, was wounded, but he was able to treat himself. He helped himself to the sulfa drugs and bandaged himself up, and the same thing with Bill Rand, the other waist gunner, he was able to take care of himself. Henry Puto was hit a little more seriously. He was in a lot more pain. I tended to his wounds as best I could. I gave him a shot of morphine. I remember giving him the shot because at those high altitudes you couldn't pull his pants down and give it to him in the leg, you had to go right through his flying suit. Heated suit and all. I gave him a shot of morphine, and it quieted him down.

And then, really, I had nothing to do until we discovered we were over water. Dale and Krivik had a hasty conference. They assumed that we were over the North Sea, which was a correct assumption, and if we just keep heading west we'd hit England. Which we did. But in the meantime, we stripped the plane of anything that could be stripped out of it. The guns. Ammo. Anything we had was stripped and dumped in the ocean.

I was in constant touch with air-sea rescue. I'd give them an SOS and a signal and they'd plot our course in case we did go down, they'd come out and get us. And I remember it so clearly because while I was in touch with air-sea rescue, the rest of the crew was trying to throw the radio out and I had to fight them off. If you're going to go down in the water, I'd like to have somebody coming after me.

When we got down around 1,200 or 1,000 feet, not much higher, we came over England, and immediately Krivik noted where we were. It wasn't far from where we'd normally come in.

He then headed for the air base, with his course set on the runway. Of course, at the sight of land everybody cheered. And I guess Krivik thought he could get it down on the runway. We didn't have any hydraulic fluid or brakes so we'd probably run off the end of the runway but that was better than bailing out. We didn't have much altitude left, 800 or 1,000 feet.

The big thing then was to get the wheels cranked down, and we had no problem with the main landing gear. It came down and locked in place. But we couldn't get the nose wheel locked in place.

At that time, everybody who didn't belong on the flight deck went back to the waist to get ready for a crash landing, including the navigator. The radio operator and the engineer stayed up with the pilot and co-pilot. We all had positions we'd take to brace ourselves for the crash. Mine was behind the co-pilot.

I don't think we were much more than 500 feet off the runway when Bugalecki finally got the nose wheel locked and he came up, and I thought – everybody thought, I guess – I thought he was liable to be down there when we landed and he'd get crushed.

So we felt pretty good. Braced for the crash. We knew it would crash. And next – there's a little window by the radio set, when you're back behind the co-pilot on the left hand side of the fuselage down by your knee and I was looking at whatever scenery you could see going by, and all I could see were trees. I had never noticed trees on our approaches before to the runway. All I could see was trees, and the next thing I knew, Krivik was pulling me out of the wreckage.

In the hospital, he came over to see how I was doing, probably the same day that he told me that when he saw me covered with hydraulic fluid he thought it was blood. He said when he got down to the runway, he could see it was covered with lorries and British wreckers. He didn't say how many. He said "lorries," though, not just one, it was several. And he said he didn't want to kill everybody on the runway so he had to overshoot it. He couldn't get back up and go around. He had to keep going, and he overshot the runway and crashed. He crashed in a farm. And when I was in the hospital, when Krivik came over and we were talking about everything, I asked him, "Gee, I thought we were gonna at least hit the runway before anything happened."

He said, "I couldn't put it down on the runway because it was shut down for maintenance."

I remember seeing the trees, but I don't remember anything beyond that. And the next thing I knew I was in the wreckage. I could see the sky, but there was stuff all on top of me, on my legs. Everything was on fire. I don't think we had much gas but there had to be some gas, and there's still .50-caliber bullets. I'd thought we threw them all out but they were going off all over the place from the heat. Plus I was in one of these fur-lined suits. I think I would have had a lot of severe burns if I wasn't. I was hot, but it protected me from being burned. I didn't inhale any fumes because it was wide open. I was looking at the sky.

I was conscious at the time, and I heard Krivik pulling Trotta out. I think he took him out seat and all. Krivik was probably the strongest person I ever saw. He was a bull. Matter of fact, I don't think many pilots could have kept that plane in the air, because he had no hydraulic fluid, and you had to be pretty strong to handle that thing without hydraulic fluid, and he flew it all the way back that way.

He pulled out Trotta, and then I heard somebody yelling that "Cadden and Bugalecki are still in there!" So he came back in and grabbed me and yanked me out and got me away from the plane. And I took about two steps and fell. Then he went back for Bugalecki. I think at this time that Bugalecki was half out but he wasn't out yet, and he pulled Bugalecki out. So I was very happy I was flying with Krivik that day.

The gunners landed all over the field. I guess what happened is the waist gunners and the tail gunner and the navigator and the nose turret gunner, they set up a net in back of the fuselage, across the fuselage, and they lean into that so when the crash comes they're braced by the net, they won't go flying up into the wreckage. And I guess everybody but Dale took advantage of that during the crash. He just acted as though it was going to be a normal landing, and he just sat down on the floor of the plane, and I guess when the plane crashed it broke in the middle and they all flew clear of the plane, and ended up scattered on the field with no injuries, really. Dale ended up going into the bomb bay, and he got killed.

He was the navigator. He was new, too, he had only flown two or three missions with us. We trained with a fellow by the name of Jackson. He had gone to Reg Miner's crew. He never hit it off well with Krivik. As enlisted men we were not aware of the friction between the officers. I knew there was some friction, but most of the enlisted men loved Krivik, because he took care of us and looked after us. I guess Jackson managed to get off the crew, and we got Dale as his replacement.

Paul Pouliot

After a while I got out of my seat to inspect the damage (the interphone had been out from the first). In the bomb bay gasoline was leaking badly. Our main tanks must have been hit, and gas was coming from the seams. The fuel-transfer pump was out and the cross feed leaked badly. Kribs told me he thought the self-sealing line would plug itself up, so there was some hope of saving gas. I went past the bays back into the waist. The boys had had a rough time there, and the sides of the ship looked like an old-fashioned potato grater. (Later we counted 70 holes.) George Noorigian, the bombardier, was on the right waist gun and Harry Wheaton was on the left. They gave me a slight grin but not the usual smile. Both remained at their guns and were on the watch for more fighters.

I noticed the broken oxygen bottles and George told me that when the bottles were hit the waist got full of white smoke. One of the 20 mms had exploded in a box beside George, and only the stout box sides had saved the boys from shrapnel. George told me how he had been practically sitting on the floor trying to get a fighter that was coming in high, when a 20-mm shell came through and missed his rear by about four inches.

I went to see the tail gunner, Harry Lied. He smiled a little and said he was all right, although he had been without oxygen for five minutes during the battle. I noticed the tail was shaking badly. Next I went forward to the nose to talk to Milton Fandler, the navigator. Everything was all right there, and he was figuring the shortest way home for us. After spending a few minutes with him, I went back to the cockpit. We passed Isom's ship to let him know that we were going to another field. Milton put his head up into the astrodome and made some queer motions. I caught on that he meant that we were over the Channel and should keep that heading to reach an emergency field.

Two P-51 Mustangs offered to see us in, but we signaled that it was unnecessary. We let down below a layer of clouds and saw England in front of us and the field ahead. It was really a beautiful job of navigation.

We had to use all the emergency procedures to get the wheels down and to lower the flaps. Kribs, the engineer, checked everything. One wheel refused to lock until Jack snapped the ship slightly to one side. We made a normal approach, Jack using the ailerons and elevators and I the automatic pilot with which we had to to control the rudders. The landing came out very smoothly, and we taxied to a waiting jeep. Then out of the plane to get down on hands and knees and kiss old mother earth.

A survey of the battle damage showed how much of a wreck the plane really was; to top everything off, we discovered that we had a 20-mm shell in the No. 2 gas tank. If it hadn't been a dud and failed to explode, we'd never have come back.

Bennett, the radio operator, brought out a little box that had dropped down from somewhere and hit him during the flight. He had picked it up and discovered it was a New Testament. We found out later it belonged to one of the ground crew armorers who had left it on the flight deck, but Bennett kept it to take along on his next mission. The boys went over the battle. In all our score was a total of seven fighters destroyed and one probable. Ted got two, Kribs got one, George one and one probable, Wheaton accounted for two, and Lied, one. If the whole crew hadn't really been on the ball we wouldn't be back. They didn't talk much. What we had seen was getting on their nerves. We called our home field to tell them we were all right.

Jack Mercer

Pouliot and Kribs reported that the crew was "all shook up" but OK – nobody hurt. Lied had no oxygen in the tail turret so he had gotten out of the turret and connected to another outlet which permitted him to stand just outside the turret and maintain a lookout.

As for damage – we knew we had no rudder controls, no radios, no hydraulic pressure, low oxygen and the No. 2 engine was running very rough. Kribs and Pouliot found a major leak in the bomb bay cross feed (gas transfer valves) along with a hydraulic leak. Kribs cranked open the bomb bay doors about a foot to reduce the danger of explosion and fire, and warned each crew member about no smoking. He said the waist and tail sections looked like a sieve from shrapnel damage, and jokingly told of a 20-mm shell that exploded in a box of chaff which was stacked immediately behind George Noorigian on the floor with no damage.

Both Kribs and Pouliot were concerned about the amount of gas we were losing, and could not make an estimate of how much flight time we could expect.

As soon as we got this information I asked Paul to go down to the navigator's table and ask Milton Fandler for a course to an RAF emergency field at Manston, England. I knew a route to Manston would put us over friendly territory quicker than a course direct to our home base, giving us a better opportunity to get on the ground safely if we ran out of gas or some other emergency developed. I also liked the idea of Manston's 12,000-foot runway over an up-and-down terrain for a "no flaps, no brakes landing," and that they were well equipped for emergency landings.

We increased power to catch up with Isom to let him know we were OK even if we could not contact him by radio – just to wave and say "bye." Since we needed to get to lower altitudes soon because of the low oxygen supply, we began letting down at 500 and then 300 feet per minute. This enabled us to increase our airspeed considerably and then to throttle back to save fuel. I didn't want to feather No. 2 thinking we might just need that little bit of additional power in any further emergency, but we did throttle No. 2 back further and reduced the RPMs to reduce the vibrations to a minimum.

After a suspenseful two-plus hours on needles and pins (at least in the cockpit) about the condition of the ship, we all let out a big cheer when Milton poked his head up in the celestial navigation bubble and made swimming motions – we had no trouble interpreting that we were over the English Channel. At that time we were down to 3,500 feet just above a layer of broken clouds. And then a sight to behold when we broke through the low clouds – there were the cliffs of Dover and beyond lay the long runway at Manston. Milton had done his job well – Manston right on the button.

With help from Wheaton, Kribs began cranking the main gear down, then kicked the nose wheel out. We did not get a "green light" on the instrument panel that the gear was locked, and could not tell for sure with our visual check. As we circled the field once for landing we tried to shake the gear into a locked position by wiggling the wings but still no "green light." The crew prepared for a crash landing.

Successful landing? You bet! Paul worked the autopilot rudder control to assist in lining up and the landing was almost normal except for the excessive speed required for a "no flap" landing. Touchdown was relatively smooth, and when we rolled to a virtual stop we found there was sufficient pressure in the brake accumulators to set the brakes one final time. We all knew we were very lucky and that someone had been looking over us, but were even more reassured when a small Bible fell on Bob Bennett when we touched down. We later learned one of the ground crew kept the Bible in a small space in the radio equipment on the flight deck so he could read it in his spare time. Needless to say – he didn't get the Bible back. Bennett appropriated it.

Battle damage? Maintenance records from the Manston Repair Depot covered more than six full pages – over 300 items. Over 275 shrapnel holes in the waist and tail sections (90 percent on the left side), damage to approximately 45 percent of the stringers in the waist. A 20-mm dud in the No. 2 gas tank, a six inch by half-inch sliver off the trailing edge of one No. 2 prop blade, severed rudder cables, shattered elevator cables, damage to the gasoline transfer system and gas lines in the bomb bay, shrapnel in both main tires, replaced No. 2 engine and prop, replaced left vertical stabilizer and rudder, replaced left horizontal stabilizer and elevator, replaced left bomb bay door, etc.

We were so happy just to be on the ground safely we didn't even gripe about our overnight stay in an RAF billet awaiting transportation back to Tibenham. Not that we particularly liked the evening meal of "boiled mutton," two small potatoes, three small tomatoes, a slice of dark bread (tasted like sawdust) and some awful English tea. Breakfast was just as bad.

Only upon our return to Tibenham about noon the next day did we learn the gory details of Kassel, and that we had not hit our assigned target of Kassel but dropped our bombs about 30 miles NE close to the town of Goettingen. All of these terrible losses just because the lead navigators and bombardiers apparently misread their radar scopes which were used for navigation since the mission was flown above an overcast. Their navigational errors placed our return route from the target to England virtually over at least five German fighter bases in the vicinity of Eisenach.

To me, the highlights of this mission include: 1) The excellent performance of each crew member operating under conditions for which we were not trained, i.e. how to operate without intercoms during air battles, emergencies, etc. 2) The difficulties of operating effectively on the flight deck while wearing oxygen masks with no intercom. When you need help you need to tell someone what you need. 3) On a personal basis I felt badly that I couldn't keep each crew member personally advised of our minute-to-minute situation, particularly regarding the condition of the airplane while we were in such a precarious situation both during the attack but even more while en route to Manston in a flying time bomb. It was their lives in jeopardy and they needed to know where we stood at all times. 4) Crew members were credited with five kills and two probables. And best of all, the next day after returning to Tibenham I was informed we would have to fly only 30 missions – one more for me and two for most of the crew. Good news for a 21-year-old newlywed.

One more than then home!!!!!

Crew members: Pilot – Jackson C. Mercer; co-pilot – Leo Paul Pouliot; Navigator – Milton Fandler; Bombardier – George Noorigian; Flight engineer – Kenneth Kribs; Radio operator – Robert Bennett; Tail Gunner – Harry Lied; Waist Gunner – Harry Wheaton; Nose Gunner – Ted Hoiten; Waist gunner – Donald Selway (not flying this mission).

Bill Dewey

I was busy trying to fly the plane, as it was shaking and shuddering. I had to make a decision now: Were we going to make it back across the Channel or North Sea or are we going to ditch possibly, or is it better to crash land in France? So that's when I called – we had four channels, very high frequency channels, Channel A was our squadron frequency, Channel B was for command between the various groups and wings and division, Channel C was for fighters, Channel D was for distress – so I turned to Channel D and called Colgate. That was the code sign for Air Sea Rescue in England, and I identified our plane and our problem.

Colgate told me to give them a long count so that they could vector in on our plane. I gave them ten ... nine ... eight ... seven ... six ... five, so forth, and they gave me a heading toward Manston, south of London, on the White Cliffs of Dover. And they asked me to check in every fifteen minutes. We were still two hours into the Continent, and in the meantime we were trying to do the best we could with our crew, take care of them, and after about an hour and a half, two hours, we dropped down through the clouds. We were gradually losing altitude, and it seemed like we were going to be okay, we were gonna make it across the Channel.

We dropped down through the clouds, and there was that beautiful runway, 12,000 feet, just over the White Cliffs of Dover. To see that runway was the most beautiful sight in the world. And the miraculous thing was that the No. 3 engine was the one that had the hydraulic pumps, and yet everything worked perfectly. The gear came down and locked, the flaps came down 20 degrees and then full flaps just before we touched down, and with that long runway how could you help but make a nice landing with fully inflated tires?

With all that firepower not one of those tires had been perforated. It was amazing. But when we taxied in finally and got out, there was a 9th Air Force photographer there, and he'd evidently been taking pictures of 9th Air Force planes. The 9th Air Force had been transferred to the Continent, but they still brought their damaged planes back to Manston when they were all shot up, B-25s, A-26s, P-47s, whatever, if they were shot up, they were directed back to Manston, which had a long runway, if they could make it. He was there taking pictures of 9th Air Force planes but he saw our plane and had never seen a plane so shot up, so he asked Boykin and Bailey and myself if we'd go back and act as if we were just coming out of the plane again, so he took a movie of us. And some stills. I never got his name. I don't know what happened to the pictures.

When I got out, that's when I got shaky. I was okay until I took a look and saw that huge hole in front of the right waist, and all the holes in the side of the plane, and then walked back and looked at that tail. The rudders were as if two giant can openers had been taken to the trailing edge. They were just shattered. There was nothing there. So it was the rear end of the plane that was really in bad shape. The upper surface of the right wing was the only one that I can recall had taken any damage. We were okay in the front completely, as compared to Paul Swofford in the Sweetest Rose of Texas whose windshield was completely shot out.

Paul Swofford

The problem was, we knew that we were going to have to crank our gear down by hand. We knew we had to crank the flaps down. But the flaps weren't as critical as the gear, because the gear puts tremendous drag on the plane when you're flying on three engines. We had been descending, and we had descended almost to traffic altitude by the time we got to the base. We've got the base straight ahead. We've got to get that gear down.

All right. It's locked in place. I have no radio. I can't call the tower and say "I'm out here, get everything ready for me." And then we've got to get the flaps down, because with flaps it slows your landing speed. We got the gear down. We got full flaps. And I had said to my co-pilot and engineer, "I don't care if we land in the grass, we've got no brakes. We've got to get on the ground. We don't have time to make a normal traffic pattern. I see the base. Whatever I see, I'm gonna land on."

I didn't care if it was a runway or what it was. Well, here I get down to a hundred feet. We've got everything under control. And they started shooting red flares from the control tower. I never saw so many red flares in my life. Because I wasn't landing on a runway. I was landing on a taxiway. And do you know, those SOBs up there, with no radio communication – the group commander should have been up there in the tower telling them – you don't send anybody back – but they waved me off. I was lined up on the taxi strip. It was dangerous, but I don't care how many airplanes we hit. The lives of my crew were important.

There were no planes on the taxi strip, they were parked on the sides. But they waved me off at my own base on three engines, back from a combat mission, knowing that everybody was shot to pieces. It wasn't just the engine. Everything was shot. All systems. Radio. Empanage. We had holes all through us. Only one man had an injured leg. They waved me off. It's 55 years, I still get angry. You don't ignore red flares. You don't ignore them.

I didn't know what was ahead, but what the group commander is saying is, "You can go and crash on the outside but you'd better not land here." I still had maybe fifty feet. Maybe fifty feet. Full power. So I yelled to my engineer, "Start cranking the gear up. Crank it up and crank it fast! We need full throttle!" And we came right down but I didn't touch down. He got the gear up. He managed. We'd already crossed the field boundary, just brushing the treetops. Three engines. Gear down. Flaps down. You can't do it. But the engineer managed to get the gear up. That was the important one. You can leave the flaps down but you've got to get the gear up, because that's a drag you can't compensate for. And when he told me he had the gear up, it was a sigh of relief to me and to my co-pilot. We went straight ahead and I tried to get some altitude. I could get to a hundred feet maybe. And then I told the engineer, "Start lifting the flaps up slowly. Do it by hand."

He managed to get the flaps up. And we might have gotten to 200 feet, but I know we didn't get any higher. And when you make traffic patterns in a military aircraft, all traffic patterns are counterclockwise. You always make a left, rectangular traffic pattern. You fly a base leg, a downwind leg, left turn onto the base leg, it's always a left turn. My bad engine was on the left side. It wants to droop anyway. You're in a terrible fix. But we managed. So I said to my crew, "Now we've got to crank that gear down again." I said, "Watch for the wind sock. See which way the wind is blowing, and we'll pick the runway, and get the runway this time, it's into the wind."

We moved off a few miles so that I could get headed straight in. Then I got the engineer to crank that gear down, and then get those flaps down. And I was able to land right at the end of the runway. And with no brakes, that airplane just rolled as straight as a die right down the middle of that runway, but there's nothing I could do except pull the power back, let the nose fall down, roll straight. And we knew it was going off, but fortunately, we had slowed down to just a few miles an hour by the time we reached the end of the runway and went straight off the end of the runway.

I could have landed on that taxi strip. It was dangerous I know, but that was a case where you didn't do things by the book. What you have to do is save the crew. To hell with the airplane. Any airplanes on the ground, to hell with them. The crew's what's important. But we got that on the ground, right off the end of the runway, and the airplane sinks down and it stopped pretty quick when it got off in the soft ground. But only after I got out and was talking to some of the people, that's the first time I learned that we'd lost all those airplanes. I had no idea what had happened. I thought they were just kind of scattered.

My crew performed admirably. My engineer's dead now, he lived down in Key West and he and his wife died in an automobile accident about three years ago. And my co-pilot was a chemist after the war with the Firestone Rubber Company in Akron, and he died in 1987. But those two were my right arms. But that engineer, by doing all of that work that he did, and thus able to keep an airplane on three engines going around – I never would say I deserved any medal or whatever, but I would say that my engineer and my co-pilot deserved recognition, that never came. We never got any recognition, not one atom. Never heard one word from the group commander, from our operations officer, no one, absolutely no one said one word. If we'd all piled up and have been killed they'd have given us a Purple Heart. That's a tremendous job, cranking those gears down. Those gears weigh thousands of pounds. And he had to get them down and lock them in position, and then crank them back up and wait till we get around there and do it again. It's an extremely difficult job to fly an airplane that's crippled like that, trying to get your nine man crew down on the ground safely. But having said all of that, it should never have happened. But we got back.

It was said that any crew going into action over there during the war with the 8th Air Force, flying 35 missions was impossible. Every time you went out there was a certain chance that you wouldn't come back. You can look at the 35 missions that my crew flew. We probably lost at least a hundred airplanes. Well, that airplane that went down on each mission, that could have been mine. So you have on any mission you go out over enemy territory, and you're exposed to enemy fire and enemy ground attack firing at you, or something mechanical happening to your airplane, or you're running into some midair collision, you get your gas tank shot out, get your oxygen system shot out and you've got to drop down to low altitude, there are so many things that can happen on each mission that the odds of anyone going over there and flying 35 missions and coming home without any injuries were very heavily against you.

Jack French

The navigator, Timms, gave us a heading toward Rheims, and as we got over that way we spotted a P-47 base. We were low enough at that point to be able to determine what was going on on the ground, and it was a P-47 base we found out they had just flown their very first mission from and were returning to, and we let down and circled the base. We had fair control of the airplane, so we circled and made a downwind leg and shot off some red flares, and they gave us a green one, so we came in and made the approach and put down what flaps we could, and of course the gear would freefall, but we never got the nose wheel out. The engineer went down and tried to push it out but he couldn't get it to go out, so we got him back up out of the nose.

We were coming down on final approach, but we didn't obviously have an awful lot of control of the ailerons and rudder, we didn't have any rudder control to speak of, but we landed and I held the nose up as long as I could because I knew what was going to happen with no nose wheel, so we held it off as long as we could, and finally just lost all kinds of control. And I tried to kick it off the side of the runway; there wasn't anything over there but dirt. It wasn't really a runway. It was one where they put down grates on the ground, that's all it was. So when the nose came down I tried to steer it off where they were using for a runway and I didn't get it all the way off; unfortunately, the back end of the airplane was still sticking out. But we got out of that thing. We were just darn fortunate that when the nose came down we didn't get lots of sparks because we would have gone sky high with all that gas.

Where the guys got off I don't know; they got out of the back. We must have gotten out the escape hatch overhead in the cockpit, those of us who were up front, and jumped down off the nose. Then we got away from the airplane until we were sure enough that it wasn't gonna blow, because that's what our first thought was, and there wasn't much else after that.

After we settled down a bit and looked the airplane over, it was pretty well shot up. The wings were full of holes. The rudder was gone. Anywhere you looked in that airplane you could see through the other side. Why nobody got hit I have no idea. You could stand there and look up through that airplane and you could see right up through, anywhere. I just don't understand how nobody got even a scratch. Not a scratch. Not even on the landing. Then when we finally got up to the headquarters building there, they called Tibenham and told them that we were there, and Tibenham wouldn't believe them. They said, "No, that isn't them because they got shot down. We have nine witnesses that that airplane went down."

They said, "No, they're here."

And later on, I forget whether it was later that afternoon or the next morning, it must have been later that afternoon, things run together a lot at this point, the radio operator that we had was pretty sharp, and he went back to the airplane and somehow or other, he rigged up something and he called the base, and he told them where we were. They finally believed him. They sent an airplane over and picked up other people around. We got back to the base, it seems to me it was the next day, and we went to the usual long briefing. Then we didn't do much of anything. Our missions were over.

We hung around for a while at the base. I did a little formation when the new boys came in, because they flew a Kassel mission the next day. But as the new crews came in, they had fellows like myself kind of initiate the guys to the new deal of wartime flying, formation flying and that sort of thing as instructor pilots for a while, because there was almost nobody left there that had been on several missions. So for the first couple of times I didn't go on missions, but we'd go up and I'd explain formation flying and staying close and that sort of thing. But I didn't stay there very long.

Herb Schwartz

We all got a little relieved feeling when we heard a bunch of shots. Pilot called back and asked who was firing their guns. We called back and told him it was flak. Our ship was too battered up to put the ship into evasive action. We were only at 13,000 and by some luck we received only a few holes. We knew now that we were lost and knew not where we were. About this time a P-38 came in about 20 feet off our left wing. We could not radio him so we motioned with our hands as best as possible.

Fiske, our radio man, started to flash the signal "Can we land here?" And just as he flashed the words "Can we" the P-38 pilot pointed his fingers down and peeled away. We figured that it was friendly territory, but still were not sure. Pilot asked Timms again where we were, and we discovered that Timms' compass was broken but pilot's compass was working all right.

Timms was directing pilot and both compasses had different readings. Only way we could hope to locate ourselves would be to lower beneath the clouds, and so we pulled down to 8,000 feet. We were pretty sure we were in Belgium and we knew that a large airfield was located on the outside of this city. So our next problem was to get to Brussels. Gas was running very low and even by pointing out rivers and railroad tracks we could not affix our position. From time we believed ourselves to have left Germany, we figured we finally flew 1 hour and 20 minutes before discovering a suitable landing place.

Every town we passed was left in ruins by our dive bombers, and we knew now where our planes had been going. We spotted a dirt landing strip with a wrecked FW-190 on it. We circled the field to land, but French didn't want to land on the field as he figured it was too short for a B-24 to land. We continued on looking for Brussels.

After a while, Timms popped up and said he thought St. Quentin was only 50 miles to the left of our course. We had carried groceries from England to this St. Quentin airfield. We charted our course for St. Quentin. After a 30-minute flight we spotted an airfield which had a fairly long landing strip, and we decided to bring her in. We noticed about 75 Thunderbolts on the field so we knew it was a friendly field.

We gunners, by the way, all the time were in the rear trying to spot a field and help the navigator spot places that might appear on his maps. French told Greenly and Timms to hurry to the flight deck as we were going to land and could not afford to circle the field. Greenly and Timms hurried up and Greenly told pilot his nose wheel was not in the "down" position. We had already checked the main gears and we reported them secured in the down position. French said it was too late to kick her down so we came in.

I removed my Mae West and parachute and braced my body as we expected a rough landing. We were mostly worried about the gas within the ship igniting when we hit the ground, and, if so, we would have blown up. We landed a beautiful landing; and ship fell to the ground, and nose fell down.

While ship was still sliding a little, I jumped 8 feet from the camera hatch and started to run as I was still afraid she would blow up. Greenly and Timms jumped out of the top hatch and ran down top of the ship before props had even stopped. I could have kissed the ground, I was so happy and wringing wet with perspiration. Major came over to me and first question asked was "How many injured?" When I told him no one, he stood there in amazement. Everyone complimented French on the landing. It was a remarkable job, but I can honestly say I had full faith in him. About 500 of the field's personnel were out there and they questioned us until a major picked us up and took us to chow.

Before I continue about our experiences on the field, I want to tell the feats of the other men. All the ships accounted for shot down were done by the men in the rear of the ship: Corman, left waist, knocked down 3; Huddleston got one and one "probable." Corman got one ship that came up from the bottom and when he made his breakaway, he got him. I, at this time, wanted to be in my original position, "the Sperry ball," but when enemy pilots saw turret was removed, they made attacks at our belly. Another FW had come in about 40 yards off our left wing, and let his ammo go at the lead ship which our C.O., Major McCoy, was flying. He got McCoy as French saw two of his propellers flying through mid-air.

Let's hope Major McCoy will rest in peace with a satisfied conscience. He was a real pilot. Corman's third feat was one of the FWs I missed and he got him on the breakaway. Huddleston's feat and "probable" were both breakaways from my tail. Our navigator verified these ships as he said that he lost count of the burning ships he saw go down. He was more scared than any of us and I could hear him tell Greenly over interphone – "steady boy."

Our radio man, also unarmed, was going through fits. Heitz, whom I first believed to be flying off our ring wing, was one of the crews that returned safely. I could have sworn he was shot down, but thank God he wasn't. Three of his men, Palm, Watson and Ochesky, were wounded. This being my original crew, I took particular interest in them. Louis Ochesky was wounded severely, receiving wounds in the left shoulder and right leg. Drake tried to quiet him with morphine but he went into hysterics. Palm was hit in the leg – Dr. pronouncing it broken; and Watson, who was only man in crew who got credit for a fighter, was blown clear out of his turret and wounded in the back. He stamped the fire out, however, and might have saved the entire crew. They landed in Brussels. Mack stayed with the wounded in Belgium and rest of the crew returned to the field.

Going back to our landing in France, we came down near Rheims – Metz – and come to find out we were in Southern France instead of near St. Quentin. There were many things that ran thru my mind while in the air. But thinking I was going to be a POW, I looked to see that I was wearing my dog tags, that my parachute was all right, that I should only give my name, rank and serial number in case I was captured.

Timms told me on the ground that he saw five men fly past his window and he felt like waving at them. After dinner at this field we radioed our field to tell them we were safe and stayed at the ship as we planned to sleep in the ship that night. We were kept quite busy as everyone came out to the ship and questioned us until I got a headache. They had kicked the nose wheel out and moved the ship off the runway. The body was all sprung and skin wrinkled from one end to the other. I don't believe she will ever fly again safely even if she is repaired.

At 12:00, MPs picked us up at the ship and took us to their quarters for coffee. Everyone treated us like kings. They wanted to give us a jeep to go to Rheims – wanted to fix us up with girls. This was all well and good, but I was so tired I couldn't move. Our officers were taken to the club and returned the next morning with several bottles of champagne. This particular field was where some of the famous World War I battles were fought and some of the old trenches still prevailed. Food was good and everyone went out of their way to treat us nicely. We took souvenirs from wrecked German FW-190, Me-109 and Heinkel IIIs.

We retired at 1:30 having not had sleep in 23 hours. Greenly, Corman and I slept in back, and though I was as tired as I could possibly be, I couldn't sleep thinking about our bombers with my friends in them on fire. Many of our boys are POW and damn glad to be such. I know I would have been. I got out of bed after laying there for 6 hours and woke up all the boys for chow. At 10:00 a ship from 96th Wing picked us up and took us back to our base. Elmer Caulk, an old schoolmate of mine, by coincidence was navigator on this ship.

We landed, but before we left the ship we all noticed that the ships on our base were all brand new ones. We knew something was wrong. I saw Hines, crew chief of 4F (166) and he told me we lost 32 ships out of 36 and 27 crews. Four ships aborted. This was the most sickening news I have ever heard. One ship from our squadron returned, and none from 702 squadron. [Author's note: The Krivik crew from the 702nd made it back to England, although it crash-landed about five miles from Tibenham.] Four crews from our squadron got back. These without their ships: Heitz, Hunter, French, our departing lead returned. Brainard, my old co-pilot; Abraham, my old navigator, and Panconi my waist gunner, were lost and as yet have not been heard from. We were the only group hit by fighters. This day 42 lost in all; rest going to flak. 8th Air Force has sent us all new ships and we already have replacements. Bruce and Heitz's crew from our barracks are not here. Two new crews have entered our quarters.

John Tarber, friend of mine, is reported missing. He was to become a father in the next week or two. We proceeded to operation and everyone was anxious to know about our experience. We were questioned by several officers before returning to our lockers to change clothing. We then went to S-2 where we were interrogated very closely and made our claims for enemy fighters. Major complimented us all and said only reason why we got back is because we gunners did such a good job of shooting. When asked by the Major if I was scared, I told him that upon landing in France, I had to defecate but when I got to latrine, all I did was wipe. He was satisfied then. Men in my barracks had taken all my clothes, but put personal things in a bag. They returned all my clothing and I got settled again.

When I walked in, the boys all thought they were seeing things as we were reported down. I thank God every chance possible for bringing us back. Few boys got back. I can honestly say that our base looked beautiful to me. I went over to see some of my friends and had long talk with Lt. Heitz and crew. They were happy to see me, but they weren't nearly as happy as I was.

George Spera
(This account was written by Staff Sgt. Thomas G. Spera, who flew as a photo observer in Terrible Terry's Terror. It was written in late September of 1944, shortly after Spera's return to Tibenham.)

We were one of 10 crews out of 35 to get through a bitter battle fought recently in the air four miles above Kassel, Germany. It all happened after we had dropped our bombs. Up until that time, I had chalked up the mission as a "milk run." Then suddenly all hell broke loose, and the interphone was busy with urgent voices calling out formations of Focke-Wulf 190s. From my station in the waist, I could see the air full of exploding shells being lobbed at us. Then they came right through our formation. In less time than it takes to tell, the sky was full of debris from exploding ships.

The leading Liberator, on fire from nose to tail, came swinging toward us like a severely wounded animal, then peeled away as if to pick a spot away from us to die. The next bomber moved up in its place. Then we were hit ourselves. A 20-millimeter shell tore through the bomb bay, ripping off the doors and severing fuel lines. Two fires started simultaneously in the bay. What strange mystery of fate kept us from exploding I'll never be able to fathom. The engineer, Technical Sergeant Robert N. Ratchford, Gastonia, N.C., threw off his parachute, grabbed a fire extinguisher, and put both fires out before the 100-octane gas had been ignited. Then he attended to the leaks from which fuel was pouring out like water from a fire hydrant. Gasoline had saturated the three of us in the ship's waist, and we all had a difficult time moving about. The two waist gunners were slipping and sliding as they sighted their guns. A large bubble of gasoline accumulated on the camera hatch blown in by the slipstream outside.

Things were happening so fast that it's hard for me to relate the events in any form of sequence. The Liberator with the engines on fire on the left wing came up from below us to explode after it had reached our level. A human form fell out of the orange colored ball of fire. As he fell through space without parachute or harness, he reached up as if to grasp at something.

In our ship, a bullet from a Focke-Wulf probably saved my life. My oxygen mask had become disconnected, and before I realized it, I was losing consciousness. A 20-millimeter shell came through the waist above the head of the waist gunner, Staff Sgt. Joseph M. Selser, Germantown, Pa., and caused Staff Sgt. Robert J. Cannon, 14300 Maiden Ave., Detroit, Mich., to look around from his position at the right waist gun, notice my trouble, and connect the oxygen line again.

I gained consciousness to find the battle continuing. Seconds seemed like hours, minutes like days. Enemy fighters came rolling through the formation so close that one could almost see the color of the fighter pilot's eyes. One FW who seemed to hang by his propeller only a few yards off our left wing was riddled by fire from our top turret guns, manned by Staff Sgt. Robert W. Sarber, 1012 Beaver Avenue, Pittsburgh, Pa. Another kill was made by Staff Sgt. Fred C. Schaffer Jr., 3203 Spring Garden Avenue, Pittsburgh.

One wave of fighters followed another, until after six minutes the attacks ceased as suddenly as they had started. Where there had been four squadrons of bombers before, now 10 ships were all we could see. Those who could closed in as if for company on the three-hour flight back to England. (We later learned that three of them landed in France, three crash-landed in England, and only four made it back to the home field where those on the ground waited in vain for planes to find their way back.)

Despite the loss of one engine, our ship managed to keep in contact with the others for a while. When the navigator, 2nd Lt. Robert H. Kaerns, 1502 South Denoms Street, Tulsa, Oklahoma, informed us that we had reached friendly lines, the sickening feeling relaxed its hold in the pit of my stomach but left a muddy taste in my mouth. It proved impossible to stay with the other bombers for long, and an escort of P-51 Mustangs picked us up in answer to a call from Technical Sgt. Jake S. Monzingo, Minden, Louisiana, the radio operator.

We were approaching a landing field in northern France when the second engine on our left wing cut out, and a third engine spit and sputtered. Those of us in the waist rushed to crash landing positions in the nick of time. Loss of a second engine had made it impossible to reach the landing strip, and our pilot, 1st Lt. William F. Hunter, Essex Junction, Vermont, cleared a clump of trees by inches, clipped a set of high tension wires, and brought the ship down on a potato patch, skillfully jumping several ditches, only to have one wheel catch in a hole, buckle, and dig the right wheel into the ground. We all took a severe bouncing, but our only casualty was a cut hand for the bombardier, 2nd Lt. George E. Smith, 7000 Ozark Avenue, Chicago.

Civilians from a nearby town were hesitant at first, but once they recognized us as Americans, stopped at nothing to make us comfortable. We were invited to their homes to wash and eat. Hot coffee and gifts of beer, champagne and wine were presented to us. Elderly folks brought us fruit and gave it to their youngsters, urging them ahead to offer it to us.

The friendly welcome was marred only by the disappearance of my aerial camera with pictures of the battle. The French police and half the crowd that had gathered set out in pursuit of it, and succeeded in retrieving it from a man who claimed it had been given him as a souvenir. He was promptly handcuffed and led away as the crowd jeered "Boche!" at him and made motions as if to cut his throat. They applauded us enthusiastically, kissed us and shook our hands.

Toward evening, we were on our way to an RAF base, leaving Terrible Terry's Terror under the guard of English soldiers. Weariness had dulled our realization of the day's tragedy. We left France still marveling to find ourselves alive.

(Lieutenant Hunter's crew eventually became a lead crew, and was transferred to the 389th Bomb Group. On a raid to Munster in March of 1945, they were shot down by a direct flak burst in the wing fuel tanks. The entire ship was engulfed in flames immediately. Only Fred Schaffer, the tail gunner, and a recently assigned radar man, Lt. Howard Hoestery, were able to escape the plane. Both were badly burned. So perished the heroic crew of Lt. Hunter.)

George Noorigian

Finally we got fighter support and then the Luftwaffe got the hell away. And we didn't know whether we'd have to dump the plane or not. One bomb went into the gas tank and all that hundred octane gas was leaking into the bomb bay. It's a good thing nobody smoked. There's one thing about our crew – nobody smokes on the plane. I had to take someone else's place one time on a mission, and the guys in the back are puffing cigarettes at altitude. I didn't say anything. That's a hell of a thing, they were on oxygen.

After that, there were just two planes flying, where normally we'd have ten or twelve in our squadron. The lead plane, they never shot him down. So they told the lead plane we're gonna stop at Manston, because we had a lot of damage and we didn't know how much gas we have. And at Manston you could land a plane any way. The runways were just as wide as they were long. It was a British base, right beyond the White Cliffs of Dover. Do you know why they call them the White Cliffs of Dover?

Aaron Elson

No.

George Noorigian

All the pigeons that roost on it. (Author's note: He's kidding. I think.)

When we came in for the landing, we didn't know what the hell was going to happen, because they shot out the hydraulic system, and we didn't know how much brake we had. But they had just enough brake to stop the plane. It came in, and boy, we watched the thing coming down. We were in back, and he did a nice job of it, coming in, Mercer. He and Pouliot, because you had to have two guys up there, not just one. We came in on wheels, but they had to hand crank them down. And finally we came in to the landing, and boy, they had the fire department following us. They didn't know what the hell was gonna happen.

Finally the plane stopped. Boy, I got out of that plane. It's the first time I ever kissed the ground. Honest to Christ, just to be on the ground. And you should have seen the mess. We had so many bullet holes, and that one hole on the side, and oh, Jesus, the tail was … and that was almost a new plane. See, normally people think that when you go over there in combat they issue you a new plane. You don't get a new plane until you fly about 16 or 17 missions. What they do, the old planes that were flying, you had to take one of the old planes. And a number of times in the beginning when we had the old plane, we had trouble with the plane and had to come back. But it wasn't until the 16th or 17th mission that we were assigned a plane. And the plane we were assigned had a problem with the engines, so they gave us a new plane. And what a mess. It's too bad in a way we couldn't go back to our base. I wanted them to see the plane the way it was. They never did see it at the base.

Gene Crandall

You know, after we lost all these airplanes on this raid, the next day we had 31 brand new airplanes. And I thought to myself, thank God for the civilians that are building this stuff. And I guess Ford built them so fast that they had to slow him down because he

224

was making one an hour. As far as I know about B-24s, any airplane that was built by Ford we could take the tail section off of any Ford plane and put it right there on another, everything was a perfect fit.

I think the civilians did as much to win the war as we did. Because one time we had a bunch of construction guys screwing around with our runway and they spilled crushed rock all over the ground, and we had to ground all our airplanes because they were running over these damn crushed rocks. And within 36 hours, airplanes were arriving with loads of tires. And the people in the United States were really getting it together.

Paul Dickerson

Paul Dickerson was a waist gunner on the Isom crew, one of four crews that made it back to the base at Tibenham. He sent this account to Bill Dewey, who published it in the Kassel Mission Reports.

Everything seemed to go as briefed until bombs away plus about 15 minutes. We made our final turn and were headed for home. Raymond Phillips, our tail gunner, called out fighters at 6 o'clock high. They seemed to be headed our way.

In waves of ten and fifteen, FW-190s poured in on us. Machine guns were firing … everywhere B-24s, Me-109s and FW-190s were falling. Some were blazing, some were smoking, and some were blown to bits. The air was full of parachutes, pandemonium reigned! A German with a black parachute drifted by our right waist window. Bill Wagner took a bead on him, then looked at me. I said, "No," and Wagner let him drift by. An Me-109 drifted up on our left wing. I could see the pilot plainly. He was that close. One burst and I had him. Ray Phillips, the tail gunner, got one FW-190, as did Art Shay (riding in the nose turret) and Wagner. Kyle Bailey, top turret gunner, got two FW-190s.

Then all was quiet. We waited for the kill. We knew that we could last no longer. We were dead men and we knew it. By now there remained only about seven of the original formation. Three of the seven were too crippled to fight back. We were helpless and hopeless.

But the Germans didn't come back. There wasn't much left of them either. Then we saw the most beautiful sight and we knew then why the Germans had not come. The sight of our fighters was unmistakable. Of course there wasn't much to rescue. At 1000 hours we were a squadron of ten. At 1006 we were a squadron of two.

The trauma, this lifetime, this eternity lasted only five minutes.

When we returned to our base we found the plane in front of us firing red flares for an emergency landing. There were injured aboard.

The tower wanted to know where the rest of the group was. They wanted to know why we were alone and asking for landing instructions. We told them that WE WERE THE GROUP. By the time we landed and were getting our gear from the plane, we were surrounded by MPs. We were told not to talk to anyone. They whisked us off to a debriefing room and locked us up. We were asked question after question, as if they were trying to catch us in some kind of lie.

Colonel Jimmy Stewart arrived from Wing and took charge of the meeting. Since he was a veteran of many combat missions and had led us on missions, he was aware of what could happen and seemed to understand as he calmed the meeting and listened intently.

It was time for the evening meal when we were told we could leave the debriefing. When we went to the chow hall, where food had been prepared for several hundred, there were only about two dozen of us that went to eat. Again there was disbelief when we told them that we were all that was left. Our meal was a quiet solemn one in that big empty chow hall. No one was talking.

Things were quiet in our almost empty hut. God only knows why we were there.

The next day we sat quietly and watched them inventory and remove the belongings of those who did not return. We were more stunned than before, as we realized that they were really gone – that they would not be back.

On the 28th the 445th put up ten planes on a return trip to Kassel. Our plane, "Patty Girl," was the only plane from the previous day's mission to Kassel that was airborne for this mission. We didn't fly it.

Yes … war is Hell!

Chapter 21: Terrorfliegers

Peter Belitsos

I came down on a farm and was surrounded by German farmers, men and women, who had watched me on the way down. Except for a very old man who punched me a few times, I was not harmed. The local constables came and walked me a short distance to a small town. I was placed in a local lockup of what appeared to be a home. The lockup was a small room with brick walls and a heavy wooden door with a small opening that was barred. A wooden bunk was attached to the wall.

The next morning I was taken upstairs into a room filled with people, some of whom looked official. A woman gave me an apple which was the only food I had since taking off from England. After a while a young German soldier in a uniform with Afrika Corps insignia came in. His legs appeared to be permanently damaged and useless. Everyone looked stern and spoke in low tones. No one addressed me. I was afraid that they might take some retaliatory action, but they did not.

I was then taken outside, handed my parachute to carry, and led down a street. I was joined by one and then another POW carrying their chutes. We were given orders not to speak and walked for most of the morning to a railroad station. I remember that the parachute became heavy to carry. We were taken to the main interrogation center, where we stayed two or three days. From there we were taken by train to Barth by the North Sea. The train was filled with New Zealanders who were captured in the battle for the Arnhem Bridge.

Ira Weinstein

I walked into a town and I looked like Murder Incorporated because our plane was on fire, I was covered with soot, and I hadn't shaved for a week. And I'm walking through the center of town and a kid about 17 years old sidles up alongside of me and says, "You're one of the American flyers they're looking for, aren't you?"

I said "Yeah. How come you speak such good English?"

He said, "I went to high school in Milwaukee."

I said, "What's going to happen to me?"

He said, "I'll take you to the burgomeister."

He took me to the burgomeister, and the burgomeister's wife gave me a bowl of potato soup, and that was the best thing I ever ate.

There was an SS battalion in that area, and the burgomeister said, "If I turn you over to them, you're going to be dead. So if you don't try and run away, I'll call the Luftwaffe and they can come and get you." About two hours later, two guys in beautiful Luftwaffe uniforms showed up, and they took me to a little garrison. They threw me in this room; there were maybe 20 other guys in it. George Collar was one of them. There were two badly wounded enlisted men, and I was the ranking officer.

These two guys had had no medical attention, and don't ask me why I did this or how, but I was always cocky. I got hold of the guard, and told him I want to see the commanding officer. So he took me in. And it would have been a joke if I wasn't so scared, but that guy looked just like Erich Von Stroheim, remember him? First I saluted him, and I gave my name, rank and serial number, and I said, "Sir, according to the Geneva Convention, we have two very badly wounded men. They're entitled to some medical care."

He came out from behind his desk with a riding crop, and he hit me across the cheek. And he said, "I'll tell you about the Geneva Convention. You're bombing out schools and our churches and you're killing our people and blah blah blah." Then he told the guard to take me away, and I went back to the room. About two hours later they came and took the two injured men away.

After you flew enough missions you thought you knew all the tricks, and one of them was that the electric shoes on the planes hardly ever worked properly. So I'd put on two or three pairs of heavy woolen socks, and then I'd put my flying boots over them. That way my feet were pretty warm.

When I bailed out, my flying boots came off. I was running around in the forest for a couple of days with no shoes. But I cut a piece of my flying suit and made a pair of moccasins. I used the electrical wires that were in the flying suit to tie them on.

So now I'm in this little room they had us in. Pretty soon the guard comes and says, "Kommen Sie mit Mir," and he takes me back to the commandant's office. My parents never spoke Yiddish, but my grandparents did when they didn't want us to know what was going on. So I knew a little bit. But a little bit of knowledge is dangerous. This is what I think I heard the commandant say to the guard: "Take him out and schussen him." That means Take him out and get him a pair of shoes. What I heard was schissen, which means take him out and shoot him. So this guy marches me out of the little barracks we were in into the compound, and about 50 yards ahead of me there's a gate. I thought if this asshole's gonna shoot me, he's gonna shoot me in the back, because I'm gonna make a run for it when I get to that gate.

Maybe 25 yards from the gate was another little room. He took me in there and got me a pair of shoes. That's how close I came to being killed that time, let alone getting out of the airplane or in the battle.

Sammy Weiner

I landed at the edge of a clearing and immediately picked up the chute and hid it along with my helmet and goggles in a nearby brush. Just before hitting the ground I had espied another chute floating into the forest directly ahead. I must know who it was. There was a small house in the distance but seeing no sign of human life I boldly started to cross the clearing. Halfway across, an Me-109 buzzed the ground around me and I hit the dirt fast. I remembered too late the briefing to go around a clearing instead of the way I had so unwittingly chosen. The Jerry had evidently only wanted to signal my position for he did not return. I quickly got to my feet again and started for the forest, when I saw two figures three hundred yards away. They had seen me too and were motioning me toward them. I studied the men intently for a few moments and from that distance I could have sworn they resembled two members of my crew.

I had not gone more than a third of the way when I realized my mistake. There was no turning back now. As I approached closer I perceived one was a tall, burly man with small eyes placed closely together under bushy eyebrows; the other was short and stocky with a heavy mustache predominant on his pimply face.

Their garb was tattered and not too clean. However, they appeared friendly enough, as the tall one spoke:

"Englander?"

I shook my head.

"Americana?"

I nodded. They conversed between themselves in German and then motioned for me to follow them. They led me to a farm house in a hurried secretive manner. Thinking I might be in the hands of the underground I went submissively. I was still dazed from my miraculous escape and my throat was dry and parched.

I did not have long to ponder on German hospitality for upon our arrival at the house the tall man grabbed a double barreled shotgun and threateningly pointed it at me. He then marched me to a small congregation that had assembled around the wreckage of my ship. A German officer was already there. He began shouting at me in loud, staccato, German monosyllables. Perhaps, he thought, if he yelled loud enough, I would be bound to understand his questions. I understood enough of his language to know he was asking me about the plane, our base, and what happened to the remaining crew, but I kept shrugging my shoulders, and shaking my head, "I don't understand."

I saw the bodies of two of my buddies in the wreckage. It made my stomach turn upside down, but gritting my teeth, I stood, bewildered and dubious of my own fate, giving a silent prayer for my two friends. The scene will be imprinted on my memory forever.

The officer shouted some order and vanished. After much conversing in German among the farmers, an old man insisted upon being my personal guard. He kept talking to me slowly in his guttural tongue until I finally made out that he was asking me for news of his son who was a prisoner in Texas. "A young man like you," he kept saying.

My leg was still bleeding and I was beginning to feel faint. Suddenly I realized I had had no food all day, except for the cup of coffee at three that morning. It seemed like such a long time ago. I lay on the ground for hours, and then was locked in a small, broken-down shed in the rear of my guard's house.

Alone at last, I began to take stock of my ramshackle surroundings and plan my escape. I looked around in the semi-darkness and my heart jumped with hope when I grasped the wooden handle of a hammer. Quickly replacing it, I then felt my way to the rear of the shed. The large boards could easily be pried open. I lay down to wait for nightfall with high prospects for a successful break.

It was not long, however, before the old man returned, bringing with him his wife and small child. The woman gave me a small square of dark stale bread, a nip of cheese, a hot cup of ersatz and a pear. It was a grand feast to me and I thanked her effusively. The child began to cry hysterically when she saw me, and I can't say I blame her because I must have looked an awesome sight with my dirty, unshaven, burned face and long hair draping over my forehead. They soon left me to my own troubled thoughts. The day was an endless one.

About five-thirty my guard returned, accompanied this time by a German intelligence officer. They marched me down the street to another house where here again a crowd had assembled. A young German girl stepped out of the crowd to act as interpreter for the officer. She was plump as a dumpling with a pleasant chubby face and an infectious laugh. The questioning began:

"What kind of plane; how many engines; how many men in the crew; how many bailed out, etc.?"

She giggled foolishly after each question and each of my replies, "I can't answer that." The officer looked on in disgust. Her eyes opened with awe when I remarked my home was Hollywood. Becoming bolder, I said, "You're kind of cute." She burst into a fit of laughter, ending the interrogation.

As I sat on the ground, I looked up to see a familiar uniform advancing toward me under guard. I drew a long breath, overwhelmed with relief at the sight of a friendly face. He was a first lieutenant, a pilot of one of the planes that had bombed Kassel that morning.

Our guards were to accompany us on foot to a town twelve kilometers away. At first they kept the lieutenant and me walking at a considerable distance apart, but after the first hour we had decreased the distance enough to talk to each other in pidgin English. It was four hours before we met five military police of the Luftwaffe. Thus for the first time the lieutenant and I were officially prisoners of war.

Glen McCormick

As I descended in my parachute and was nearing the ground, I saw many chutes already on the ground. It was obvious that several airplanes were downed in this immediate area. The general area from my vantage point may be described as a small village with a railroad passing through the eastern part of the village. Just east of the railroad there was a small river approximately 15-20 meters wide. Then further east of the river the terrain changed abruptly into a wooded bluff. This bluff rose rather sharply – I landed in this wooded area. At the foot of this bluff (on the village side), there was a secondary road. There was a bridge crossing the river and this was located basically northeast of the village

If I may interrupt the train of thought – I was to learn later through a contact I made just two years ago – the village is Neustadt and the river is the Werra. Neustadt is just inside the border between East and West Germany.

Further west of the village there was an autobahn with a large curve that turned in a southerly direction. During my scouting, I did not see any traffic whatsoever on the autobahn. That appeared to me as a good place to start my journey from the area.

Above the bluff or further to the east, the wooded area cleared and the ground was fairly level. At that time, the field was used for growing potatoes. Also, between the secondary road at the foot of the bluff and the river there was another field of potatoes. This is where I dug some potatoes and put them in the lining of my flight jacket. I still had some when I was captured.

After dark, I crossed the bridge over the Werra and made my way to the autobahn. I started walking on the autobahn in a southerly direction. I hadn't walked too long before I passed another village east of the road. I was to learn later that this was the village of Gerstungen.

After passing that village, I left the autobahn and went into the forest. By that time, I was extremely tired and needed to rest. It had been a long, long day! I slept until noon the following day. Rather than going back to the autobahn at night, I stayed in the forest and headed in a westerly direction.

If I may interrupt again, I would like to mention a human interest story. On the afternoon of the 27th, I was scouting the area and I came across a small lean-to made from small branches and limbs. This was obviously a project of a young lad. I know because I built one very similar as a youngster. This appeared to be a good place to spend the time waiting for darkness. As I waited, I could hear voices and the sound of horses and a wagon. I checked on this on the topside of the bluff and found that there were women digging potatoes. In late afternoon, I heard the wagon go by, evidently going home. The edge of the woods was a scant 15 feet from the shelter I had borrowed. After the wagon passed, I heard someone approaching. It was a small boy about 8-9 years of age who was probably checking on his secret retreat. I stepped from the shelter and said "hi." When he saw who I was, his jaw dropped and his eyes got as big as saucers! He took off on a dead run and needless to say I did too.

This was my first eye to eye contact with a German citizen!

Now back to my trek through the woods. I walked generally at night and slept or rested during the day. One day, I spent the daytime hours in an old fire watchers' tower. A civilian was plowing a field with a horse-drawn plough (single horse and single bottom plough) and every time he made a round he would pass right below me. Wouldn't he be surprised to know he was being watched. Another day, I holed up in a pile of timbers that had been stacked for drying. I heard voices and it was three older women in the forest picking up small limbs and branches. One of them passed within 30 feet of my little home. Again, wouldn't she have been surprised!

After being loose for several days, I started gaining confidence, and on the day I was captured I had been walking in the daytime. I was in heavy forest and walked in fire lanes and had not seen anyone all day long. I came to a valley containing a small village. To get a closer look to decide how I would cross the valley after dark, I was working my way closer. I came to a clearing and rather than taking the long way around in the woods I started across the clearing. I had not gone more than 50 feet or so when someone shouted at me. Discretion won out over valor and I stopped. A soldier and a civilian came up to me. The civilian had a bicycle with a rack of some sort built on it. I suspect that they were in the woods to get them a deer. They took me to Bebra and we arrived well after dark.

The village I was scouting when captured was Weiterode and I was caught about one kilometer south of Friedrichshutte and just west of the road leading to Friedrichshutte.

Frank Bertram

I landed in the trees, and we really received no training as far as parachuting that I can recall. I tried to manipulate the chute when I was coming down, and on the way down I saw a fighter plane in the distance coming closer and I thought, "Oh, boy, what's this?" As it turns out it was an FW-190 and he went by me – maybe a couple of hundred yards – and he waved to me, and he kept right on going east.

I was going east too, because the wind was very strong, west to east, so I thought "My god, I'll probably drift to Russia." I probably drifted four or five miles farther than if I'd held my pull string another five or six minutes, as some of the guys did.

As I came down I could see there was a lot of beautiful green and I saw some little villages, and I could see these woods, and I thought, "Oh, boy, I'm gonna hit those trees just sure as hell," and I did. I tried to manipulate into a little meadow nearby, but no way, I couldn't budge that chute. And I hit the trees. I would say they were anywhere from 60 to 80 feet high. The chute spilled, and I tumbled straight down, right through the trees. And right now as I'm talking to you I can hear those branches snapping as I hit them. I hit the ground with such force that it knocked me out. I don't know how long I was out. But when I came to I couldn't move my legs or my back.

Now I'm panicked again. Here I am and there's branches of trees all around me, the chute's around me, my feet are killing me, and then all of a sudden the feeling is starting to come back. I start moving and pretty soon I could feel everything and I thought, "I'll see if I can roll over and get up," which I did, and oh, my feet are sore. My knees are sore. My back hurts. But particularly the ankles and feet.

Fortunately, all the branches and stuff on the ground had probably saved me from bad damage. But I'm really paying for it now.

So I start off. I gathered up the chute as best I could; Jesus, it was a struggle. I could hardly move my feet. I threw branches over the chute and I took off for the west. I didn't go 150 yards and I heard the damnedest noise. It sounded like a V-1 rocket, putt-putt-putt-putt, or a motorcycle. I could hear German voices real loud. I was walking down a forest road, and I ducked off the road and all of a sudden this truck was coming, an old, old, truck, and blowing smoke. I think they had a coal burner running it.

I dove, and I hurt my feet more from the movement I made, and got behind something where they couldn't see me. There were a bunch of German soldiers and civilians in there, and I thought, maybe they're on their way to work or something. Darn it, they were looking for me, I never even thought about that. I didn't think about that for fifty years, and then I realized those guys must have been looking for parachutes.

I kept marching a little more, and I was just dragging. One time I heard a very guttural sound, which you hear a lot of in Germany, and I thought, Oh man, I'm moving into an army camp, it's like a sergeant directing the troops, and I picked my way over through some trees, and down in a little valley I saw an airplane. I couldn't tell if it was a Messerschmitt or a Focke-Wulf, and then alongside, further away, there was some guy with his mules, there were horses plowing the ground, and he was yelling at the horses. I ignored that and went my merry way through the woods. I came to a point where there was a big, broad autobahn. It was getting dark so it was probably around 4 or 4:30 in the evening, so I had walked about three and a half hours at that point. I think our combat was about 11 o'clock.

Now I'm really hurting. I don't know what I'm doing. I'm scared. I'm getting real tired.

In Germany, they have these towers where hunters go up and they sit up there and they shoot the deer. So I slept under one of them that night, put a lot of branches over me, and damn near froze to death.

I got up the next morning and started hiking. I found some pieces of our airplanes that I recognized. I found a motor embedded in the ground, the propeller all bent up. I wondered what happened to all the guys. And I'm going from forest to forest, some were birch, some were beech and some were aspen, they're beautiful forests over there, and I'm thirsty. All of a sudden I come across a pool of water and it's dirty, but I had this escape kit that had this little deal in there with the pills and you mix with the water and they make it drinkable. So I'm down there on my knees, and all of a sudden I hear a noise. At this point I still have my gun, and I think, "Oh, Jesus Christ, if I'm caught with this thing," so I threw it away. Of course it couldn't do any good anyway, there's no bullets in it.

I'm frozen. I hear this noise getting closer and closer, and I'd just got the water put in this little tube where you put the pills in — all of a sudden out comes the biggest stag I'd ever seen. Big rack on him. He took one look at me and he split and I split. We both got out of each other's way, but it was just one of those little things that stay in your mind.

I kept on walking. Some of the trees were aspens, and they were so big and close together I had to go sideways to get through them. They weren't big in circumference, but they were close together. I'm going along, and as it turns out, I'm headed toward the Werra River, which I found out later.

As I go there, I hear an airplane, then I hear an explosion. And I look out. And on the other side of the river, here's trees going, and dust and dirt and wood and everything. The whole ground shook, and I thought, "My god, what happened?" I figured that a B-17 got its bombs hung up after a mission and came by and just dropped them right there. Toggled them out, and I thought, "My god, this is the most terrifying thing," although it was a mile away from me. I could have been over there. How can these people even survive a thing like this? And they went through this a thousand times worse than what this was, but it sure scared me.

Now I know I'm near the river so I'm staying in the woods, still being able to look out and see the river. So I follow this river to see where it goes. I'm going through the woods and here's a field; a farmer had just plowed and there's potatoes there, so I go out when nobody's looking, and I grab a whole bunch of potatoes. I must have had between 15 and 20 potatoes in my pants pockets. Then I'm going along a little further, and I see what looked like men with pickaxes hitting something and my first thought was, "My god, they've got one of our men up there and they're beating him to death." It was actually our lead ship that went down right in that area, that blew up. This is the plane that led us to this debacle.

I walked right by them. I presume that motor I found was off their ship. And I guess they were just chopping up the pieces that were left there. I went by the area and I went a little further and then all of a sudden I came to a beautiful valley. I'm looking down this valley and the river's over to my right, but a little creek comes off this river and goes to the left and there's a railroad track up there, and up the hill there's some more woods. So I thought, I'll lay low and go up through those woods, because I knew there was a town nearby; I don't know why I knew but I just felt there was.

Oh, in the meantime, let me tell you what happened. Even before I got to this point of seeing that deer, actually before I got to sleep the night before, I came to this autobahn I was mentioning and forgot to finish. It was about six lanes, and there's no traffic in either direction. So I start across, and I get halfway across — there was a section in the middle — and I hear a noise. And I look down in the distance on the right, and here come some lights. So I started to run, and I couldn't run because of my feet; I was just hobbling across the road, hoping they didn't see me, and they didn't. I fell into a ditch. And boy, they went zooming by. I thought, "Oh, man, this is nervewracking."

To continue my story, now I'm down in this valley. While I'm looking out at this valley, I hear another airplane and I hear explosions. I look up and see all these pieces flying down. What they turned out is, they were little letters sent in German, propaganda. And money. Counterfeit money. Great Britain and the United States decided if they couldn't ruin Germany with bombs they'd ruin their economy with phony money. So I laid low for a while, before I went across this little meadow, and then I decided, well, I'd better do it. So I went across. Then out of the corner of my eye – I'm about two-thirds of the way across – I see a movement. All of a sudden here's a bunch of kids. There was a little bridge there that went across the creek I was headed for and I knew I couldn't make that because I'd be out in the open, so I turned and went straight to the creek. And I got down behind a tree.

Because of the injury to my leg, I had to have one leg straightened out, and it was hanging in the water. I'm lying there the best I can behind this tree, and all of a sudden I look up and I see this one little kid. As it turns out it's Walter Hassenpflug. He looked down at me, and he doesn't know that I see him because I've got my eyes half-closed. He jumps up and runs back and he comes back with another kid, who turns out to be another good fellow, Willie Schmidt, who worked with Walter years later. Then they both split and they came back and there was a bunch of them; there were a couple of girls, real cute girls. As a matter of fact, years later I met one of them; her name was Rose Marie Neuman. But those girls were 15 and 16 at the time and most of the boys were younger. And there was a tall, thin fellow who came over and looked at me and he said, "Sir, are you hurt?" I didn't answer. I thought, "Oh, this is it. I'm dead." And he kept repeating, "Sir, are you hurt? May I help you?" In very broken English. And I finally said "Oh, yes. I'm hurt."

He said, "Let me help you up." He came down, he stuck out his hand and I grabbed it and he helped me up. Now all this time, all these kids are running around there, and they're oohing and aahing because they've probably never seen a guy with a four-day beard and hair standing straight up, beat up like I was. And all this time, I learned years later that up on the hill, a little further on, I saw an SS man up there, who was in charge of all these Hitler Youth, who were out picking up the pamphlets and phony money. And apparently this SS man could have caused a lot of trouble, but he just let them go on and do what they did and kept his nose out of it. Fortunately for me.

So this young gentleman that had me; this 18- or 19-year-old, said, "I'll have to take you to the authorities."

I said, "Yes, okay, I understand that."

And we walked across this little bridge and onto the railroad track, and maybe after 15 minutes walking, here come two fellows toward us, and they've got uniforms on that looked like major domos. I thought, "Holy mackerel! Is that Heinrich Himmler or Hitler himself coming to see me?" So I asked this guy, "What is this, Gestapo?" And he laughed.

He said, "No, no. Police. Police." And these two as they got there I could see they were older gentlemen, not quite my age today, but they were in their late sixties or early seventies. And very nice. They didn't speak any English. But they took me to a two-story house, and the lady of the house had a little baby and she fled, because the propaganda had it that Americans beat little children, or something to that effect that scared the hell out of her. I met that guy 40 years later, the little baby. He's not little any more, believe me. Bigger than I was. But they took me in and they interrogated me, and right across the street there was a house, and I heard them say a Dr. Blom is over there.

Pretty soon this fellow comes over, well-dressed, wearing a vest. He had a napkin tucked under his chin, and he was still chewing a sandwich he had finished. He introduced himself; said he was Dr. Blom. He spoke English perfectly, and he explained the situation, that he'd have to question me. I gave him my name, rank and serial number, and that was it. Then we talked for a while. It was very pleasant. Up to that point, it was more of a party, really, with these kids and everything. But they left, and these two policemen then said, "We have to take you into town." So they took me into this little town. I remember going into this jail, and there was a woman there, probably in her late twenties. And the policemen said, "We're going to put you in a cell and lock you up here."

They shoved me in a solitary cell with just a board with some straw on it, and I'm just dying. My back is killing me. They stripped me and took all my stuff away, emptied all my pockets, my shoes, everything. Down to my underwear. Then they let me put my things back on and dress up. I had a prayer book. And as we had intended that night to go out, I still had my navigator wings on, my first lieutenant bars. I had my nice green shirt on. I was hot to trot once we got back. So if they had any brains at all they knew that I was a navigator.

After 10 or 15 minutes in this cell I hear, "Pssst. Hey, Yank."

Up above my bed is a little window, and I hear a voice coming through: "Hey, Yank. Come up to the window."

I think, "They're not gonna get anything out of me, they're just trying to give me this phony stuff."

In the meantime – first, let me go back. Two civilians came and interviewed me, and they were downright nasty. Those are the guys that made me strip – of course the girl was out of the room – and they kept telling me that I was a sergeant, not a lieutenant. I would say "Nein. Nein, Oberleutnant, Oberleutnant." They were very solemn-faced, not at all like the two police officers, who were very nice. These guys were strictly business. I called one Mr. Moto. He looked like Peter Lorre. And the other one was Sidney Greenstreet. One was big and fat and the other was short and thin. Finally they left after getting all the information they could from me, which was nothing. I guess they went back to start the paperwork to get me out of there. That's when I heard these voices, and it was these two Englishmen. One said, "Hey, Yank, wait till those two civilians go. We'll cook you up some hot cocoa and cookies."

I thought, "What the hell is this?"

By god, about a half-hour later the door flies open and here's one of these police officers and these two other guys. It turns out they were two British officers who had escaped from their prison camp. One of them had been captured at Dunkirk. That means he was in his fourth year as a POW already, and the other one, as I recall, was captured in Norway, which is about the same time. And they were jolly fellows even though they were a little as we say around the bend.

They said that they had been free for three or four days and got captured and were just waiting for their guards to come get them and bring them back to their camp. Everything was done on the up and up in those days. The Germans had a certain system and that was it.

So these guys, sure enough, they hold out cocoa and start to make hot cocoa, and we had cookies that they had. They had all kinds of food which they had saved up for their escape, which was confiscated but given back to them, and they in turn gave it to me. They said, "Our guards are gonna be here tomorrow, they're gonna confiscate this stuff and take it away, so you take it." But in the meantime, everybody laughed because when they had examined me, I had all those potatoes in my pockets, so they took my potatoes away from me.

The two British guys gave me their names and addresses, but when they wrote them down they said, "Don't let anybody see it. If anyone's coming in, they'll confiscate it." And I ended up chewing on it and swallowing the paper when that young lady came into my cell. I woke up in the middle of the night, and the door flew open and she threw something on my chest, and here was my little baseball mitt. This young girl must have known it was a souvenir-good luck charm and wanted to see that I got it back, probably with the approval of the police officers. But they had it turned inside out. All the stuffing was hanging loose and I had to shove it back together. I still have it in front of me, hanging on the wall.

A few hours later, in the wee, wee hours of the morning, the door opened and a sergeant from the Luftwaffe came in. Tall, thin guy. He talked to the British officers because they could speak

German. And they explained to me that I would be taken to another place, and from there I'd go to a camp.

I remember walking down this cobblestone street with this sergeant, across an old stone bridge over the Werra River. There was a full moon and I can still see it reflecting off the water there. On the other side, we hopped into a car or a truck and then drove off, and he took me to a Luftwaffe camp. Guys were Heil Hitlering all over the place; everybody's saluting everybody.

He took me down to a barracks and I came into like a dungeon, and as I walked in and went down this hallway, lo and behold, coming toward me and being led by a guard was the navigator that was in Jim Schaen's ship, Corman Bean. We just looked at each other, never said a word. Didn't even blink an eye, like we never saw each other before. And here we had breakfasted that morning together. He got shoved in a cell and I got shoved in a cell. I have no recollection of how long it was before they came and they got me out, but pretty soon they took me outside and Corman Bean's there along with ten or fifteen others from the group.

We all were taken from there to a railroad station, and when we were standing at the railroad station we heard these guys talking marching, in German, eins, zvei, drei, vier, and here comes a whole bunch, maybe 35 guys, American, assorted sizes and shapes and guys beat up. I recognized some right away. George Collar was right in front. His face was swollen. His nose was broken. He had black eyes. They'd beat him up.

Now we sat down and we were taken from this railroad station and put in railroad cars. I remember one fellow, he had been a football player; we thought he had a broken back, but I guess he just had some broken bones, and he was in such misery. We're in this railroad car and it was moving, and boy, were these guys surprised – they were all pretty hungry – when I opened up my pockets and pulled out this food. It didn't last very long, but the little bit that there was was most welcome. There was some cheese, butter, powdered cocoa, crackers, probably spam too; I never could remember the names of those British boys.

The train took us to an interrogation center for all airmen in Oberursel, it was called Dulag Luft. And you go in one at a time to these inquisitors and they ask you, "What group are you with?" So you'd just give them the name, rank and serial number, and then they said to me, and probably to every other one, "Until you give us some more information you're just going to stay here in solitary." And you just shrug your shoulders and think, "They're not gonna keep us in solitary too long; there's too many of us because a lot of planes went down." Twenty-five planes over the target.

Also, what happened when this was taking place, at the same time the battle for the Bridge at Arnhem was going on. A complete Polish parachute regiment had been captured by the Germans and they were in Dulag Luft with us, but they were on the other side of the fence and the Germans were just meaner than hell with them. They didn't bother us too much, but they were using bayonets on these guys' fannies if they didn't double time, it was just terrible. I'd hate to have been a German when those Poles got loose because they were the toughest looking guys I've ever seen.

After about a day there, we were sent to Stalag Luft 1. We were shoved into a train that had compartments, six seats on each side and a luggage rack, so they put ten of us in each compartment and they gave us a Red Cross parcel each, which contained a week's rations.

It took six days to go 350 miles to our camp. We went through air raids. We'd pull off at sidings. They were strafing and bombing ahead and we had the heck scared out of us in Frankfurt. When we went through Frankfurt an air raid was coming on and they abandoned us and let us sit there at the siding. Fortunately they were B-17s, they couldn't hit the mark I guess.

We had a German guard on each end on the railroad car. I don't know how many cars we had but we did have a commanding officer, and he was Lieutenant Colonel McArdle, a British paratrooper, who was in charge of the operation at Arnhem. He had finally surrendered, because they were running out of ammunition and out of men. So consequently, there were a lot of paratroopers, and these were all officers – we were all officers headed for Stalag Luft 1 – so there's quite a few British officers from the paratroop regiments, and then us, plus others who had been shot down.

One of the fellows in my compartment was from the 15th Air Force; he was shot down in Italy on a B-25. His name was Richardson. He had been burned; the top half of one ear was burned and his hair was burned off, but he was jolly. He had a big bandage wrapped around his head. He had a few cuts and scabs from when he bailed out. Talk about walking wounded, we looked like a fife and drum corps. Everybody in different clothes, some with shoes, some without shoes. And you didn't know what's happening when you're going to a prison camp.

On the train, three guys would sleep sitting, two guys on the floor, and then the next night we would switch off. It was very uncomfortable. You didn't get much sleep. It's very demeaning. You're a prisoner of war. You've got two guys with guns at each end of the car glaring at you. You can't describe it unless you're there. And you never think about this when you're home until suddenly, bingo! You think of what happened. And the hard part is worrying about what happened to the other fellows. We didn't know what happened to Virgil Chima, the co-pilot, or Omick, or the enlisted men at that point other than Joe Gilfoil. We knew he was hit; they announced that when they threw him out of the plane, hoping his parachute would open and he would be treated on the ground. And we were misinformed by someone that he was okay. One of the enlisted men came up to us right after we were captured and said they managed to get a doctor which they didn't. George Collar ended up picking up his body.

Eugene George

I used to swim a lot, and when I came out of the airplane I was afraid I would hit some obstruction so my safest bet would be to get into a cannonball position. I didn't know whether I had a parachute or not. And there were three things. One, I'd been off of oxygen for quite a while and I wanted to get lower. Two, I knew there were a lot of German fighters in the area and chances are they wouldn't shoot someone in a parachute but I was afraid of getting rammed, or run into, by a fighter. We had been briefed on the fact that the Polish fighters in the RAF would have no hesitation shooting a German in a parachute and that the Germans would retaliate. And the other thing was, in training films we had a Navy character named Dilbert. He was a cartoon. He was a cadet, or a pilot, who goofed in every possible way. One of these cartoons showed Dilbert in a parachute with a target painted on his chest and a duck sitting on his head and a Japanese aircraft lining up his sights, and I had that vision, of Dilbert.

243

I was tumbling and in the cannonball position. I thought I'd better get out of that, and I stretched out into a swan dive. And I reached for my ripcord to see if everything was still there and I started spinning, so I got back in the swan dive.

There was solid cloud cover underneath me. I thought when I get into those clouds, I'll pull my ripcord.

I went right through the clouds, and I could see the ground. But I was still in a freefall situation, and I was curious as to whether I had a parachute or not, but actually, the swan dive situation, it's almost exhilarating. It was fun!

So I fell most of the 23,000 feet, and I pulled my ripcord, and I was jerked up into the proper parachute position. My parachute worked. That was the great news. And I was coming down on some trees, which I later found out were beech trees, and my canopy covered the top of a tree, and I was swinging in the tree.

I was kind of reconnoitering. I could hear an air raid siren, and I could hear impacts of aircraft crashing. And I could hear a lot of small explosions, which I think were ammunition on the aircraft.

I was able to swing over to the trunk of the tree and I discovered that my boots had snapped off when the parachute opened.

Now, I don't know what sort of a religious person you are, but in the tree, I got over to the trunk and could climb up so I could reduce my parachute, which I left in the tree, and while I was in the tree I looked down and there were two foxes. They were beautiful. Red foxes with white tips on their tails. And they were obviously frightened by all of this activity. I thought, they would know where to hide. I mean, they would go to a dense place. So I watched their direction. I never saw them again, but I got on the ground and headed in that direction, and I did get into a very dense undergrowth. I could see the sky but I was pretty well concealed, and sort of took stock of things.

I opened my escape kit, and it had been rifled. There were hard candies, some halizone tablets for water purification, but someone had been through it, and the map was not there, which was really the one thing I wanted. I had a little pocket Bible, and with it a New Testament with psalms, and I just opened it up. It was about ten o'clock in the morning, and it fell open to the 91st Psalm. So that was very reassuring. That was a miracle, I mean the foxes and the psalm.

I waited for quite a while. I did see three Me-109s flying low, they were in formation, they were probably returning to base, but they could not see me. There was a path not too far away and I heard some people talking. There were three men, all senior citizens, and they had a little fox terrier with them, and I was really worried about that. But I was downwind from them. I was enough of a Boy Scout to know about this sort of thing, and the dog never caught me. But they were sort of talking to the dog, the dog was looking up at them, they went right on by.

My plan was to head for Switzerland, walk all night and sleep all day, and before the sun came up I would find a place to dig in.

I ran into Corman Bean, and we were together on that first night, or maybe the second night, I don't remember. It was pretty chilly, and he slept all morning and he kept talking in his sleep about Millie, his wife. He would talk about her and it was quite a touching encounter.

We didn't have any food. He didn't seem to have an escape kit. Well, he must have because we both had these little plastic water bottles that folded up and we purified our water. We had plenty of water. We tried eating raw potatoes. It was fall and there was fruit on the trees, but the German dogs were really friendly and they would start barking, and we didn't want to risk that, so we didn't eat.

But there were two things. Corman's stories may match up here some, but I think most of what I'm going to tell you was solo on my part. Somehow we got separated. We didn't dare make a fire, or even if we wanted to I don't think we had any matches or anything to make it with, but the raw potatoes were just not possible. At any rate, I found myself alone, still headed south. It was about six days before I was picked up. I lost count. I knew it was into October some.

It's amazing how your senses sharpen up under these circumstances, and I realized walking in the dark that I was not alone, and you freeze. I had made shoes for myself out of part of my heated flying suit. I had a very sharp pocket knife and I used the wires in the heated suit to tie the shoes together, so I could move very quietly. So I just froze, and there were two lovers, I was very close to them. They never knew I was there. They were focused on each other.

Another time I found an autobahn, the main autobahn south, and headed toward Switzerland. I was very concerned about bridges, because I didn't want to get caught in the middle of a bridge. So I would walk all night and hide out all day.

About the sixth day I ran out of cover. I was down in a valley, an agricultural area, there were no trees, and there was a bridge. I thought if I could get under that bridge I could stay there all day. So I did get under the bridge in some high stuff, but I didn't reconnoiter.

There was a path under the bridge also on the other side of the stream, and the Germans went to bed fairly early but they got up very early, and there were agricultural workers walking on this path. I knew they'd see me. I knew I was burned about the face and looked horrible, but I didn't have a mirror, I didn't know what I looked like, so I thought my best plan is to just get up on the road and act boldly, and if I can find a bunch of bushes somewhere I'll go in there, but surely they've seen me. I think they were so-called slave labor. I don't know that they would have said anything. But I got up on the road and walked.

A couple of military cars went by and didn't stop. And I was getting into central Germany. I'd been walking like crazy. I put myself down as four miles per hour, because I was used to that pace. But I ran into an overseer of these laborers, and he saw me and he looked very stern. He said, "Englishman!"

I said, "Nein, nein, Amerikanische." I was pretty hungry and tired by this time. My right eye was really hurting and I was afraid I might lose it from the burn. I could feel my face, and part of my oxygen mask had melted on my face. He looked at me and looked horror stricken.

And we had been told that the SS were dangerous, to never give up to them; that the Hitlerjugend were kids and they were dangerous, but to give up to the Wehrmacht. So I asked if he could take me to the Wehrmacht. He said yes, he would. He took me into this little town, I don't know where it was. He took me into what would be the equivalent of the administrative office, and I had an olive drab uniform with insignia and stuff under my flying suit which had been burned in places. I took off my flying suit to show that I was in uniform. Finally they sent for someone who spoke English. So he came up and he said, "Are you from Chicago?"

I said, "No, I've never been to Chicago." And I told him I had walked for six days without food, did he have anything to eat?

He said, "Oh, you'll get food." They never did.

When he asked this question about Chicago I thought he was thinking about gangsters, American flyers were gangsters. So I told him name, rank and serial number, that I was a student, an architectural student, and they were amazed at how old I was. They thought I would have been much older. And that I was from Texas.

He said, "Well, I lived in Chicago."

And I said, "You must not have liked it because you're here in Germany."

"Oh yes," he said. "I'm going to go back there as fast as I can when this war is over."

So they put me in their hoosegow, which was a little room at the top of their church. And I was so exhausted. And they sent for a Wehrmacht guard and a truck to take me to the railroad station.

That little room in the church was so filthy. I slept on the floor. But I was dead to the world, I was so tired.

So I got on the train in the baggage car headed for Frankfurt. I didn't know where it was going. And they had a guard in the baggage compartment, it had bicycles and baggage, and he was a Wehrmacht soldier. Do you remember the Milton Caniff cartoons? You remember that he was very accurate in his drawings, and he would show Germans with Mauser rifles, and his drawings of Japanese landing craft were so accurate that those were used as training aids. But one of the things he was very accurate with was his weapons, and the German Mauser was one of them. And this guard was a young guy.

I looked at him, he was very curious about me, and I think the word had gotten through to him that I was from Texas and that I had been without food for six days and had walked all this distance. I did ask him how far I was from Switzerland. He said about 50 kilometers. And I went back and checked that distance later from Bad Hersfeld to see if it was possible, and it was plausible at a four mile per hour pace. Now, I don't know whether I'm exaggerating or not, but at any rate, that's what I believe I heard him say. Another two nights I could have done it.

But anyway, I saw his rifle and I said "Mauser?" I looked at it, not trying to get too close, and he handed it to me. I looked out the window, and I lifted his rifle and very carefully handed it back to him, and he realized what he had done, and then he was a little uptight. I was whistling, which I think just passed the time, and I was whistling the Marseillaise. He asked me not to do it. He didn't speak English. So I tried Lili Marlene and asked him to sing Lili Marlene, so we got into Frankfurt eventually. I still hadn't eaten. Actually, with water you can last a long time. But those peaches I had back several days before had to last a long time. At any rate, I was taken into where there were a lot of German enlisted men, and they had all known that I had walked this distance and had been without food, and that I was from Texas. And being from Texas, it really turned them on. One or two of them spoke English, and they said "Did your father fight Indians?"

And I said, "No. My great-grandfather did, not my father." And that I grew up on horseback, and with cows and oil wells. So we talked about things like that. The big question on their minds was, "When is the war going to be over?"

Corman Bean

We had been trained back in England about what to expect in the event that we got shot down. And one thing they emphasized was that if you bail out at a high altitude, don't pull the ripcord. Freefall for a long way.

Well, during that freefall you can assume any attitude you want to – physical attitude, not mental – so I remember rolling over on my back and looking back up and seeing the planes flying over, the fighters, and the shells exploding. I remember seeing some of the bombers, and seeing a lot of smoke; the 20-millimeters made a little puff of smoke when they exploded. I saw a lot of other parachutes. And saw some planes smoking and on fire.

So then I freefell and I went into a cloud bank, and when I hit that cloud bank I figured I'd fallen far enough, I'd better slow this thing down. So I did, and I landed in the top of a tree.

I suppose I was 40 feet up. I didn't get hurt at all. And we were told, get your chute and hide it. Well, that was a crock, you weren't gonna get a chute out of a tree. In fact, you had to crawl up a little bit in order to take the tension off so you could unhook the straps, and then shinny on down the tree once you got free of the parachute. And when I got to the ground, there was another lieutenant, he was a co-pilot from another airplane in our group; I don't think he was in our squadron. And when I got to the base of the tree he was standing there waiting for me. He had seen me come down.

It's interesting, because his account of our time after we met at the foot of the tree and my account are very different. You say about the same event and two people see it different.

He and I were together right after we both landed. I knew where we were, pretty close to where we were because I'd been the navigator, I ought to know where we were. And I had a couple of compasses, little ones. So we thought, well, we'll get the hell out of here, we'll walk back. So we started off in the right direction.

We walked near an autobahn, and followed the autobahn a little bit, but even before we got to the autobahn, the ground was being covered by German soldiers looking for us. It was like a bird hunt, and we were wounded birds all over the place. So he and I were "evading," and we were in the brush alongside a road, and the Jerries were on bicycles and or automobiles looking for us, and we just stayed hidden and waited until they went by and then we'd walk.

We stayed hidden pretty much during the daytime and tried to do our walking at night. But after we'd had about 48 hours of that we knew that there's no way we're going to get out of here. If the Jerries don't shoot us the Americans will if we ever get to the front lines. So toward the end of the second day, we were less careful in our hiding, and we literally allowed ourselves to be spotted by a group of farmers working in the field, and they "arrested" us, and took us in. They took us to the local Wehrmacht office.

They questioned us some, but they had no authority over us. But I was able to communicate with them enough to say that, well, they knew we were American flyers and that we should be prisoners of the Luftwaffe, not the Wehrmacht. And they loaded us on a little truck and took us over to the nearby German air force base. We had been told back in England, if you're shot down and captured, try to get to be a prisoner of the German air force, because they'll take better care of you than the German ground troops will, let alone the SS.

The Luftwaffe took us to a Dulag Luft, that's a temporary interrogation center. And this George and I had been separated by the Germans, according to my account, and he was badly burned, so they took him in one direction for medical help, and I was hale and hearty so they just shipped me off to this Dulag Luft, and they threw me in a cell. I was the only one in the cell, and I was dead tired. I hadn't slept in two or three days. I lay down on some straw and went to sleep. And when I woke up there were six or eight other prisoners that had been picked up in the same raid.

Within a day or two they started interrogating us. The first interrogation session that I had was with a German officer. He was sitting behind a desk, and his first question to me was, "What do you think Mildred will think of this?"

Now that's kind of jarring.

He had a file, which, he said, "we keep on all American flyers because we get so many of you down here." And he knew all about me. He knew where I was in England, which bomb group I was in, and the crowning blow if you will was, he pulled a picture out of that file and it was a picture of our airplane, the one that we had finally been assigned to, sitting on a hardstand in England.

There wasn't much more he could get out of me, and he knew it. But they kept me there for about two weeks, and their interrogation went just the way our instructors had told us it was going to go. Very nice to you to start with, and friendly, and they'd say, "You give them name, rank and serial number, and they'll respect that. But they'll feign anger after a week or so when that's all they've got, and then they will have you in this room and you'll hear some rifle shots outside and they'll say, "Well, those guys wouldn't tell us anything, so we got rid of them." We were told they would do that and it was all a hoax.

At each step along the way, things happened exactly the way our people had told us it would happen, so you start getting pretty confident that hey, I've got a little control here. But then after about two weeks, and all they got was name, rank and serial number, and I think they knew that a poor little navigator doesn't know anything about the conduct of the war other than where you're going this day. So they loaded us on a train and headed us off toward our prison camp.

Doye O'Keefe

The air battle was from about 10 a.m. until 10:15 a.m. or so. I now had to get away from this area. I paid strict attention to my woodsmanship and squirrel hunting experience. Birds chirped and sang. No one around or coming. I moved out to try to locate myself. Very quiet. Alert and fast. I saw a lookout tower that was empty. Went up quickly and looked for anyone. Lay flat. No one in any direction. Moved into a brushy area and hid on the ground the rest of daylight. Don't move in Germany in the daytime, don't travel in France at night, was our training.

It finally became dark. I moved toward the highway I had seen after the chute had opened. In an hour or so of cross-country walking (mostly hiding. Moved very little) I found it. Stayed off to one side and kept moving west and alert. A sign, "Kassel 120 KM." I was northeast. Now head west, away from houses, towns. Cross-country.

In a short time I found my problem. Heading west in Germany, all the creeks and rivers ran north to the sea. Think now. To cross rivers you must use a bridge. If all are guarded, I have to ride across, on a train.

I spent the night cross-country trying to find the railroad tracks I saw falling. I finally did. Walked up to a crossing and a voice in the middle of the night said something in German. A watchman at the crossing in a little house. I assumed he was telling me to be careful of a coming train. He said "octung," which means "attention."

I said, "Ya vol," meaning "yes sir," about all I knew. Nothing more was said. Nothing happened. The train came by. I turned and walked down the tracks west. Kept on walking. It worked. I walked the rest of the night on the tracks, to the edge of a freight yard, and hid for the whole day. I thought I was freezing. Terribly cold, stiff, and hungry. Get the mind used to this. We're just getting started. Trains came by during the day, would stop to switch and pull out. In the evening I went over, caught a freight train, hid in the switchman's cabin and rode west for several hours. We pulled into a yard on a side track and stopped.

Soon along came another train. We had sidetracked for – God! The train was filled with German tanks and halftracks. It had to be going to the front, in France, fast. Exactly where I was headed. I jumped off my boxcar freight. Jumped up on the car opposite me, a big halftrack, anti-tank job. Dark as a coal mine. Reached in my pocket, took out a book of matches, lit one and looked around. It was brand new, soft seat and map reading table. It was warm inside. I sat in the seat, leaned my head in my arms on the map table and fell fast asleep as we were now speeding west to France, over all the rivers. We were really moving.

When I woke up it was gray, turning daylight, as we had pulled into a freight yard on the edge of some town. I didn't want to be sitting here in daylight. I've bombed too many of these to know they are no place to stop.

I peeked out. Guards, walking the train one on each side. If I could get them walking in opposite direction, I could get away. They come to the center and did an about face. I could make it easy as they both walked away from my position. Count their steps toward me as I peeked out a gun port. About face. Count their steps away. I had at least two minutes. Then for some reason I laughed, and pulled the greatest practical joke I've ever done. I reached in my pocket, pulled out the book of matches, and carefully laid it on the map reading table. Opened the door on top, quickly slipped down and disappeared into the long lines of people leaving the town to work in the fields. Still to this day I get a regular chuckle and smile nearly each day as I think of ol' Fritz or Hans climbing into a brand new anti-tank halftrack and there laying on the table is a book of matches from of all places, "The Top Hat Club, London, England."

It was beginning to get light. I continued to walk past the working fields and on into the country. I found a hiding place and lay down in tall weeds and brush to spend the day, waiting for night. I was lucky to be off the train. I'd surely have been shot if I had been caught. I didn't think the day would ever pass. Damn, I was miserable. Cold, tired, hungry. I had a long way yet. Think of home. Think of Sara. Think of anything. Get really tough about this. Wait till full dark.

It was nearly dark. I could start. I could see no one. Hadn't all day. I'll cross that field, into the heavy woods. I struck out for the evening. Not quite dark, but the sun was down. Head into the sunset. As I came into the woods I ran flat into a ten foot cyclone type fence. Barbed wire. Buildings in the woods with netting over them. A path inside the fence. Armed guards on duty. Good Lord. Turn around. Go directly back where I came from. Hadn't been seen yet. Made a big circle around. Crossed the tracks. Headed west across an open field. I walked upon a bomb crater in the field and setting in the bottom were several ladies eating sandwiches. They spoke a greeting. I looked as best I could. Nodded to them. Smiled and kept on going.

I had walked to the edge of the field along a railroad track again and carefully looked back. They were talking to a soldier with a German police dog. What lousy luck to walk up on them by accident. It indeed, to them, was strange to see a tall young 23-year-old person with blisters on his face and all raw red way out here. The dog and guard soldier soon were near. The man called out at about fifty yards to me. I stopped as he and the dog came forward with a German Luger drawn. I thought I can kill him, I know, but the dog. Possibly it too. If I do, I'm really hunted and would be shot for sure. As he came up to me, a few feet away, I took out my dog tag to show I was an American flyer. I was captured, I guess, for sure now. You can't get home if you're dead.

I was taken over into the woods. Behind the fences I ran into something special, a huge ammo depot, all in this woods with netting over acres of buildings.

I spent that night being threatened to be shot as a spy near this ammo dump. But the next day I went to an airfield. There were Me-109s all over the place, possibly some we had seen in the air. I was put into a small room about four foot by six foot. Closed the door and locked it. I lay down on an old door on two saw horses and slept till they woke me the next morning.

Then I was put into a small truck with a guard and went to some headquarters. There I saw other airmen also. We were taken into a barbed wire camp, separated and placed in single rooms, no lights, a small peephole out the door. That was it. I'd heard about this and here I was, solitary confinement. Small room. Five feet by six feet about six foot six inches high. A wood slat bunk. A pot for toilet and black dark except the peep hole. Guards outside. I could see no one else.

In the middle of the day a guard with a table on wheels came by, opened the door, gave you a cup of ersatz coffee (roasted acorns or something ground up), a (I mean "a") slice of black bread with a lard type spread on it. That was it for the entire day and night. I would be taken out about late afternoon. Taken into a private room for personal interview. Stay with name, rank and serial number. And would you believe it? I gave my name, Technical Sergeant and Army serial number, 3637 0929. The danged Army made my tags read 3637 0920. That really caused a fuss for a few days. I was a spy. Didn't even know my own number. I just told the officers. This was even more proof. Strict Army screw-up. Ours was similar to theirs in many ways. They always seem to screw up something. He laughed and talked of himself. He came to Germany to visit his family and couldn't return. His family was in the United States. He was from North Carolina actually. I still have the dog tags today.

That lasted seven days. It's funny. You get just so hungry. Then after that some way the Good Lord will adjust your body. That week and the two days before capture I had seven cups of imitation coffee and seven slices of black bread. Hunger was now part of my life. I don't remember going to the toilet in any way. The body uses everything up. I might have. I don't remember it.

Chapter 22: Kriegies

Frank Bertram

Now let me wander back to that train ride, on our way from Oberursel up to Stalag Luft 1. We were scared to death because of the bombings and things that were taking place, and then some guy came along and says "Hey, we're safe, you don't have to worry. They're not gonna strafe us. It's all marked on top of each car, POW."

And some wise guy said, "Yeah, but suppose they come in from the other side. Spell that backwards." And everybody howled. "Oh man, we're really gonna get shot."

One night, we pulled over from the main railroad to a little siding, and it's probably 10 or 11 at night. Jackson and myself couldn't sleep. We were up shooting the breeze and all of a sudden we heard THUD! You could feel the stuff hit the ground. I think we had been dozing, and that woke us up. And we wanted to know what was going on. We looked out the window, and in the distance we could see searchlights, explosions, you could feel them. The RAF was raiding this town. And the town was Berlin. We were on our way to Barth, which is 100 miles north of Berlin, and we're probably right now 25 or 50 miles south of Berlin. And we're sitting there watching them bomb Berlin. Here we're prisoners of war. And we see explosions, we know an RAF plane has been hit, and these big blockbusters kept hitting, and all of a sudden the German guard comes up to Jackson and me and says something, and Jackson says, "He said something about an apple for some cigarettes."

I said, "An apple? Let's do it!"

They gave us five packs of cigarettes on that Red Cross parcel. We gave this German guard three or four American cigarettes, and the guard gives us each an apple. Holy mackerel! Next thing we know he comes back and Jackson says, "He said he can get us some beer."

I said, "How's he gonna get us some beer?"

And through sign language or whatever – Jackson never did speak German, but he could communicate better than I could – about a hundred yards from the train were a couple of very dim lights, and he came back with a German canteen full of beer. And if you've seen a German canteen it was about twice the size of an American canteen. It must have been a liter. And we're sitting there chewing apples, drinking German beer, and watching them bomb Berlin.

I had to remind Jackson about that the last time I saw him. He completely forgot about it. I'll never forget it, because a day and a half later we ended up in our camp. When we got to Barth they dropped us off at the station and we started marching. It was in the evening. We had these guards with these monstrous German shepherds and Doberman pinschers. They were big and they were mean. Three or four hundred of us marched about three and a half miles, and some of us were in bad shape.

I had received a little medical attention at Oberursel. I got to see a German doctor there in this hospital. There were a lot of German men there who were going into the service, and I felt sorry for these guys because they were in their fifties and they were being taken in the service. Some of them were in worse shape than I am now. When I got into this room, this German doctor took one look at my back, and he said, "Not much we can do," and then he just bandaged my feet. He said, "Your back is pretty bad. Do you want to see what it looks like?"

I said, "What do you mean?"

He said, "Take a look." And he had two mirrors. That's the closest I came to fainting up to that point. My back was just the color of tar. It was solid black, all the way across the lower back, where I had been injured. The doctor and his aides gave me a heat treatment which made me feel a lot better. I thanked him very much. At the same time, I remember them saying an American nurse was in the hospital there. She wasn't injured, but she was taken there with some of the injured. She was flying in the plane and was shot down outside of Aachen. It was a hospital plane carrying troops out, and she was captured as a POW. And the funny part of it is, about three years ago there was an article in the paper about this nurse up in Sacramento who had just passed away, and it was her. The only Army nurse that was ever captured over there. And I thought, my god, here I am 40 miles away. I never saw her over there but just the thought of all that was going on, what very brave young ladies they were.

Malcolm MacGregor

That night they got us, on the way to Eisenach I had a couple of soldiers that were with me because I couldn't walk very well, so I was going much slower than the rest of the guys that were going down the road. We went into a little field, and there was a German brownshirt with the red swastika on his arm, and he motioned me over. There were three or four Luftwaffe officers there and a couple of cars, and he started hitting me with the back of his hand, and that's when I fell down. Then he kicked me, and then I got up and went on down the road with the two guys taking me. I wasn't badly hurt. I got down the road a ways and out of a little house came a very short German old guy with white hair all around the fringe like I guess I am now, and he came out and kicked me in the fanny. He had rubber boots. It would have been kind of funny except I had a piece of shrapnel back near that, and that aggravated it.

Then I went to Eisenach, and we were put in a long barnlike building with a shelf, and I spent the night there. Got up the next morning and saw the 8th Air Force going over. The sky was just black with bombers. I don't know how the Germans ever put up with it.

From there we went to Oberursel. That was their interrogation center, and they put me in solitary confinement, where I stayed for I think it was three days, and you got a little ersatz coffee in the morning and then a piece of bread and then a little soup in the afternoon. About 11 o'clock both mornings – I was interrogated twice – they took me into an interrogation room, and a very nice gentleman talked to me. He told me all about the mission. He knew more about it than I did, and of course I just told him my name, rank and serial number. But he knew how many planes there were, how many guys there were.

There were some that still hadn't been caught. I think Ammi was still evading; I think Ammi evaded for a couple or three days. And we just chatted awhile. There's nothing particularly one way or the other, they didn't blindfold me or handcuff my hands behind my back or do any of the stupid stuff we're doing today.

Prisoners of war are the most helpless people in the world. They aren't usually individually violent people. They're there because they're soldiers and that's their job. So you know you're not going to have a lot of trouble with them. And the Germans never had a lot of trouble with any of us. I suppose there was an occasional guy that tried to cause trouble, but in general you just want to get on with what the next thing's gonna be. So interrogation was very gentle. And I really didn't know anything that he didn't know. He figured that out pretty quick. So I stayed there three days and then I went to Metzlach, and that's the Dulag Luft, and that was overseen by the International Red Cross. I don't think Oberursel was. But I didn't see any signs of anybody being tortured.

Solitary is a terrible thing. You probably have never been in solitary. The room was probably seven or eight feet wide and maybe ten feet long. And it was totally white. The inside of it was painted totally white. It had shutters on the window. They were all totally white. And a little slot in the door that they could put food in. And you had nothing to do. Nobody to talk to. Nothing to read. Nothing to watch. No scenery to look at. Just white walls. You can only think your own thoughts for about so long and then you wonder what am I doing here?

It made me be very appreciative of freedom, even a lot moreso than any other part of my prison experience. I mean, it wasn't great the rest of it, but I was in a compound that probably had 1,500 other guys in it, so you could play bridge and you had somebody to talk to. But when you're in solitary it's just you. And I don't know what happens when you're in solitary for a long period of time, but something's got to shut down. But with me, it was just a very unpleasant thing. They weren't mean to me or anything. So that was my experience with solitary.

In Oberursel I saw a Britisher who was captured at Arnhem. He told me that there were three or four of them in this little house, and it was nighttime, so they stayed there overnight. And in the morning they heard ch-ch-ch-ch, and they looked out the window, and here came a Tiger tank up over the brow of the hill in front of them, and it lowered the gun down and aimed at them. And they said "We surrender."

When I got to Stalag Luft I, I put what little stuff I had in the barracks that I was assigned to, and I turned around, and the guys gathered around and they said, "Okay. Sit down. Tell us your horror story." So I told them what I just told you, about the specifics of the shootdown. The thing that impressed them the most was the 20- and 30-millimeter cannons exploding in the bomb bays when I was right in the front of the bomb bay. They thought that was pretty neat.

Then they told me their stories. There was one guy, I think he was a pilot, no, he couldn't have been because he had a chest pack, so he must have been a navigator or a bombardier. Anyway, the plane blew up and he didn't have a chute, he was just out in the air. He wasn't hurt. And all of a sudden a chute came by, and he reached out and grabbed it, hooked it onto his chest pack, and that's how he got there.

There was one guy there, I think he was either the pilot or co-pilot, I think it was a B-17, they had a top hatch on a B-17, and the plane was all shot up and going down and it was over the Zuider Zee or somewhere in Holland. It crash-landed itself as he was climbing out of the top hatch, and hurt his hip. I thought that's pretty amazing. There was a P-38 pilot and he was shooting up an airport, and his indicator was 350 miles an hour as he's going down and shooting this place up. And the ground fire shot his controls out. So here he was, right on the deck at 350 miles an hour in a P-38 with no controls, and the plane crash-landed, went up and did a snap roll he said, and came back down, then skidded to a stop, and he jumped out of the airplane. He said he jumped out and ran about fifty feet, and then he collapsed. And his back was broken, right in the middle. It's amazing he even got out. And they put him in a German hospital with a German fighter pilot that was also in the hospital, he was there three or four months, and you could run your finger down his back, and there was a U in his backbone, you could feel it. But he seemed to be doing all right. But that was pretty amazing, to crash at that speed and walk away from it.

George Collar

All day long we went up hill, down dale, picking up bodies and parts of bodies. We came back with two haywagon loads, and we came into the cemetery at Lauschreden. We unhitched the horses and left the two wagons standing next to a stone building. Then they marched us into town and we went up to the village pump, and we drank water until we thought we were gonna die because we hadn't had a drink of water all day. All we had to eat all day long was a couple of apples that some kid gave us. So then they marched us over to the little jailhouse again. Pretty soon – this must have been a little after dark – they brought us a big mug of ersatz coffee and some white bread. That's the last white bread I saw until I got back to the United States.

We'd just got to sleep, and they rousted us out again. There was a Wehrmacht truck outside, and it was full of wounded guys, and oh my god, we drove all around the country till about 3 a.m. We'd stop in a village and they'd take us into an old barn, there'd be a wounded guy laying there. We'd bring them out, lay them in the truck, and I remember one guy, he had a 20-millimeter hole right through his thigh. How the hell he was alive I don't know. We brought him back, and all these guys are in there, and Jerry Cathol was laying near the tailgate and he thought his back was broken. It wasn't, but his hip was dislocated.

Jerry Cathol is a big guy. He played end at the University of Nebraska. And I carried that big guy up two flights of steps. Three o'clock in the morning in Eisenach at the hospital. And after we got all these wounded people unloaded and in the hospital, they took us three guys that weren't wounded over to the Wehrmacht base and they took us downstairs and there was a guardroom down there. There were rows of wooden shelves, about six feet deep, and they had a raised end like a pillow made out of wood. And about 25 of our guys are laying on these shelves. One of them was Weinstein. One of them was McGregor. And two guys that were wounded were laying on stretchers on the floor. They should have been in a hospital. One of them had a Polish name, he was a guy by the name of Galuszewski. One of them, I think he was on Brent's crew [this would have been Constantin Galuszewski], had a leg wound and it was bad. The other guy was wounded and they couldn't walk, we had to carry them.

We were there a couple of days. You couldn't tell whether it was daylight or dark because we were down in the basement. In the morning they'd bring us a bowl of barley, and at night they brought us some black bread and ersatz coffee. And they took us one by one and the guy tried to quiz us, and he took our wristwatch. If it was a private watch he gave it back. If it was a government issue watch he kept it. But he gave you a receipt for it. I've still got the receipt.

There were about 25 of us. One day two guys showed up from the Luftwaffe. They were feldwebels or something, high-class sergeants. They had Walther submachine guns. And they said "We've been delegated to move you to an air base at Ehrfurt. We're gonna go by civilian train." And they said, "We'll protect you, but keep a low profile. Don't say or do anything that would stir things up."

Also, when we picked these wounded guys up, they put a bunch of loaves of bread underneath the blankets. That was supposed to be our food on the trip. They said under no circumstances show that bread to the civilians.

So we marched down the street in Eisenach. We got on a civilian train, and had a whole car more or less to ourselves. We went through Gotha and got up to Ehrfurt. And Ehrfurt at that time had never been bombed. It was quite a picturesque town. That's one of Martin Luther's old hangouts, quite a historic place. So we got off the train there and marched up the streets. We had these two guards. And it was hot, and we weren't in too good a shape. You get tired carrying these stretchers; they're heavy. So we had to keep changing off all the time. It was almost all the way uphill. We got to the top of that hill and we just about died. So we set the stretchers down and we all sat down on the street. One of the guards stayed there and the other one went over to the beer joint and had a beer. And about that time a lady came out from a house and she had a big can full of cold water. Boy, did we drink that water.

Pretty soon somebody showed up with a two-wheel pushcart that had rubber tires. Boy, that was swell. We put those stretchers on there and we pushed and then pulled them. We just about got out of town, and we blew a tire. Then we had to start carrying them again.

Along about suppertime we come dragging onto that Luftwaffe base, I mean we were dead. We came in carrying the stretchers and went right in this barracks. We all flopped down right on the wooden floor and went right to sleep.

Finally they ordered us all out and we got out in the street and there was a big truck waiting for us. A staff car drove up and I don't know whether he was a colonel or something, he called the roll. And when he called the roll, he said "Weinstein."

There's little old Weinstein, about five foot tall. "Vainshtein," the guy says. "Das is Jude."

I thought, oh shit, they're gonna kill old Weinstein. He did, too. But that's all he said, "Das ist Jude." And the next thing you know we're all on the truck heading for the Ehrfurt station.

We get to the station, and we're standing in a column of twos on the sidewalk, and a couple of SS guys come out with black uniforms. Meaner then hell. And they start in on us when they find out we were terrorfliegers. They were ranting and raving and getting the crowd all worked up, and it was looking pretty ominous. About that time the staff car drove up with this colonel in it. He got up and stood in the back seat and he read the riot act to those guys, you ought to have seen them scram. He was a Luftwaffe colonel.

We got on the train about midnight and we finally arrived at Frankfurt am Main. The old railroad station looked like a skeleton; all the glass was laying in pieces all over the floor. But the trains were all running in and out. They pulled our car on one of the tracks, and we're all sitting in it, and away goes the engine. It left us sitting there.

Pretty soon somebody in the goddarn crowd discovered there was a POW train over here with a bunch of Amerikanisch terrorfliegers. So they started getting hostile. And they started picking up paving bricks and they were threatening the guards. The guards told us to get back and lay down on the floor, and they held their burp guns on these guys. And I'll tell you what. All it would have taken is a rock hitting one of the guards' heads and we'd have been dead, because that was a mob.

You know what saved us? The air raid siren went off, and everybody skedaddled for the air raid shelter except us. We're sitting there. And pretty soon we heard a plane coming, it was a Mosquito, and he dropped a great big bomb about two blocks up the street. Oh, man, did that shake things up.

By the time the all clear sounded, an engine came in and hooked onto us and pulled us out of there. And they took us to the little town of Oberursel. It was an interrogation center. Finally we come to this camp, and when we pulled in, the courtyard was full of Polish, Canadian and British paratroopers that had been captured at Arnhem. And I stood there, I was right next to a Polish colonel, and we're standing there with our thumb up our hind end not knowing what to do, and jeez, I was hungry.

Pretty soon efficiency took over and they took several of us to this room and several to another room and they had us down in a basement room, there was a little window about ground level. And the next morning they came along with a big pushcart and they had a big canister of Purple Passion, that's what we called it, it was cabbage soup. Boy, that tasted good. Then they said, We're gonna take you one by one for interrogation.

They took me down to this room and there was a guy sitting there, he had an Afrika Korps uniform on. It was a light summer uniform. He spoke perfect English.

"Here, have a cigarette."

"No thanks."

"Have a seat."

He starts talking real friendly. The he starts quizzing me a little bit.

"What group are you in?"

"Can't tell you."

"What kind of plane were you flying?"

"Can't tell you. Not supposed to do that."

Finally he says to me, "You don't need to answer any more right now, but I can tell you a few things. You're from the 445th Bomb Group." He knew all about our group. For crying out loud, he knew more about it than I did. "Now," he says, "if you want to go to a permanent camp and be with your friends, you're going to have to answer a few questions. Otherwise you may be here for a long time."

I said, "I'm not allowed to say that. I'm just supposed to give name, rank and serial number."

"You do as you please," he said. Then he dismissed me and they took me out. They put me in solitary confinement in a room on the second floor. It had a single bunk and a pallet filled with excelsior. That's when I got the fleas in my shoes. No window or nothing. There was a window but it was frosted over.

The next morning they roust me out and I got out in the hall. There must have been 200 guys standing in the hall, mostly all from our gang, and there were some from the 15th Air Force. They took us out into a courtyard and there was a barracks out there. We went in there, and there had to be 200 of us at least. British paratroopers. Polish paratroopers. Paratroopers are taken care of by the

Luftwaffe, because paratroopers are part of the Luftwaffe in the German army.

We're all in this room, and they took all our shoes off and tied the laces together, threw them in a pile on a blanket and away they went. That's so you wouldn't escape. I was kind of hoping I'd get a better pair but I didn't.

Boy, were these paratroopers rough guys. They held out for two weeks up at Arnhem and they were only supposed to hold out for seven days, and they got captured. And this one British guy, tougher than hell, he says, "Wait till we start winning the war," he says.

The next day, they came along with that big blanket full of shoes. We all fished out our own shoes and put them on. Then they marched us up to the railroad station, put us on a train, and we're heading for Wetzlar, that's what they called Dulag Luft. And Wetzlar was the hometown of the Zeiss Camera Company. Also they had a 20-millimeter antiaircraft gun factory there. So on the way up, there were planes strafing, so they backed us into a tunnel.

When we got to Wetzlar and got out of the train, we're all standing there next to the engine, 250 of us, and the guards have got burp guns on us. At about that time the air raid siren sounded and along came a flight of P-51s. We were sweating blood. The guards went over in the entrance to the air raid shelter and held their guns on us and made us stand next to the engine. And these planes circled around and they came back, and I thought oh, jeez, this is gonna be it. They made one circle and they took off. The only thing I can think, they knew there was a prison camp there, or it's possible it said POW on top of the train.

Doye O'Keefe

As we moved across Germany, it took a week or so packed in box cars. We would be let out once a day and then locked in again. By this time men became sick, depressed, and generally, more or less, the strong survive well enough as an animal would. We all would be mistreated, abused, taunted, degraded in nearly a constant manner. Now it was beginning to be burned into my system what the meaning of "freedom" really was.

We pulled into a suitable yard north of Berlin, and I guess changed engines and serviced the train. We were let out for a few minutes and loaded and locked back in. Then it happened. American P-47 fighter planes attacked the yard. Strafing machine gun bullets up and down. Run after run. Right over us just a few feet off the ground. Every attack, men would scream, pound the walls, yell trying to get let out. I tried to quiet the fellows in our boxcar and did. We all said the Lord's Prayer out loud together. The planes continued their runs over us, shooting away. We sat and I'd tell when we couldn't be hit by the sound of the attack. They began to understand. We were not hit, others were. From then on two things happened. The Germans took out their bitterness on us in treatment to pay for the attack, and I was automatically the leader of men in very trying situations.

After seemingly forever we stopped at a side track way in the country. Lined up and started to walk. Then a "Raus mit you!" or run with you. We started running with guards jabbing with bayonets. We ran a couple of miles to our new home, Stalag Luft IV. I was okay, exhausted but okay. I felt to hell with them. No way would they get the best of me. Many were in bad shape. Hit, stuck. I had shoes I jumped with. The rest had boots, heavy, or lost them and were in stocking feet. We were a terrible looking group when we arrived. Police dogs were allowed to charge and bite you as you ran. Many were wounded, hurt. It was bad all the way.

We were taken into the receiving area and processed for POW life. Stripped naked and all clothes searched, even the seams. Amazing what they found. They would rough up the person, push, laugh, degrade, and generally make the person look foolish. This area was called for vorlager. We were fingerprinted, photographed, and given K.G.F., or Kriegsgefangenen (number) meaning war prisoner. My tag number was #3741. Still we were not fed. After a few days of hunger it became part of a person. Finally we were taken into our area of the camp.

The camp was divided into four compounds, each separate and self-contained. All arranged in a square and bisected by a road from which a single gate led into each unit. There were twin barbed wire fences about nine or ten feet high running parallel about the same distance apart all around each of the compounds, as well as the entire camp. Along the outside area were log guard towers about 100 yards apart all around the camp. Searchlights and machine guns were mounted on each tower. Guards on foot with police dogs were outside all of this.

There were ten POW barracks, five on each side of a large open ground, for roll calls and exercise area. Each barrack had a latrine pit, washroom, and water. Another building was for the kitchen and offices. The barracks were about 40 by 130 feet, having ten rooms from a central hallway running lengthwise of the building. Each room was 15 by 23 feet and designed to have 16 men. Later there were eight wooden bunks, double decks. The bunks were very crude, containing six slats with a mattress we stuffed with straw. We got two blankets and a straw stuffed pillow. That was a blessing, because for the first several weeks we slept on the floor on a pile of straw we fluffed each morning.

There was one table in the center, only four chairs, and a small coal stove at one side. We got one small bucket of coal when they got around to it for heat. We would endure far below zero weather this season. The room was never warm enough.

Food was brought to the rooms by a 10-quart, galvanized bucket, the mop bucket type. For breakfast there was nothing, ever. For noon usually a bucket full of barley soup most of the time. Supper was plain boiled potatoes. Always one bucketful to divide up. Sometimes a substitute of cabbage soup, stewed greens, boiled kohlrabes. Sometimes a boiled dehydrated vegetable mix. I know of no meat that could be identified, but at times something stringy would be in with the potatoes. Red Cross packages were rare and very precious. Maybe one a week per room to be divided among all the men.

Escapes at the time were not allowed by our own advice. Too dangerous and too near the war's end. Inside was organized with committees, for news, smuggled in daily by a camp doctor. It was always delivered in each barrack with our own men watching for Germans. Our news man was a small-time actor and he was more dramatic than the real news, I'm sure. Everyone waited for his every word.

I was the room leader. My job was to see that we operated. No arguments. Settle any disputes. Divide the food evenly. Keep the card game going (I still have the cards). Fortunes of make believe money changed hands regularly. Everyone began to lose weight. I tried to keep everyone taking walks in the compound and exercising regularly, not to weaken.

Days became weeks. We would all fall out every morning and afternoon regardless of weather to be counted. My birthday had passed. Thanksgiving had come with much snow. It's true, Thanksgiving meant so very much. We were alive. We had done much and were still looking forward. We all tried to save bits of fruit from Red Cross packages to make a dried cake patty "thing." Something anyway. We celebrated Thanksgiving. As room leader I said our Thanksgiving grace, read from a Bible from the Red Cross. We did well, but were all sick at heart for home. More snow, ice. So cold. As we waited for Christmas to come and go we tried to exchange presents which were good words and encouraging conversation. We sang Christmas songs and had a camp program. The New Year celebration was better. We were positive from news of the war we would be home this year, 1945.

Every night as we were locked into our barracks and all doors and windows were shuttered and bolted, I would go to the west end and slide back the small peep door for the guard to look inside from his rounds. I'd first look for the guard. Then, on clear nights, I would look for the evening star, Venus, I believe. As it glistened, I would make my wish on the "first star I see tonight." Always something at home. I'd wonder if Sara or someone at home also would see the same star this night and be at least that near. It was so lonesome day in and day out.

John Ray Lemons

If I had to describe my interrogation it was like I was in there watching the movie that I had seen for the training film. The same routine they told us you would face if you ever got to be a prisoner. In the training films they show you what you're going to face, name, rank and serial number. But they wouldn't accept that routine. The guy that got me said he was originally from Buffalo, New York. He said he came to America and was there until 1939 and lived in Buffalo, and he knew a lot about that part of the country. And he said, "I can listen to your language and tell you where you're from. You're from Texas." He knew where I was from because he had my dog tag, and I'm sure he already had figured out who my crew, the crew he thought I was on. He was wrong. Then he said, "Have a Lucky Strike."

I said, "I don't smoke." I did smoke but I didn't want one.

"Well," he said, "you've got to tell me something. What happened today? What were you guys doing?" He finally said, "You're not telling us anything. We're going to put you in solitary."

I said, "I've told you what I can tell you. You know what it is. It's name, rank and serial number. Do you need me to repeat it for you again?"

He said, "I'm gonna bring the big man in here in a minute if you don't do something, because we're gonna put you in solitary."

And sure enough he did. He took me out and put me in a room with a guy I figured was a plant. He probably was, but he had on a GI uniform.

The other guy, before he turned me loose, he finally said, "I know everything about you. I know everything about your group. I can show you what crew you're on. You're on the Johnson crew." Well, we had a guy named Johnson.

I said, "I don't know what crew I was on." He thought I was on the Johnson crew. So he gets the book out and opens it up, my god, it had more information than I knew we even had. They had names in each squadron, 701, 2 3 and 4. And how they got that I don't to this day know. But anyway, he put me in solitary like he said he would and I stayed there about two days. But what really surprised me later, when I got home, Baynham says, "I saw you at Wetzlar. Your face looked like you had been beat to hell." Well, I knew I'd been beat up because they clubbed me with a pistol.

I said, "I didn't see you."

He said, "No, but I saw you."

So that kind of brings you to the point of what happened to the crew. Knox and Boldt were both in Obermasfeld hospital. When Knox was liberated, he and Boldt were both sent home. Knox was in a body cast still. He weighed 60 pounds. And they put him on a hospital ship, flew him to New York, and then his wife to be, they hadn't been married yet, got him to have an interview, and got him in the headline in the paper there when he got home. And Boldt went straight to the hospital when he got to the States and he was in the hospital for two years. So Baynham and I and Bosquet were really the only ones that came out more or less OK.

Glen McCormick

On the road to Bebra, our little party was joined by a horse-drawn wagon full of potatoes – a woman was driving the wagon and her son was with her. The boy was about 12, and he was practicing his English on me. He quizzed me on everything. When we got to Weiterode, the only ones left of the little group were me and the soldier. He took me to the burgomeister's home where they searched me for the first time. I was taken to the local jail where I spent my first night in captivity. There was a co-pilot there from the 445th Bomb Group who had an injured hip and he had been in that cell for many days. He was glad to see me.

Early the next morning, we were taken to the railroad station and boarded the train. Two Wehrmacht soldiers then took us to a Luftwaffe base. We were there for about three hours and then the same soldiers took us to Frankfurt on the Main. From there, we took a streetcar to the interrogation center just outside Frankfurt.

The railroad station at Frankfurt was nothing but a shell. We evidently bombed the tar out of it.

I spent the night at the interrogation center and the next morning an unteroffizier came in and questioned me. Your name, rank and serial number was all you could talk about. After a lot of questions, he finally showed me a notebook that had the names of the crew members, tail markings of the airplanes, etc. All he wanted was my verification that I was on Chilton's crew. He didn't find out.

That same day we went to Wetzlar, Germany, and were there overnight. I saw our radar operator (Johnson) and our pilotage navigator (Hudson) at this Dulag. The next day we shipped out by rail for what was to be our permanent camp – Stalag Luft IV. This was a special railroad car made specifically to transport prisoners. Two older Luftwaffe soldiers were our guards. We developed a speaking acquaintance with them and both of them showed pictures of their families, etc. The train pulling our prison car must have had the lowest priority possible. It seemed we were always being put on a siding and had to wait for hours to go again. Several times during these waits, the guards would go get their canteens filled with beer. Mind you, only one guard would go at a time. We shared the beer – it was usually a light, sweet beer.

We arrived at Gross Tychow where Luft IV was located. After the usual searches (which by the way were pretty damn intimate), we went to the compound where we were to stay for a while. I was in Compound "B." The room I was in was completely full and we had a straw tick to put on the floor. After about a week, our waist gunner, Merle Briggs, showed up. He and Howard Sturdy met in the woods one dark night after bailing out and were loose for nearly a month. Though we weren't in the same barracks, we were in the same compound and could visit during the daylight hours.

Life at Luft IV was rather uneventful. Our days consisted of walking the compound, standing for those infernal roll calls twice a day, and worrying about food. It snowed in late October and that same snow was still on the ground along with more snow when we left there in late January 1945.

On the 29th of January, 1945, we were loaded into boxcars (40-and-8) and finally pulled out two days later. That was a miserable trip! There must have been over 60 people in our car – one five gallon bucket (the potty) for all of us – one half-gallon pitcher of water for the whole car per day. We arrived at Nuremburg a week later. When we got out of that boxcar we could hardly walk.

Nuremburg was an old concentration camp and prisoners were moving in from all over. The penetration of the Siegfried Line had been accomplished and the Allies were sweeping across Germany. We had it pretty rough there. The biggest problem was food – we didn't have any! This is where I lost most of my weight – I went from 146 pounds down to 95 while in prison and I think most of it was at Nuremburg.

We left there April 4, 1945 on a forced march to Moosburg. That wasn't an easy journey either. We would walk during the day and bed down at night in the villages in their barns. You see, in that country, the farmers lived in villages and would go out to their farms during the day. The barns were really part of the house. I said "villages" – the number of troops being marched was tremendous. I heard it was over 10,000. One village couldn't quite handle that mob!

The second night out we didn't make it to a village and we camped out in the woods. It rained – and rained – a typical early cold April rain. By morning we were miserable and started moving out without benefit of our guards. We were leaning up against the rail of a bridge crossing one of the many streams. A German guard (goon) was standing there with us. Finally, he started off stomping his feet to get them warm and left us standing there – one small detail – he forgot his rifle! One of the guys picked up his rifle and dropped it in the stream. It made a very pleasant "glug-glug" sound. Later that day the Unteroffizier in charge of the column was riding back and forth on his bicycle asking if anybody had seen a missing rifle. Too bad, too bad!

You would think that a bunch of POWs would try to make a break for it. Not so – the column was being followed up by SS troops and we heard of some of the attempts to escape – they ended up getting shot. Besides that, there is protection if you are in a group.

We arrived at Moosburg on April 16th, a journey of about 160 kilometers (100 miles),

We were liberated one day before Germany capitulated. From there, it was back to France and on our way home.

I received my honorable discharge on September 19, 1945.

Nearly six years of military service and I am proud that I could serve my country. I have no regrets whatsoever. During the course of discussing my experiences, I seemed to gloss over the fate of our crew when we were shot down.

We lost five good men during that battle on our crew alone. I only wish their outcome would have been like mine. War is a serious matter and lives are to be lost to achieve your goals. Why must it be?

Major Don W. McCoy, Command Pilot – lost in the attack.
Capt. John H. Chilton, Pilot – lost in the attack.
1st Lt. Raymond E. Ische, Navigator – lost in the attack
2nd Lt. Harold E. Sutherland, Co-Pilot – lost in the attack.
S/Sgt. Robert L. Shay, Gunner – lost in the attack

1st Lt. Parker S. Trefethen, Bombardier – Anacortes, Washington
1st Lt. Carlton V. Hudson, Navigator -- ?
2nd Lt. Cloys V. Johnson, Radar Operator -- deceased
T/Sgt. Howard L. Sturdy, Flight Engineer – deceased
T/Sgt. William J. Sloane, Radio Operator -- ?
S/Sgt. Merle H. Briggs – gunner – deceased
S/Sgt. Glen S. McCormick – gunner – Wichita, Kansas

S/Sgt. Donald W. Mills – gunner – Fresno, California

Johnson was reported as killed in an auto accident shortly after returning to the U.S.

Briggs had a heart attack (approximately 1977)

Don Mills received a letter from Howard's wife about 1954 stating he had been killed as the only occupant in a civilian aircraft crash.

Sammy Weiner

We rode for hours, passed a large airfield, stopped in a small village where another American prisoner was taken aboard, and eventually reached a Dulag camp.

At the dispensary there I received some inadequate medical attention and was taken to the guardhouse, stripped and given a thorough search. Here I consumed a cup of cold ersatz and one small morsel of black bread, and was pushed into a cold, damp cell for the remainder of the night. Almost immediately, I fell into a dead sleep.

Early the next morning the other two prisoners and I were taken to the Commandant for questioning. The interview must have been far from satisfactory to him. When later I received a ration of black bread and an inch square of margarine and Limburger cheese, I ate ravenously, not giving a thought to my next meal. But I was to soon learn the secret of subsistence by saving morsels of food from one "meal" to the next.

During a bombing raid on the nearby village that morning, we were hustled to a bomb shelter. Twelve other Americans had arrived before us. The raid appeared to be an everyday occurrence, for the Jerrys' reaction was unusually calm to the shattering din of bombs.

An hour after the all-clear signal sounded, we were hauled in army trucks to the railroad station of the bombarded village. The raid had been a disastrous one and the civilians, now bitter and resentful, shouted vituperously at us. Some even threw stones. There was an hour's wait on the railroad platform, five guards standing a close watch who presently herded us into two small compartments of a waiting train. We were twenty in all, counting the guards. There was no food and only two cigarettes between us.

Just where our final destination lay, no one knew, but our route was through innumerable towns that had already felt the mighty arm of the Air Corps. Many of the marshaling yards were completely demolished. The most thorough destruction was visible at Fulda and Frankfurt. On a siding we saw forty-five locomotives put out of commission by air strafing. What a pleasant sight to our sore eyes!

After eleven weary hours we arrived at Frankfurt where we were to change trains. What a relief it was to stretch one's legs again and breathe deeply of fresh air. By now I felt I was the dirtiest, thirstiest and most hungry man alive. But most of all, I longed for a cigarette. Here we received a cup of German soup.

I had the misfortune of being the last one to board the train accompanied by two surly guards. The mad scramble for space had begun when the air raid sirens sounded, and we were forced to change again to another train on a different track to get out of the path of the actual bombing. There just wasn't any space left in either of the two compartments allotted to us, so I was pushed along to a small section where I sat with one guard alongside of me, and the other sitting directly in front, both holding rifles across their knees. I made up my mind right then and there that I didn't like these two Jerrys or the malevolent glances they bestowed upon me. Almost immediately they began talking between themselves, clucking their lips, and shaking their heads tragically, pointing at the skeleton frames of 15 and 16 story apartment buildings stretching into the skies. One guard turned to me balefully, saying:

"Vhy Americanas come here to kill our women and children?"

What could I say to these two SS men? That we did not come to Germany to kill women and children, but to put an end to the dreadful purge Hitler had begun in the world?

"Vhy?" the other kept repeating.

Boldly, I decided to counter with a question.

"What about your destruction of England, Czechoslovakia, Poland, and other countries?"

Whether or not they actually understood what I had said I did not know, but they continued to mutter between themselves at each new sight. I eyed them cautiously. I would not have a Chinaman's chance if they decided to do away with me. I spent three of the longest hours of my life sitting in that tiny section with the two guards addling me – three hours of suspenseful watching and waiting. My face was a veiled mask and I said nothing.

We arrived at Oberursel at one o'clock in the morning of September 29. We were to begin immediately the four kilometer march to the Dulag Luft. Two of the fellows were unable to walk so we took turns carrying them on boards. Outside the Dulag barracks a huge German wolfhound was paraded before us. It was a ferocious beast, snarling and barking as it strained against its leash. We whispered among ourselves, "What's the keeper trying to do – scare us?"

Haggard and worn, footsore and hungry, we were marched across the compound into a cell, five feet by eight, which was locked securely on the outside. The 15 of us in that tiny space fell asleep where we stood. Tomorrow there would be other difficulties to encounter, but now sleep completely overcame us. It is still a wonder to me that the fellow on the bottom of the pile had not suffocated during the night.

Interrogation began at 6 o'clock the next morning. Each man was examined separately. I was given a long questionnaire. I filled in my name, rank and serial number and handed it back to the SS guard. He sneered and led me into the Commandant's office. Then began a 15 minute third degree examination. My answers were all the same, "I cannot answer that." (I learned later that the Germans had a complete record of the history and background of each of us, compiled presumably by their Secret Service in the States.)

I was then put in solitary confinement in a dirty, small, dark cell. The only light was from a tiny aperture near the ceiling. After my eyes had become accustomed to the darkness, I noticed various groups of markings on the wall, which I imagined signified days of imprisonment by others before me. I counted as many as 56 scratches in one group and still another of 75. Right then and there I thought I "had it" again.

Hours passed and then to my astounding surprise the door was opened and I was led to a room where a group of fellows were assembled before a desk behind which was a German officer. We were to be quartered in the barracks for the night. I felt almost as though I had been saved from the hangman's noose. It helped considerably to wash up as best we could with the bit of soap they gave us, and to smoke cigarettes that an English chap passed out, my first in 36 hours.

Next morning we entrained for the processing camp near Wetzlar which was under German supervision with an American colonel as the American Man of Confidence. Here we were allowed a shower and given a small American Red Cross toilet kit. I had my first shave in four days and cleansed and rebandaged my leg wound. I could see my wound was not healing properly. Here, too, we received our first Red Cross food parcel.

Jack Erickson

My chute carried me over to a clump of woods where I descended into the trees where my chute snagged on the top of a pine tree and the canopy collapsed. I was left dangling about 20 feet above the ground. Grabbing the shroud lines with my right hand, I tried to lift my weight off my harness so that I could unsnap the leg harness straps with my left hand. Without warning, the limb that had snagged the chute suddenly let go and I fell to the ground, chute and all. I landed so heavily on my feet that my knees were jammed up under my chin.

I apparently passed out for a few moments and when I came to I had a terrific pain in my lower back. When I stood up the pain was more acute and it was difficult to walk. I got down on my hands and knees and gathered up my chute and buried it beneath the pine needles and leaves that I gathered from around me. I then crawled to the edge of the woods where I could see the clearing and saw the other chutist walking across the field. I picked up a dead tree limb that was laying on the ground and using it as a crutch I stood up and yelled at him. I hobbled out of the woods toward him and it was not until I had exposed my position that I saw a uniformed man holding a shotgun some yards behind the other airman. It was too late for me to change direction as the armed man had seen me. He waved his arm motioning me to continue over to his location. As I approached I was very surprised to see that the other chutist was Lt. Bob Christie, our co-pilot.

I now took a closer look at our captor. He was wearing a funny shaped hat that was curved to fit the rear of his head like a skullcap and it had a circular crown in the front. The front of the hat was embellished with a large silver like sunburst badge. He wore a greenish gray military like tunic over riding breeches and polished knee high boots. He was an elderly man, probably in his sixties. He

275

appeared to be very nervous and his shotgun shook as he covered Christie and me. With one hand he gave us a pat search but could find no weapons. Air crewmen in the 8th Air Force did not carry side arms at this stage of the war. We had all turned in our Colt .45 automatics in early August this year. He did pull the ripcord from my pocket and by the expression on his face I could tell he was puzzled as to what it was. Perhaps he thought it was some kind of secret weapon. In a somewhat shaken voice he said to us, "For you der var is uber."

As it turned out, he was the local policeman. In fact, he was the only one in the area.

He motioned to me to put down the limb I had been using for a crutch and for me to sit down on the ground. He then took Lt. Christie into the woods where I had landed to retrieve my parachute. They shortly returned with it. Apparently, I had not hidden it as well as I thought I had. He motioned for Christie to carry me piggyback while he gathered up both chutes that he half carried and half dragged, and we started off for the local village about a quarter of a mile away.

Upon arrival in the tiny village, we were taken directly to the local jail, which consisted of one small cell with a barred door and window. The cell contained two straw ticks on wooden frames.

The jailer was a jovial, robust woman about 40 years old. She and the policeman quickly searched us and confiscated all of our belongings. In my case it included my G.I. issued wristwatch, a pack of Camel cigarettes and my cigarette lighter. The jailer was quite friendly and after the policeman departed, I coaxed her into giving me back two of my Camels that they had confiscated. I learned that the Germans called them zigarettens.

Christie and I sat down for a much needed smoke, the first since before take-off that morning. As the longest day in my life came to a close and darkness settled in, the jailer brought us each a bowl of very thin barley soup, after which we settled down on the straw ticks to try and get some sleep, wondering what tomorrow would bring.

The entire air battle that day had lasted less than five minutes. Twenty-five of the 445th's Liberators had been shot down at the scene of the attack. In addition, two B-24s had crashed in France, two more at Manston in England and a fifth had crashed in the vicinity of our home base at Tibenham.

The original Group casualty list showed 1 killed, 13 wounded, and 236 crewmen missing in action. By the time the war was over and the 445th was departing England the status of the 236 MIAs indicated only 15 officers and 63 NCOs were prisoners of war. Only 13 were officially listed as killed in action. The Group never learned the fate of the remaining 145 MIAs and it must now be presumed that most of them had also been killed in action and their bodies never recovered or identified.

American P-51 fighters responding to the SOS finally appeared on the scene, too late to provide protection or cover for the 445th, although they did manage to destroy a number of the Luftwaffe fighter planes.

According to news reports, American P-51 fighters of the 376th Fighter Squadron, 361st Fighter Group responded to my SOS, too late to protect the bulk of the 445th Libs. The P-51s led by 1st Lt. Victor Bocquin was able to intercept several of the heavily armored FW-190s of Stormgruppe II JG4 and its Me-109 escorts. In an air battle that was fought between 24,000 feet and the deck, the 376th pilots in their yellow- nosed P-51s shot down 18 of the enemy aircraft and probably prevented the complete annihilation of the 445th's forces. One pilot, 1st Lt. William Beyer, shot down five FW-190s and Lt. Bocquin destroyed three. The total of 18 credited victories by the 361st Group set a record for the total number of victories by a single group on a single day's operation.

Reg Miner

At first we were in the north compound at Stalag Luft 1. We had a mess hall there, and we got Red Cross parcels, more or less every week. And the kitchen would take the staples, like if it was roast beef, and make meals of that. Then you're left with your D-bars, candy bars, peanut butter and things like that you'd snack on. It was fantastic. Tobacco, some cigarettes. We were there until after Christmas, then all of a sudden they said, Hey, you guys are moving.

They took all the guys whose dog tags indicated they were Jewish and they put them in that barracks, and they took us and we filled in the places that they left. That's where all of us were together in my crew, in the south compound, and there was a guy by the name of Schlossberg, and he was upset because he didn't have Hebrew on his dog tags and his buddies were gone, and he felt guilty about it. But the worst thing that happened there, they had old guys as guards. The younger guards probably were sent to the Russian front. These old guys were quick with the trigger and they killed a couple of guys in our compound. One guy came out of the barracks next to us during an air raid not realizing there was an air raid on and they shot him. And another guy across the compound jumped out of a window to get something, and he was shot, for no good reason.

In the period after the Germans left, they abandoned the camp, and we were all on our own, and Hubert Zemke was trying to keep us in the camp. He didn't want a bunch of guys roaming this frigging countryside. The war is on, they're liable to get killed. But I went out in a field. We were kind of on a peninsula, and I was walking out towards the water and I'll be damned, there's a German family that had committed suicide lying out there in that field, several people.

They were terrified of the Russians, those goddamn Russians were like animals, and created havoc. It was four or five people. Young kids. A woman. Older man. I thought, "For Christ sake, the war is over practically." As a matter of fact, when we got into camp, we were telling everybody, the war's going to be over pretty soon. Patton was going like a bullet through Europe. He bogged down just as we got in there. So we were overly optimistic about how long it would last, but at least it probably helped more than it hurt, to have some optimistic points of view coming in.

Ira Weinstein

Before I left, I had a cousin who was older than me, he was already flying his own plane, and he was my hero. His father and mother invited me to dinner, and he gave me a watch. It was a Longines Weems watch, which was the watch that all the commercial and other aviators wore. And he said, "I want you to take this. It's a great watch for you, and you bring it back safe." That's the watch I wore on all my missions. So when we got to the interrogation center at Dulag Luft, they threw us all in cells, and first they'd run the temperature way up, then they'd turn it off, but I was only there two days as I remember, maybe just overnight. And then they brought me in to a guy to interrogate me. We had seen a movie that showed just what to expect when you were going to be interrogated, and it would be laughable because it was just like that if you weren't so scared. They told us just give your name, rank and serial number. Don't try and outsmart them or get in a conversation with them.

I stood my ground. Finally, he brings in a guy, and he says to me, "Lieutenant, you don't have to tell me anything. I know all about you. Your mother is Lillian Seligman. She lives in Rochester, New York, with your sister. She lives at 47 Rutledge Drive. You were born and raised in Chicago. You worked for Goldblatt's." They had a dossier on me that was better than the Americans had; they knew everything about me. "You were with the 445th Bomb Group. Your mission was to Kassel. You were in the 702nd Squadron. Your squadron commander was Lieutenant Colonel Jones." So I didn't have to answer anything, I just kept giving them my name. "Now, all you have to tell us is, where were you flying that mission and what was your target?"

I'd say, "Name, Ira P. Weinstein, first lieutenant, 0694482." So finally he got pissed off. Then he says to me, "You are not an American. You're a German. Your name is Weinstein. You were my neighbor in Frankfurt. You're a 'shpy.'" If you're a "shpy," you're gonna get shot. I didn't give. Finally, he calls in a guy. A guy comes in, about six feet tall, in a black body suit with a rubber hose. Then the interrogator's asking me questions and this guy's slapping that hose. But we saw that in the movie. I was plenty scared, believe me, I wasn't going to laugh like I can now. And the interrogator finally says, "Well, if you don't want to tell us what we want to know I'm going to have to turn you over to this guy." I stuck with it.

Then they sent in a German officer in a flying suit with a lot of ribbons. He said, "Cigarette, Lieutenant?"

I said, "No, I don't smoke."

So he sits down on the couch. He says, "You know, you're a flying officer. I'm a flying officer. I'd just like to talk to you about what it was like. Can we discuss it?"

I said, "No."

"You know, we're compatriots."

"Sorry."

So he left.

After I was interrogated, they took all our clothes off and deloused them, and they gave us a shower. As I was marching down this long hall on the way to the showers, before they took our clothes, another group was coming back, and a prisoner from New Zealand said "Hey Yank, if you've got anything you don't want them to get, you'd better get rid of it now because they're confiscating everything that's on you." So I took the watch off – it was on an expansion band – and I threw it to him and said, "Here, you take the watch."

"Okay."

Two days later I'm in a boxcar in Frankfurt, in the marshaling yards, and the RAF comes to bomb the marshaling yards. It's night, and the Germans lock us in the cars and they go to the air raid shelters. On the next track is another set of boxcars with POWs. There's the New Zealand guy. He sees me. He says, "Hey, Yank, you want your watch back?"

I said, "Yeah."

So he threw the watch through the slats – and I caught it. And I kept that watch all during the time that I was a POW and I brought it back. That story is in Roger Freeman's book, and I wrote it up for the 8th Air Force newsletter, "The Watch that Went to War."

George Collar

I never smoked but I chewed tobacco. And these guys that had been prisoners for a long time were starting to get tobacco parcels from home, food and tobacco parcels. Right away they saw that in order to protect their interests, they had to form cartels. And they had the tobacco cartel. Everybody who got tobacco, they got together and they set the price. I had a friend named Henry Fry, he was from my hometown, and he chewed tobacco. And this one guy had a whole carton of champagne plug. It cost about ten cents a plug in the United States. They set the price at a D-bar. And a D-bar was the gold standard. A D-bar was supposed to be worth ten bucks in prison. So every time we wanted a plug of tobacco we had to save our D-bars that we'd been saving from the Red Cross parcels. I'd put a half of one up and he'd put a half, and we'd get a plug of tobacco, and we'd cut it in half-inch cubes. And every morning we'd walk the perimeter, and each chew a half-inch cube till it was gone. Then we wouldn't chew again until the next day. Yeah, those tobacco tycoons we called them. Hey, they could get their laundry done, they could get all kinds of stuff because they had the money.

We didn't do too bad up at Barth until the first of the year of 1945. Right after Christmas. We used to get a Red Cross parcel a week per man, and eking that out along with your German rations you could just about consider you had about a square meal a day. It would keep you alive. But when the Red Cross cut out, we lived on 800 calories a day till Easter, maybe longer. That was tough. I went down from 170 to 135 pounds. And you don't have much ambition and pep when you get hungry. You're tired.

Sometime in '45 they rounded up all the Jewish guys and took them over to the North 1 compound and put them in a single barracks. And Bertram and those guys had to move out and went to the south compound. There was a funny thing about that. They never got Weinstein, but yet they took an Irish guy. They didn't hurt any of them. I heard, it might be that somebody saw the war was coming to an end and they wanted to protect them. I don't know whether that's true or not. But I know when things got really hairy, we could hear the Russian guns. They were approaching Stetin, that was 60 miles away. So the Germans gave permission to dig slit trenches, which we did.

When things were really getting close, we knew where the lines were because there was a secret radio in camp and everybody got the news every night, the real news. Colonel Hubert Zemke was our senior Allied officer. He was head of the 56th Fighter Group. Colonel Zemke was approached by the German colonel, and he said, "We're going to have to perhaps move this camp." In other words we'd have to march to the west. And Zemke said to Colonel Warnstedt, "Look," this is supposed to be true, he said, "We are not in any kind of shape to be marching. We've got people here that have practically been on a starvation diet for four months. We can't march very far. What are you going to do if I give the order, everybody sits down in the middle of the compound? Are you going to kill us all?"

"Besides that," he said, "you know and I know the war's pretty near over." Warnstedt did know that, too.

So Warnstedt says, "I don't want to see any bloodshed, so I'll tell you what I'll do. When we get ready to evacuate, I'll let you know and you can take command of the camp."

This is all going on unbeknownst to us guys because this is high level stuff. So on the evening of the 30th of April, 1945 – we got locked in every night, the lights went out and the power was shut off about 10 o'clock. We could open up the blackout shutters and get some air. So we're laying there, some of them sleeping. About 2 o'clock in the morning, the word got around to take a look at the guard towers, they're all empty. And the dogs aren't in the compound. They had dog patrols every night.

Somebody broke the doors open and we got out and sure as hell, the Germans left. So Colonel Zemke sent word, "Everybody stay put in his compound. Don't move." Because we didn't know where the hell the Russians were. See, the Russians are coming, but we don't know exactly where. So at 6 o'clock the next morning, the first Russian guy showed up at the gate. He was some kind of officer but he was drunk. And he was on a white horse. And he's raising all kinds of hell. He said to Zemke something about "What do you mean, aren't you happy to see the glorious Red Army? I don't see anybody cheering. I don't see any towers being burned down."

So Zemke thought, "I'd better give this guy a little show," and he passed the word, "Burn down a couple of guard towers." Jesus, they lit some guard towers and everybody took off over the hill. They all went to town. Zemke was fit to be tied.

They came back the next day, and you should have seen what they brought with them. My god, there was a full tracked vehicle, brand new. It drove in. And there were horses, there were sheep. Rabbits. They took everything. And this guy Crotty, a friend of mine who was in our room, he was quite a drinker – we always told him the only thing that kept him alive was getting shot down – he went in town, the Russians were all drunk because it was Mayday, and they'd uncovered a bargeload of Holland brandy in the harbor and everybody had bottles sticking out of every pocket. And they were all drunk and they were making everybody else get drunk. Oh Jesus, it was a shambles.

And old Crotty, they carried him in on a shutter.

And what happened, the Russians had a policy of automatically killing the burgomeister and anybody that's connected with him.

That was their policy. Bloodthirsty policy. So the burgomeister of Barth went out on the dike and took his family with him, and he shot them all and killed himself.

I think Warnstedt got away, but there was another German major that wasn't a bad guy that was captured there, I imagine they killed him. But I'll tell you what they did. Probably a couple of months before we were liberated a whole contingent of Ukrainian partisans came in town, they were fighting on the Germans' side, and they were like irregular troops. They had all horse-drawn vehicles. They were driven out of Poland or someplace, and they came into our town. So the Germans let them come up on our peninsula inside the compound and they built a little tent city. And I heard that the Russians rounded those guys up and murdered every one of them. See, Stalin was the most ruthless, bloodthirsty sonofagun that ever lived.

If one of our guys would go to town, he'd liberate a bicycle from somebody and he'd be riding along, if a Russian saw him and wanted it, you either gave it to him or he'd blow your head off. The Russians went in the jewelry store and they shot the jeweler. I saw Russians with wristwatches up and down both arms.

We got sick of the Russians pretty quick. Some of them were all right. Some of them were just ordinary guys like anybody else, but some of them were real rabble rousing communists if there ever was one.

They finally came in and got us on the 13th of May. We were liberated the First of May and they flew in with B-17s in the Barth airfield and picked us up and took us to France.

Frank Bertram

I don't want to go into too much detail on the stalag. We were there for eight or nine months and it was hell. You're feeling just rotten, and when you're injured you feel worse. And your mental condition isn't the greatest. The winter was miserable. The food was poor. We lost a lot of weight. I lost 30 or 35 pounds. All of us were pretty skinny. And one thing about it: When you're hungry you don't think about anything else. It's always food, food, food. You dream day and night of food. And escape was not advisable. They said, "You know, it's not a game anymore. You're going to get shot if you get caught." And at one point, Hitler issued orders to take the American Jewish boys and separate them, and there actually was an order out to shoot them.

Common sense at least prevailed and they realized that if anything like that took place there would be an interaction in the United States and we were holding a lot more of their prisoners than they were of ours. That's the general thought, anyway. But nothing came of it, fortunately. We had this one Jewish guy, his name was Gerber, and he was very swarthy, almost Arabic looking. And he was so funny. He said, "They're not gonna get me, because I just changed my religion."

And we said, "What did you change to?"

And he said, "I'm gonna say Hindu."

Everybody just howled. But they got him; they put him in the other barracks.

Our liberation in the camp came by the Russian army. We could hear them cannonading down the road about three miles away toward the town of Barth and the guns firing, the tanks rumbling. We still had German guards, and then all of a sudden one morning we woke up and we had American guards. I guess Bernie Levine told you that story about Henry the Butcher Boy's daughter. I felt sorry for her, because Henry was one of the ferrets we called them; he was a snitch who would do everything to just annoy all the Americans, really a nasty fellow. He set dogs on them. I think he was really hated more because of the fact that he came from the United States, as did one of our commanding officers over there, from Long Beach, Colonel Von Mueller I believe it was. He was a Long Beach Nazi. Most of these people were of German descent or had been born in Germany and had come over here and then went back to the Fatherland.

I'm looking in my mind at Colonel Von Mueller, who was a pretty nice fellow, I thought. He interviewed me when I first went into the camp. When I walked in there this man said, "Ahh, Frank Bertram. You're married. Your wife's name is Mary. And you went to Commerce High School in San Francisco, graduated in 1938."

Now he's telling me this and I'm sitting there thinking, "What is this?" They knew all about me, as they did most everybody else. And he said, "You have no children."

I said, "We didn't have time."

He said, "Ahhh, that's the trouble. In America, not enough children. In Russia too many children. But in Germany, just right."

Then he said, "You know, I could have you shot as a spy."

I said, "What?"

He said, "You write down your name as Bertram. But the dogtags you gave me said Bertrum."

He said, "Take a look."

And sure enough, they had misspelled my name on my dogtags, and I never knew it.

Then he said, "Of course, we wouldn't do that. We know who you are."

Charles Graham

Sollien told me as much as he could before we were separated, and then I was in this Dulag camp for about five days, sleeping on benches. They knew more about us than we knew about them. The next thing we knew we were in the 40-and-8 boxcars heading for our camp. They put us in a marshaling yard at Frankfurt, and the RAF would bomb at night. It was terrifying, but fortunately we weren't hit.

Then they moved us up to Stalag Luft IV. And prior to that, we didn't realize it at that time, but maybe a month prior to our capture, the prisoners had been at some other camp and were brought there by boat and unloaded there, because they were too close to Berlin at the time, and that was when they had to walk or run between the columns of soldiers and German dogs, it was called the Heydekrug run. They were in our camp also, and several of them were still in the hospital when we left there. I think one boy said they had about 42 dog bites and 18 bayonet wounds. So I fortunately wasn't in on that.

But they treated us okay while we were in prison camp. What potatoes we peeled, that was what we got to eat. At night, there were 24 of us in our room, there were Australians and English, New Zealanders, all different nationalities. And the English were smart. They would parade and exercise during the day around the compound, and we'd lay in their bunks because we had to sleep on the floor at night, and read books. And we got soft, not realizing that one of these days we were going to be liberated, and maybe forced on a march. Nothing like that crossed our mind.

After about seven months had gone by, they started to have rumors going around that there was going to be a forced march, and some of the boys were in such condition that they wouldn't be able to walk. Ammi Miller was one of them. His feet and legs were real bad. So consequently, he went by train with I don't know how many others to Barth. And I didn't see Ammi after that until I got back to the States.

I was issued an English RAF uniform, which was very wooly. I wear a 10 and a half shoe and they issued me a 9 and a half boot. Then prior to that, they had dropped a soldier where he could be captured, because he had been trained to take over a camp to keep from using all the Red Cross parcels. We got one Red Cross parcel a week, between four men. So if you got 48 prunes, you got 12 prunes for the week. And we would take those four prunes, say, for three days and peel them from the seed and then use the klim milk and the water and make like a little syrup with it, and that was our breakfast, along with the millet, which was birdseed, but it was good at that time.

Outside of that, and the potatoes like I told you about, once in a while we would get Jerry jam, that was just about all of the food we would get. And again, of course, the Americans were dumb. We would trade the English our D-bars, the chocolate bars, for their cigarettes. And the English were quite ready for a march. We weren't. And when we left, on the 6th of January, it was snowing outside, and we were given a complete Red Cross parcel per man. But it was so doggone heavy that you'd see the boys just throwing the pieces out into the ditches. You kept what you could carry, and it didn't last too long.

We ferried across the Oder, and we would stay at night in barns. About 10,000 of us they figure started out on the road march, and we got to the Elbe and we crossed the Elbe River on the bridge and stayed at a camp between Hanover and Amberg for about a week. And then Patton started his drive on the south and Montgomery on the north. When Patton got to the Rhine, he was supposed to have held up and let the Russians come in and finish the war. But when he didn't meet the resistance he thought he would, he went across and Montgomery hearing that, why, he went across in the north, but the Germans had moved us back into Germany away from Montgomery and blew up the bridge, so it was four or five days later before we were liberated by Montgomery's 2nd Rangoon Division on the road. And the night before, we could hear small arms fire in the distance, so it was definitely a violation of the Geneva convention that we were that close to the front lines.

About halfway through the march, the fighter escort of the Americans would fly and they knew where we were, but we didn't know where we were. So I guess they kept word going back to the different air force bases. But the second pass he made, this road pillbox opened up on him, and on the third pass he made he came in to get the pillbox, and with those tracer bullets going all around, we were digging in, that's when I really did get some flak and received the Purple Heart.

After we were liberated and we started to walk as a group into another transit camp to be deloused, we had on the German helmets and their guns and all that they had given us the night before, and here come our fighter pilots and they thought it was a German column, and they started coming in and strafing us. So we threw everything in the ditch and got rid of it, and they realized what was going on.

The night before we were liberated, I had two German guards with me on the march, one used to be a doorman at the Palmer House in Chicago, and the other used to make road maps for Shell Oil Company in Toledo, Ohio. They had gone back to Germany on vacation and they got stuck over there, and they had to go into the German army. They knew where Decatur was, and that it was the soybean capital of the world. And they said, "We'll do anything in the world we can for you, but if we're told to shoot you the next minute, we've got to do that. And when we get to this barn, we're to go up and get our orders." And here comes old Fritz back, I said, "Fritz, what happened?"

I never saw a man so dejected in my life.

He said, "They told us to get to the Berlin section as fast as we can, that was our reward for getting you people as far as we did." He was really dejected. I felt sorry for him. And they were in their sixties.

I never had the feeling that I'd be liberated. I always had the feeling that they'd line us up and mow us down before they'd let us be liberated. But we didn't realize at the time that we were considered hostages more than we were prisoners. When we were captured, they took our Bibles away from us, which we always carried in our flying suit, and threw them in a pile like they were going to burn them. But when the attempt on Hitler's life at

Berchtesgaden failed, they gave us our Bibles back. So we had those with us when we were on the road march. But we had very poor medical facilities. We had doctors with us, but they didn't have any facilities to do much. And then when I was liberated, I went to Brussels, Belgium, to a hospital and I was there for a month, and all I got was champagne and milkshakes, so I was bloated. I had lost 30 pounds on the road march, because the only thing actually that we got after we had used up what Red Cross parcel we had, we just sort of picked spuds and things that we'd dig out of the dirt going into the barnyards, because they didn't have any facilities to feed us.

One day they told us that if we marched 30 miles, we'd get a warm meal and a place to sleep under cover. We walked the 30 miles and we got to an open field, and they had sort of a supply wagon there, and with our little klim cans around our neck that we had for water as we'd go through the villages, we got a little can of soup, and we slept in the open fields that night. That was when Ammi left us because he couldn't make that 30-mile march. Most of the time we walked 12 to 14 miles a day. But what was bad with the march was about every hour they let you rest about five minutes, and that just got you stiff and you couldn't hardly get back up.

After the hospital thing I went to Le Havre and waited for my orders to get back to the States, and I got onto a Coast Guard cutter. The chief petty officer was Victor Mature, and he gave us a show every afternoon onboard. He was real good. In fact, one of the sergeants – at that time I was a staff sergeant, this one sergeant he was a higher grade than I was, he tried to get myself and the prisoners to clean up the decks and so forth, and Mature came down and told him, "These boys have been through this. They're not going to do that. You get your group and you do it." So I thought quite a bit of Victor Mature.

When we got back to the Brooklyn Navy Yard, we were sent to Fort Sheridan outside of Chicago, and I caught the Bluebird down to Decatur, and my poor mother, she had the feeling that anything she didn't eat I would get, so she had lost even more weight than I had, and she looked like a little peasant lady there standing on the platform as I got off the train.

Bill Bruce

We stayed at this place until Dec. 21, 1944 and then went to Sagan Stalag. On Jan. 27, 1945 we were told to get ready for a long trip. Most of the other prisoners walked to Nurnberg 110 kilometers away. They took the most severely crippled by train – we barely escaped being liberated by the Russian troops by only about five minutes.

We traveled by train, trucks and walking until Feb. 11, 1945 with very little food and no toilet paper. I was by this time able to operate on crutches. This trip was really a rotten one – the German guards were just as hungry and miserable as we were. We did nothing to aggravate them because they did actually shoot prisoners.

We arrived at Nurnberg Feb. 11, 1945.

This was a complete transition from what we had at the Sagan camp. The Germans were very nasty and actually shot two prisoners going to the latrine after 10 o'clock at night. I met several of my old pilot friends here and heard that our Kassel raid was the biggest loss of aircraft on a single mission in the war – 25 out of 37 aircraft shot down and several others crashing in France.

Stayed at this POW camp until April 4th when we were sent to Moosburg, Germany. There were 6,000 of us and 660 German guards on this march. It was one helluva trip. Myself and two friends kind of kept out of the mainstream. However, after a couple of close shaves with the SS boys we rejoined the rest of the men.

All the way to Moosburg (about 100 kilometers) – at this time we knew the Germans were close to having the shit kicked out of them. Even the German guards admitted they were losing the war. Their manners and attitude changed 100 percent for the better.

April 29th – A Big Big Day

At 11 o'clock American P-51s came in at treetop level and strafed all around our camp, causing the Germans to panic. This lasted about ten minutes and then our lovely big Sherman tanks came crashing into our camp with the infantry soldiers right behind.

Loudspeakers from the tanks told the prisoners to lie flat on the ground and stay there. They didn't have to tell us twice. With that they blew up every building around the camp – also a church that had 88-mm guns concealed behind the closed door. We as

POWs knew that the Germans meant to fire at our camp when the Americans came to rescue us. We told the tank boys that it was full of German anti-tank people with a lot of ammunition.

Our tanks called in a spotter plane for range and after three or four shots hit the jackpot, blowing up the church and everyone in it in one gigantic explosion. What a thrill for us POWs. We were no longer prisoners of war.

The 14th Armored Division of the Third Army were our liberators. I personally met and talked to General Patton and believe me, he was and looked as we all knew he would – white pearl-handled pistols and all – a real great guy.

For the next few days things were not too good – we still had very little food, no date to leave – still in Germany – and no information on when we would go home. Actually, we were practically in the front lines even though we did not know this at the time.

Finally, the Army really took hold and flew us to Camp Lucky Strike in France. They put us on a large ship for home – arrived in New York City as the first POWs from Europe to a great welcome. I called my wife who I hadn't heard from in eight months and found out I was the father of a six month old baby girl.

Chapter 23: Walter's Story

Walter Hassenpflug

This is excerpted from a life story by Walter Hassenpflug as told to and translated by Gunther Lemke.

The morning of that November day (Nov. 21, 1944), classes had been stopped because of an air raid warning as so many times before. At 12:00 noon, my father came home from work for lunch. My mother was busy in the kitchen cooking.

At that time, six families were living in the double house 25/27. Our apartment was located on the ground floor.

In the meantime, the radio announcements concerning the airspace over our area reported that enemy bomber units were returning from the central German area.

Subsequently, residents of Friedloser Strasse – most of the time the same ones — had taken shelter in the Felsenkeller (celler in the rocks) approximately 400 meters away. Mrs. Berg from our building and her five year old son as well as our neighbors the Gorges were on their way to the air raid shelter.

My father and I were standing in front of the main entrance to our house when two women came toward us from the main road. One was my aunt Katharina Hassenpflug, 36 years old, of Friedlos, and Mrs. Helene Daube, 71 years old, from Hersfeld. Both of them were on the way to Friedlos and intended to pay us a visit. While we were talking to them the roar of engines told us that airplanes were approaching.

A short while later, a group of 12 four-engine bombers appeared in the sky approaching from the south. They were flying unusually low and slowly. I could clearly recognize them as B-17 Flying Fortress aircraft.

At this moment, Mrs. Martha Rudolph, 23 years old, stepped past us out of the house with her two and a half month old baby Sieglinde to hurry to the Felsenkeller. She was already in the street with her baby carriage when she ran back inside the house because she had forgotten something.

Suddenly I noticed yellow smoke floating towards the ground near the lead aircraft. For a moment it looked like the aircraft was on fire. I immediately realized that it was a smoke bomb which had been dropped to mark bombing targets. I immediately ran into the kitchen to warn my mother and in a flash returned to my father and the two women by the front door.

Right away I observed several bombs in the sky which were falling to the ground hissing and whistling. It looked to me as if the bombs were falling at an angle to the rear. This seeming fall, as I know now, is based on an optical illusion which is caused by the fact that the bombs remain in a horizontal position behind the aircraft that flies on.

I immediately dropped to the ground instinctively without a feeling of fear or threat to my life. The two women remained standing. My father, who was standing two steps below us, lay down in front of me and thus covered me with his body in the direction of the garden.

Not even 10 meters from us a bomb had hit.

I was hardly lying flat on my stomach when I heard a terrific detonation and promptly lost consciousness. I awoke in total darkness with my mouth and nose full of sand, concrete and limestone dust, and I felt like being buried alive underneath the rubble. I was unable to move, not even an inch, and was unable to utter a sound. I did not feel any pain, though. I then heard my father moan and again lost consciousness.

The building was leveled to the ground. A direct hit penetrated the building all the way to the basement. Another bomb exploded in the garden behind the house and still another one only a few yards from our position.

I have no idea of how long I was buried underneath the rubble. Possibly only for minutes because otherwise I would have suffocated. I came to because I suddenly felt that I was being pulled from underneath the rubble. I was hurting unbearably. Almost blind, I could not see anything and only shadowyly recognized some men who were lifting me up. They carried me across the street and put me down on the road leading to Beckersgraben (Becker's ditch) next to the Fenners' residence. My father and later on my mother, too, were put down there, however, I did not know that they were dead. Mrs. Rudolph was recovered – seriously injured – but died later at the hospital. Her baby, Sieglinde, was still lying in the baby carriage in the street and miraculously remained unhurt.

(Sieglinde was raised by relatives. I never met her afterwards, but her father was a soldier at the front, and he remarried after the war. She later moved to Wiesbaden, and married a police colonel. He was two and a half years old at the time.)

I was completely dazed, unable to talk, and was barely able to see and hear. I hardly became aware of what was going on around me. Wracked with pain, I was eventually carried away on a stretcher. Then I lost consciousness again. I regained consciousness at the county hospital only the next day, heavily bandaged and with my right leg in high traction. Beside the head, chest and leg injuries I also sustained a compound fracture of a leg.

I stayed at the hospital until the beginning of January 1945. Afterwards, I was transferred to the remedial hospital at Niederaula where I stayed till the middle of February.

A delayed action cap exploded on the road to Beckersgraben, where I had been laid down, in the afternoon. Fenner's residence, which had previously been severely damaged, was now finished off.

Of the eight persons in the double house 25/27 at the time of the raid, I was the only survivor. The bodies of Mrs. Helbling (38 years old) and her daughter Inge (13 years old) were found much later. Furthermore, the remains of the two women who had been standing next to us at the entrance, they were torn to pieces by the bombs.

When I came to the following day, I immediately asked for my parents. I was told "they are also at the hospital and are suffering from severe leg injuries so that they cannot come to see you."

In the beginning, I believed them because I just couldn't imagine that they were dead. The same day, I was visited by relatives including an aunt from Hamburg. Due to the fact that all of them were weeping, I asked: What are you weeping for? I am still alive." They gave me the same answer as the hospital staff when I asked for Mom and Dad.

I was then asked if I knew something about Katharina and Mrs. Daube. A farmer, who passed by our house on a horse-drawn wagon, had observed them enter our house. So far, they had not been found yet. They, however, did not tell me anything about the extent of destruction or other casualties.

There were more visitors during the days to follow. Friends, classmates, leaders of the HJ (Hitler Jugend), BDM (association of German girls) and NSDAP (National Socialist Workers Party of Germany), as well as relatives stood in front of my bed. I kept noticing that some of the visitors had tears in their eyes. That made me suspicious. Every day, I asked for my parents. Their evasive looks, and those of the nurses, slowly made me doubt. One day, my aunt from Hamburg tearfully admitted to me that my parents were dead.

They had already been buried on 25 November. My aunt Katharina was buried three days later. Her husband had been killed in France in 1943; now her two children, Elisabeth and Artur, were orphans who had lost both parents.

I couldn't believe it and wept bitterly – also during the following days and nights. Sometimes I woke up and thought that this just had to be a bad dream. But only for a moment, then reality got hold of me again. Almost every night I was plagued by bad dreams. For months I was dreaming of air raids. Often I wished to be dead, that's how desperate I was. Despite the loving care by the nurses and relatives, I felt a deep void surrounding me.

Today, all I can say is that losing your parents at such an age is a trauma. Only those who have experienced a fate like that can really understand this. Naturally, there was no psychological care in times of war like it is available nowadays after a terrible disaster.

After this fateful occurrence I was always scared when sirens were wailing announcing an air raid warning. Previously, I had never felt that way. In case of an air raid warning while at the hospital I was always pushed to the lift, like all other patients confined to their bed, and then hauled to the basement. Sometimes, I was lying there for hours underneath big heating pipes that gave me a nightmare. I always feared to be buried under rubble again as a result of bombing.

I was now able to understand why classmates, who had already experienced the bombing raids on big cities, were trembling when American bombers approached.

When I was at the hospital, I temporarily shared a room with a 14-year-old boy from Cologne who had been seriously injured in the course of a low level attack on a train near Mecklar on October 2, 1944. His right leg had been severed above the knee. He also suffered a through and through bullet wound of the left calf. The boy, accompanied by his mother and four brothers and sisters, was on the way to Thuringia where the children were supposed to be sent for the purpose of Kinderlandverschickung (children were evacuated from big cities to the countryside to escape the heavy bombing). The mother as well as the brothers and sisters remained uninjured.

I witnessed that air raid. Seventeen people were killed and a large number were injured.

Personally, I did not know any feelings of hatred until then. I knew, however, that Allied airmen were generally hated by the population. The bombing war and the threat by low-flying planes were considered as terror by the population.

The following day (Sept. 28), around noon, heavy bomber units returned via our area. Again there was closed cloud cover. At 1:31 p.m., we were shocked by a terrific explosion on Friedloser Strasse, accompanied by a huge shock wave that made windows and doors of the buildings tremble. Approximately 100 demolition bombs struck the Zellersgrund area, where the prisoner of war camp was located, and the southern slopes of the Giegenberg, approximately 500 meters from us. Two barracks were completely destroyed. Fortunately there was only property damage because the forced foreign laborers were at work in the factories at Hersfeld at the time. My research later revealed that the bombs were dropped in this location due to a navigational error. The bombs were supposed to hit the Eschwege airstrip.

Along with the bombs, thousands of leaflets and phony, already expired, ration cards had been dropped. The leaflets drifted in the direction of the Solzwiesen (meadows along the Solz creek) of the Friedlos area.

The Hersfeld Hitler Youth immediately dispatched a number of boys and girls who were supposed to gather the leaflets and ration cards. They were burned on the spot. I also belonged to this group. We had been urged not to read the leaflets or even take them with us. We still read them but did not believe the contents; we considered it false enemy propaganda.

In the course of gathering the leaflets we discovered an American flier who was hiding in the bushes along the Solz creek. With much interest we curiously studied him from head to toe. The man was rather tall and had full black hair. He did not wear headgear and had a green overall that could be heated, and insulated brown semi boots. He had problems walking because he had sprained his ankle while landing and leaned on a heavy stick. We escorted him to Friedloser Strasse, where in House No. 130, a so-called "pilot point" in case of an air raid warning had been set up which was manned by policemen. In the meantime, our Bannfuehrer (warden leader) appeared on the scene to be informed about our leaflet search operation. He was surprised to see us approach with this airman. Since the Bannfuehrer was wearing a uniform and carried a pistol on his belt, the American evidently began feeling uneasy; however, nothing happened – there was no abuse or malpractice. The pilot (airman) was searched at this "pilot point" and questioned. He had raw potatoes in his pockets as well as a prayer book. We learned that he was a First Lieutenant from San Francisco.

He belonged to the crew of the bomber that had crashed the day before at Grebenau.

He was then escorted to the police station in town.

At that time, I had no idea that I would meet this man again some day.

Chapter 24: Death by Hanging

Kay Brainard Hutchins

This is a copy of something that went to Walter. The Archives is writing to Walter, saying that "in reply to your letter of July 10, 1986, we searched the records of the office of the quartermaster general and located missing air crew reports. We also searched the records of, according to our files, Joseph A. Lemp, Paul Kolliger and others who were tried for their involvement in the shootings of Second Lieutenant Cowgill and Lieutenant Scala and others" – see, Newell was one of the others. "If you wish to order copies…" what they say is it costs money to get them.

This is a copy of a letter from Walter Hassenpflug that George Collar sent to me: "Thanks very much for your letter of January 27th, and the enclosed newspaper clipping. The information you sent was very interesting and helpful in my recent research.

"With great interest did I read about the Blasted Event on the mission to Saarbrucken. This aircraft crashed on Sept. 27 near the village of Iba with the following crew: Lt. Carrow, who was a POW. Lt. Brainard" – and it said "DED" – and I didn't know what that meant. I had to write and ask. It means "declared dead." And these others were either killed or were prisoners of war, about evenly divided. "When the B-24 crashed it set a barn on fire. Frank Bertram took pictures of the crash site. Austin, Beluski and Panconi were buried at the cemetery at Iba. I talked to the carpenter who built the coffins, and he's now 82 years old. I do not know where and how Newell Brainard died.

"It is possible that he landed with his chute near the village of Nentershausen and was one of the five airmen who were shot to death there. This, however, is merely an assumption. Therefore, I would like to know if his sister, Kay Brainard Hutchins, knows something about it? … A few weeks ago I met a lady from Lauschroden, 77 years old, who spent a few days here visiting the West. She remembered that the prisoners were handed apples through the window in the prison. I think I'll be able to get more information this way." And he's enclosing something I marked "the alleged crash site in East Germany of your B-24" with an X – that's what Walter wrote to Collar, and Collar sent me a copy, which was the first that I learned about what might have happened to Newell – and that's March 5, 1987.

I called him right away and told him I appreciated it, and that's how we got started back and forth. I would write to Hassenpflug and talk to him, and George Collar again. But I also wrote ... here ... "We have no record of the prisoner of war status of Newell Brainard, John Cowgill and Hector Scala." They more or less denied it, although they never held back any information on purpose. It seems to me that maybe they didn't have enough information, although it was four years before they finally identified him and said he definitely was killed in action.

They still called it killed in action; they didn't call it murder. And then they said, "We referred your letter to our military field branch for an examination." And then I heard from them, something about a fire in Missouri when a lot of things were destroyed. "This agency has made several attempts to retrieve the individual deceased personnel file of Newell Brainard from the National Records. Unfortunately, that center is unable to locate the file. However, a major fire at that center destroyed or severely damaged a lot of the military records," and so forth.

That's the only information I could get. But in 1990, I was working in New York. I worked for many years for Douglas Fairbanks Jr. And he didn't have a secretary in New York that year, so I worked the whole year up there. But he had to travel, and one time when he was going to London for a week, I decided to go to Washington. My cousin took me to the Archives. So I went in and requested the files on the 445th Bomb Group, and they brought out a cardboard box with all these files in it. I started first reading a little here and there, and I would see occasionally where Newell went on a mission. They'd give pictures even, I think, of the formations up in the air. I think it would usually say that it was Carrow's crew. By then I knew that Carrow had been his pilot.

So I get to the file on the Kassel mission, and it was empty. And there was a note in it which said "This file has been missing since" I think sometime in 1973. And whether somebody had just lifted it or what the reason was, they didn't know. By the time the

Archives in Washington got them, it was already missing. The next mission, and from then on out, I could read about every mission. But it said nothing about Newell's flight.

After I'd been reading for a while, the head of the Archives, who was very helpful, came along and he said, "How are you doing? Are you finding the information you've been looking for?" And "Do you need any help?"

I said, "Well, strangely enough, the one thing I was interested in was this file that's missing."

And I told him a little bit about the story, that I had heard that my brother was killed but I really wanted to find out for sure.

He said, "You know, what you should really have is the burial file. Come with me, I'll give you their telephone number." He took me to a telephone, gave me their number, and told me to call them and tell them I would like a copy of my brother's burial file. It's in another building, or another area. And they took down the information and said it would take a few weeks, but they would send it to me. And they did. I was still in New York when this package comes. It was an inch thick.

I started at the first page. I think there were 118 pages. Some of them were duplicates. I read through them, page by page, and it was the missions and all this kind of stuff. But it wasn't until I got to page 80 I think it was – somewhere in the eighties – that I found the one that made it very clear he had been murdered.

"United States vs Josef Ehlen et al. 5 February 1948. Persons tried: Josef Ehlen, August Viehl, Reinhard Beck, Franz Muller, Martin Baesse and Paul Winkler. Gist of offenses: The accused were tried on two charges and particulars. Both charges were based on the violation of the laws of war. The first particulars alleged that the accused participated in the killing of four unknown American prisoners of war. The second particulars alleged that the accused participated in assaulting two or more unknown American prisoners of war..

"Trial data: Tried by a general military government court appointed by the commanding general of the United States forces, European Theater. Findings were made and sentences imposed as follows: Josef Ehlen, first charge guilty, second charge guilty. Death by hanging. August Viehl, first charge guilty, second charge guilty. Death by hanging. Reinhart Beck, first charge not guilty, second charge guilty. Four years.

"Franz Muller, first charge not guilty, second charge guilty. Six years. Martin Baesse, first charge not guilty, second charge guilty. Six years. Paul Winkler, first charge guilty, second charge guilty. Sentence: Death by hanging.

"Evidence: Prosecution – Four unknown American fliers parachuted to earth on 27 Sept. 1944, two in the vicinity of Nentershausen and two in the nearby village of Suess, Germany. The two flyers who landed in Nentershausen were taken to a labor camp in Nentershausen, beaten and then shot. The two fliers who landed in Suess were brought to the Nentershausen labor camp and there taken out and shot. All of the convicted accused except Beck participated in the beating or killing in one way or another.

"Defense – All of the accused denied active participation in the beating and shooting of the American flyers, although all except Beck witnessed at least one of the killings. Ehlen attempted to justify his illegal actions by stating that the Americans had attacked him and the other accused. Beck was involved in the incidents only to the extent that he went into the camp enclosure to collect a bill for bread at the time two of the flyers were being held prisoners.

"Discussion: Each of the accused except Beck was present at a killing, and although each denied that he killed or beat any flyer, the court was justified in arriving at the findings of guilty to the respective charges since there was ample evidence to show that all of the accused except Beck were eager principals in the beatings or killings and not merely curious bystanders, as each accused contended he was. The evidence was sufficient to support the findings and sentences except as to accused Beck.

"Summation: The court had jurisdiction of the accused and of the offense. Examination of the entire record fails to disclose any error or omission which resulted in injustice to any of the accused except Beck.

"Sentences: The deputy judge advocate for war crimes recommends that the findings and sentences be approved to all accused except Beck. As to Beck he recommends the findings and sentence be disapproved. War Crimes Board of Review No. 1 concurs in this recommendation except that it recommends a modification of the findings as to the particulars of Charge 1 against Ehlen and Viel, and a reduction of three years in the sentence of Baesse. I do not believe any modification is necessary respecting the findings as to the particulars of Charge 1 against Ehlen and Viel. In my opinion Ehlen and Viel participated to some extent in the killing of all four flyers, their principal participation, however, being in connection with two of the fliers. Also, I see no reason for reducing the imprisonment imposed on Baesse. He participated in the crime and took a watch belonging to one of the fliers.

"Paul Winkler, one of the accused sentenced to death in this case, has already been executed for his participation in another, similar crime. His sentence to death in this case should be approved but not ordered executed.

"Petition: Subsequent to the report of the War Crimes Board of Review on the record of trial, a petition was received in behalf of Ehlen alleging that an executed war criminal by the name of Karl Eggert exonerated Ehlen before his execution. This petition has been investigated and carefully considered by both the Deputy Judge Advocate for War Crimes and War Crimes Board of Review No. 1. Both concur in the view that it should not affect the sentence against Ehlen. I have also carefully considered this petition and concur with the Deputy Judge Advocate for War Crimes and War Crimes Board of Review No. 1. Even if as alleged the actual shot was fired by Eggert, Ehlen was present at the time and is equally guilty.

"Recommendations: I recommend that the findings and the sentences of this court be approved as to Ehlen, Viel, Muller, Baesse and Winkler and that they be disapproved as to Beck. My recommendation has been formally bound in the record of trial."

This was the missing Air Crew Report. That's where he was DED. You can barely read it. They didn't have Xerox machines then, and they were terrible.

"Report of Burial. Murdered. Brainard, Newell, 700 Bomb Squad, Nentershausen, Germany, 27 Sept. 1947. 1) Previously buried as unknown X-1535 at St. Avold. Identified through exact comparison of tooth chart obtained for X-1535 and that for Lieutenant Brainard. 2) Estimated height and color of hair for X-1535 in agreement with that for Lieutenant Brainard. 3) Clothing of X-1535 marked 'Brainard.' 4) Estimated date and place of death for X-1535 in agreement with Missing Air Crew Report for Air Crew 42 – 110022 of which Lieutenant Brainard was a crew member. 5) German Dulag record KU-3079 indicates that Lieutenant Brainard was killed in the area from which X-1535 was disinterred.

"Previously buried in isolated grave located at Nentershausen. Have fingerprints been placed on report of interment?

"No.

"If not, explain.

"Fingers missing.

"Remarks. Remains received wrapped in mattress cover in a UK box. Body intact with large amounts of decomposed flesh. Clothing found on body: Marking Brainard found once on wool undershirt. Tooth chart accomplished.

Fluoroscopic examination negative. No personal effects. Estimated weight of remains: 40 pounds. Two bullet holes found in skull. See blackout chart. Remnants of gauze head bandage found. Report of burial found with no pertinent information. The marking Brainard corresponds to the only Brainard listed in casualty book." Signed, Ernst C. Gaddy, CWO, USA"

Actually, as bad as it sounds, that's only one of many casualties like that. Maybe that's why they thought that it's better to just say "killed in action" than to give you all the details. Mother of course never knew this, which thank god she didn't.

They buried him first as an unknown, and then after they did all this investigating, they went and brought him back. Newell had had a head injury – I got all this information from Hassenpflug – evidently either he was injured by flak or hit his head when he jumped out of the plane or when he landed. They first took him to somebody's house, and the lady of the house was concerned about his head injury and had a nurse sent in – a Red Cross nurse from the town – and she bandaged his head.

But then he was taken away from that house. He was supposed to be turned over to the military authorities, but somehow or other he got mixed in with this group. They were four at first and then one came in from another area; whether Newell was that one or not I don't think they ever knew. But the person that they turned him over to – I don't know who did or how they made the mistake, but the guy was running a slave labor camp, and they said that anybody who was in charge of slave laborers was a tough guy to begin with, and so rather than turn them over to the right military people, he just beat them up and killed them. And then they removed all of their identification, they thought. There were no dog tags, no insignia, no uniforms.

So when he was brought back the second time for identification, that's when the teeth and so forth proved who it was, to a certain extent, but not definite enough for Walter's work on it. He found out that where Newell was buried, there was a bandage, and he knew that Newell had been to this woman's house and that they had bandaged him – so that's how they said, "That must have been Newell." And they also claim to have found a mark on his undershirt that had his name on it. But the thing that convinced them was the fact that the bandage was still around the skull.

Walter told me that the woman who bandaged him was in a nursing home. She was very elderly. And he was sort of hoping that we could get together, but she wasn't in that town anymore. She was probably ten or more years older than I am.

Chapter 25: Walter's Research

Walter Hassenpflug

The following is from a letter Walter wrote to historian John Woolnough and translated by Guenther Lemke, describing Walter's connection to the Kassel Mission

For approximately the past four years I have been busy gathering information about the aerial warfare events of World War II in the area of Bad Hersfeld and investigating their background. In doing so, I especially busied myself with the disaster of the 445th Bomb Group, because there are some personal experiences for myself involved in this tragedy. My research, however, is not complete yet. The work is very difficult. Many of the witnesses of those days are no longer alive and I am still trying to find out the addresses of others. It is also extremely hard to locate German pilots of those times. I think only very few are still alive. Many of them were killed in action during the last months of the war. There are hardly any documents to be found in German archives. Most likely, all reports that were made and photos that were taken by the police, military and other local authorities, were destroyed at the end of the war or were otherwise lost.

Another difficulty I kept running into with my research work is part of the events took place on the territory of the now German Democratic Republic (East Germany). Several planes crashed there and many U.S. airmen landed there with their chutes. No information is available from this border area of Thuringia (GDR restricted area about 5 kilometers).

I obtained many documents, however, from American archives. I have also been able to get in touch with a number of former U.S. airmen, who have related to me their experiences and furnished me some photos. With some of them I have established a very friendly relationship. I owe thanks to all those nice people in the United States who have assisted me so far.

Based upon what I have gathered so far, this aerial combat on 27 September 1944 is extraordinary in its dramatic and concentrated run of events. It was probably one of the most spectacular events in the resistance against the allied bomber offensive against Germany. Tragic events also took place on the ground.

In some villages, acts of violence by civilians against U.S. airmen who had parachuted to safety occurred. It even happened that airmen were murdered. Beside these outrages there were genuine cases of assistance. Many U.S. airmen tried to flee in an attempt to escape capture. Some of them succeeded to hide for weeks before they were picked up. This region is densely covered with woods so that many airmen landed in the woods. Many of them got caught in tall trees.

It is astonishing that such a disaster is only so scarcely described in the literature of aerial warfare. I only know about the short mention in "The Mighty Eighth" (Page 178/179) by Roger A. Freeman.

I presume that you are in possession of a lot of information from American sources. Therefore, the following account of mine is limited to my local research.

The 35 planes of the 445th Bomb Group dropped their bombs (1,000 pounds GP [general purpose] bombs only) on the open fields between three villages a short distance from Goettingen. There was only property damage to a few buildings, as well as garden plots and farm fields. An ox was injured by shrapnel and had to be slaughtered.

After dropping their bombs, the group returned on the same course as the other groups of the 2nd Air Division, only on a route slightly further to the east. First, the group took to the south from Goettingen and then turned to a south-westerly course approximately 10 kilometers northwest of the city of Eisenach. This course was about on a line with Hersfeld, Giessen and Koblenz.

The German fighters evidently attacked at exactly the moment when the group was flying on a south-westerly course. The ships of Lt. Fromm (No. 2) and Lt. Jones (No. 9) crashed so far away from the main course because they left the general course, after the crew had bailed out, since the autopilot was on and the ships veered off from the original course to an opposite course in the direction of Kassel/Goettingen.

The German fighter formations had taken off from the bases in Eastern Germany and were guided to the west by their Ground

Control stations in order to attack the 2nd Division which was approaching Kassel. By straying off course, the 445th Bomb Group found itself between the rest of the returning division and the German fighters which were approaching from the east. However, it is possible that the German control officers realized that the 445th BG was without fighter escort and, without hesitation, directed all German fighters to attack them.

All three assault groups (Sturmgruppen) of the Reichs Defense of the Air Force took part in the attack (Freeman mentions only the II./JG 4), namely: II./JG 4, IV/JG 3, II./JG 300.

The First and Third of JG 4 and the First of JG 300 were assigned as Me-109 escort groups. The exact number of planes is not known. American sides usually mention the number 100 to 150. These figures seem about right.

The first wave of attack was probably flown by II/JG 4 which had taken off from Welzow. Their two ME-109 escort groups were led by Wing Commander Michalski. IV/JG 3, led by Captain Moritz, had taken off from Lukau and was probably flying the second wave, while the third wave of attack was II/JG 300 under Lieutenant Bretschneider which had taken off from Finsterwalde.

According to corresponding memories by American and German airmen, the surprise attack was described as follows:

The FW-190 assault fighters were passing through the bomber formations, their 20- and 30-mm cannons blazing, and broke them up. Within a few minutes (from approximately 11:03 to 11:09 German Summer Time) all hell broke loose. The skies were full of bright flashes from exploding shells. Burning and exploding airplanes were roaring earthward. Debris from planes and equipment were spinning through the air. In between them, parachutes were floating to the ground. Explosions, blazing cannons, roaring airplane engines were causing one hell of a noise.

The center of aerial combat was located over the Werra valley in the area of the suburbs of today's community of Herleshausen and the adjacent Thuringian villages, especially Lauschroden, across the wooded area of Gerstungen towards Reichelsdorf (today called Wildeck).

The inhabitants of those villages were thinking the Germans were using a new wonder weapon because of the inferno dropping through the clouds (it was overcast). It was the time when potatoes were harvested and many people in the fields became witnesses to horrible events.

I was then 12 years old and, together with some classmates, witnessed Captain Chilton's Liberator crash. That morning, the alarm systems were sounded as on many days before. Classes in our school were recessed and the students were sent home. It was a dreary day with clouds completely covering the sky. We were outside when we suddenly heard the sound of cannon fire. Only seconds later, the debris of an exploding airplane dropped through the clouds into a wooded area. Because of the clearly visible double rudder assembly we were able to tell that it was a B-24. Also, several airmen could be seen floating to the ground with the chutes; however, they did not belong to Chilton's crew but to Lt. Miner's. Five airmen were captured in this area immediately after their landing. Three of them were wounded and were taken to a field hospital at Bad Hersfeld. These wounded men were Lt. Omick, S/Sgt Kitchens and S/Sgt Thornton.

I was at the crash site of Captain Chilton's ship, too. The debris was scattered in the woods over an area of approximately 1 kilometer. Four bodies were recovered from the front section of the wreckage. Another dead airman was found nearby. The tail section with half of the fuselage was found approximately 750 meters away. It was not burnt. We were not told anything about all the other plane crashes in those days.

The next day, September 28, I had another experience in connection with the disaster of the 445th BG. The air raid warning had been sounded again and the sky again was overcast. At 13:31 hours (German Summer Time) 100 X 500 pound GP bombs were suddenly dropped on our area. The bombs fell into a wooded area and on the open fields between the village of Friedlos and the city of Bad Hersfeld. There were no personal injuries, only property damages. The bombs had been dropped by the 324th Squadron (B-17) of the 91st Bomb Group, 1st Division, led by 1st Lt. O'Brien. The squadron was on the way back from a mission to Magdeburg and was supposed to attack an airfield at Eschwege, approximately 22 miles northeast of here. Besides the demolition bombs, a lot of leaflets were dropped.

All local youths of the Hitler Youth were hastily called together to pick up the leaflets and burn them immediately. I was one of those youths. In the process, we found an American airman who was hiding in some bushes along the banks of the Solz, a small creek. He had bailed out and, when he hit the ground, sprained his ankle and had to use a stick to be able to walk. We then thought that he was a member of the crew of the plane that had crashed the day before. We then turned the prisoner over to the police.

Three years ago, I searched for him in the United States and eventually was able to locate him. The man in question is 1st Lt. Frank J. Bertram from 1st Lt. Miner's crew. Last year, Frank J. Bertram was here again for a visit together with his pilot, Lt. Reginald R. Miner.

During aerial combat on 27 September, the German Air Force lost 29 planes, 4 Me-109s and 25 FW-190s. 18 German pilots lost their lives (one of them, and probably another one, were shot coming down on their chute). It is possible, however, that several more planes were wrecked whose pilots were able to get away unhurt.

American statements concerning German losses deviate considerably from the above figures. From American documents I added up a total of 50 claimed downings (45 FW-190s, 5 Me-109s). I assume that gunners from different bombers simultaneously fired at an attacking fighter and claimed it individually. This would not be astonishing during such a dramatic action.

Of the 25 Liberators that crashed on German soil, 22 crashed in our area. The other 3 crashed on their way back, in the area of Giessen and vicinity of Koblenz. Of the American fighters, who came to the aid of the 445th BG, Lt. Leo Lamb of the 361st Fighter Group crashed and was fatally wounded. He collided with a FW-190 in mid-air.

On Page 2 I mentioned that American airmen were murdered, too. I do not know if you know of these terrible events. In the course of my research, I came across the following cases:

In the village of Nentershausen five airmen were shot to death on September 27, one of them immediately after he had landed with his parachute. The perpetrator was a soldier on leave.

The other four were captured in the vicinity of Nentershausen. They were taken to a camp for hard labor and executed there about midnight. In the area of Nentershausen copper was being mined in those days on a rather large scale, which required a lot of manpower. Many foreigners were forced into hard labor there who were accommodated in several camps. The perpetrators were civilians; the main culprits among them were the camp commanders of the hard labor camps. The perpetrators were held responsible in war crimes trials after the war. Death penalties were pronounced and executed.

As far as I have been able to find out to this day, the murdered airmen were:

2nd Lt. John Cowgill
2nd Lt. Hector V. Scala
T/Sgt. James T. Fields
(all from Lt. Baynham's crew)
T/Sgt. John J. Donahue
(Lt. Elder's crew)

The fifth one was probably 2nd Lt. Newell W. Brainard of Lt. Carrow's crew. I am proceeding on the assumption that my guess is right. I have exchanged correspondence with the sister of Lt. Brainard, Mrs. Kay Brainard Hutchins, regarding the fate of her brother. So far, she has tried in vain to obtain detailed information from U.S. authorities as to how her brother got killed.

Another case deals with 2nd Lt. Flickner from Lt. Johnson's crew. During the night of 6-7 October, Lt. Flickner, together with another, unidentified person, supposed to be an airman from the 445th BG, was captured in a small village approximately 21 miles west of his landing site by two elderly men. The two prisoners were supposed to be locked up in a nearby village. On the way there, the unknown individual was able to escape. The next morning, Flickner was picked up by a policeman who was supposed to take him to a police or Wehrmacht station. On a secondary road, which was leading past a forest, Flickner was shot and killed by the policeman with a pistol. The policeman stated that the prisoner was shot "while trying to escape." After the war, the policeman was apprehended and committed suicide while under arrest.

In my correspondence with former airmen of the 445th BG, I was informed that 2nd Lt. Harold P. Allen of Lt. Jones' crew was also killed by civilians. I have absolutely no information regarding this. I only know that Lt. Allen passed away at the field hospital of the Eschwege airfield at 18:15 hours, 27 September from severe injuries.

Chapter 26: The Gerstungen Cross

Sarah Schaen Naugher

Do you want me to tell you about Jima and meeting those people at Gerstungen? You know, part of the trip over there in '90 was to go to the crash sites, so I was very anxious to go to the crash site where Jim's plane went down, which was one of the farthest away from Bad Hersfeld. It was way on over, I don't know east or west, but anyway, we were out at Gerstungen and Walter has said now this is where the seven American flyers were buried to start with right after the crash. And there was an East German woman and man out there to kind of direct us around. I told her, "I want to know exactly the spot where Jim was buried," because we had asked that they be left there, each of the next of kin had written to the graves registration or whoever in Washington and asked that they be left. This had been six years. And they said no, they wouldn't leave them, they would have to move them to a military cemetery.

The next was, "Can you leave the remains together and just bury them in one grave?" No, they would make every attempt at identification. So you just say where you want. So I had Jim's remains brought back to Arlington, and in January, January the 31st of 1951, Mr. and Mrs. Schaen and Dick, Jim's brother Richard, met in Washington and David and my mother and Jima and I went to Washington and Jim was buried in Arlington National Cemetery. Now, up to now, two of his grandchildren have been to his grave. In fact, Jima's youngest son, David, was there just a couple of weeks ago and had made all kind of pictures of his little girl at Jim's grave.

Okay. Back to where they were originally buried. This little East German woman through the interpreter said this is the spot where they were buried. And I said, "Are you sure?"

"Yes. This is the spot. Until they removed the cross and the remains." She said if they hadn't removed them the Russians would have taken care of it anyway so it's just as well that they had been removed. But she went on to say this is so unusual because today a German man was here looking for his daddy's grave, and it's over on another part of the cemetery there at Gerstungen which was just a city cemetery. The citizens had buried those boys themselves, no government involvement whatsoever. And so she told us about the German man. She said he lived in West Germany so he could not come into East Germany to look for his daddy's grave but he was one of the fighter pilots. And so back at the hotel Jima met Martin Brunotte and he was the German man who was looking for his daddy's grave and found where his daddy's grave was. There was no marker but he was told where it was. And so Jima met him and they became close friends, and the next summer, I believe it was the next summer, Martin and his wife Sylvia came to the United States and visited Jima and Steve in South Carolina, and Jima has been back several times to visit Martin.

The next time when she went back which was a year or so later, she met Martin, she stayed with Martin and Sylvia, and they met the son of one of the other German fighter pilots that was buried in that grave. Jima was born five months after the air battle. Martin was born about two months after the air battle. And the other fellow, and I forget his name right now, was born after the air battle too. This was written up in the European edition of Stars & Stripes, and in '06, when we went back to Germany, Jima and I did it for my last time, Martin brought his mother to Bad Hersfeld to meet me, and we had a good visit too, because we'd both been through the same thing except my husband was a pilot on the B-24 and hers was maybe the fighter pilot who shot him down, who knows? But there were no hard feelings.

Jima Schaen Sparks

The day we went on the tour in '90, out visiting the crash sites, we went to the cemetery in the little village of Gerstungen, which was in what had been East Germany. And we had gotten this little German woman and man to meet us in this cemetery so they would tell us exactly where the American graves were; they were not marked. So they were with us the whole time we were in the cemetery and they pointed out where the grave site was because they were teenagers when this happened, and they remembered where the grave was. They chatted through our interpreter, and when the little lady, from our interpreter, Gunther, told her who I was and my mother, she kept smiling and looking at me. I couldn't figure it out, and I asked Gunther what she was smiling about. He said, "She just thinks it's really strange that this morning a German man came here looking for his father's grave site, but that he had never been there even though he was German and lived in West Germany. He was searching for where his father was buried because he was killed the same day."

And I thought, well, that is kind of strange. That's why she kept looking at me. All these years nobody had ever come looking for the grave sites until that morning. She thought that was very strange.

After we finished touring, the bus took us back to the memorial to take pictures of the flowers. It was late in the afternoon. We were kind of in a hurry because we were going back for the banquet that night. And there were other people besides us at the memorial, and there were photographers and people from newspapers doing interviews, and I walked past this man that was from a newspaper. He was filming and interviewing a German fellow. And the guy was speaking English but he had a very strong accent and I couldn't understand anything.

I guess I was eavesdropping, and I heard him say the word "Gerstungen." And that caught my attention because I thought, well, I've been there, I want to see what this guy says. So I stood around, and I could pick up a few words, and this guy said his father was killed in the battle, that he was a German fighter pilot, and that he was buried in the cemetery at Gerstungen. I thought, hmmmm, I wonder if that's the guy this little old lady was talking about.

Now, you have to realize there were hundreds of people around that day. So I waited until the interview was finished, and I introduced myself to this German fellow, and asked him if he was in the cemetery earlier that day, and he said that he had been. For the first time, that was the first time they had been allowed to go into East Germany and they knew that his father was buried there along with a couple of other German fighter pilots, and they still didn't know exactly where the grave sites were, but they knew it was in that cemetery. After we introduced ourselves we started chatting, and he was going to leave the next morning, but the bus was leaving and I had to get on the bus. So I go running off to the bus thinking, I wish I had had more time to talk to this guy, and I didn't even get his address, but then I knew the photographer, or the journalist, was from the Stars & Stripes, and I thought, well, I can get in touch with him and find his address.

I got back to the hotel, and as I was walking up to go into the front door, for the banquet, he followed the bus back to the hotel, and he jumped out and asked if I was staying there, and could he join me for a drink after the banquet, and I said yes, that would be fine, because I'd like to find out more about him. So I told him, why don't you just come to the banquet?

He didn't have a ticket, but we got him a ticket, along with maybe his mother, I don't remember. So he came to the banquet, and we had dinner together and then went into the little bar area and we started talking. And everything, it was like, it was a very weird situation. He kept telling me these things about himself, like he was his father's only child, and I was as well. His mother was educated, I believe she taught kindergarten. My mother was a teacher. And his mother had remarried when he was three, and so did mine. And he had two half-brothers. I did. And everything he said I almost knew what he was going to say.

There are many more similarities in our lives. He has two sons and so do I. He was named for his father, and so was I. And I think his parents had been married just a very short time before his father went into the service, and his mother had gone back to live with his parents, that was the same situation that happened on our side of the Atlantic. So we exchanged phone numbers and we wrote letters and phone calls and found out even more about each other. And he came to South Carolina the following year, his wife wasn't with him but he came down with his uncle and his mother.

He wasn't a member of the group, he had just come down primarily to look for his father's grave. He brought his two uncles and one of his friends that I met. So when he came to the United States, he stayed with us over Memorial Day weekend and the lady from the newspaper came out and took pictures and did an interview. We had a big gathering of my friends to come over and meet him, and we had a little cookout. But it's just been a very special friendship over the years, and when we went back in '90 they had located a definite grave site for his father and the other two German pilots. I think they had to get some archeological equipment, I don't know exactly how they did that, but they did find a definite site for their graves. And this was away from the German cemetery. They buried the Americans and kept up their grave, they planted flowers. But they didn't mark the German pilots' graves.

Of course there's a reason for it, I'm not sure exactly why but there's a reason why the people of the village didn't care for the graves. But we have since met the son of another of the German pilots buried in the common grave with his father, Gerhard Metz. We met him in '94, and he was born right after the battle. Martin was born in October, after his father was killed, and I was born in February. Gerhard was born in either March or April. He grew up in East Germany, and I think they had just found out about the memorial. His mother and stepfather were there, and he speaks no English and he's legally blind. But Martin talked with him more than I did.

Ten-year-old Erlyn Jensen, Major Don McCoy's sister, after winning a swim meet while wearing her brother's wings. *Photo courtesy of Erlyn Jensen.*

Chapter 27: Gold Star Families

Erlyn Jensen

Everybody knew my brother as Don McCoy, but I always called him Bill. His middle name was William. We always called him Bill. It was Willie when he was a little boy, but he was always my big brother Bill. He was 12 when I was born, and my sister was 14.

My brother and sister were way ahead of me in school. She graduated in '37 and he graduated in '39, and I was born in 1933, so you can see they were quite a bit older than I. But he was my idol.

[As I was interviewing Erlyn at a reunion in Savannah, a veteran of the 445th Bomb Group sat down and introduced himself.

317

"Hi, I'm George Leininger."

"I'm Erlyn Jensen. I'm the sister of Major Don McCoy."

"I think he was on the Kassel Mission. I came in as the replacement crews after that, so I was there maybe a week later."

"What did people say about it?" I asked.

"We were all quite upset, I'll tell you that. When we came in and heard there were that many losses, we figured, 'What are we getting into?'"]

I grew up in Rainier Beach, just at the south end of Lake Washington outside of Seattle. It was a rural neighborhood. In fact, I have a picture, my brother sent home his wings so that I could go in a swimming meet and win it. He just knew if I had his wings on I was going to win. And I did. I was so thrilled to be wearing those wings.

We all idolized Bill, but especially our mother. Every mother loves her son most of all, I think. My sister and I used to joke about that, and then after my brother was gone, he just became bigger and bigger in her eyesight. And of course he always was in mine. He hauled me everywhere he went. My years with him were from birth until he was 18 and he went out to the University of Washington to become a law student, and I was so proud of him because he was in ROTC.

When I was really little and he was in his dating years, he used to take me on dates, and that didn't go over very well. One time he was going to pick up this young lady named Maggie, and we went up on Capitol Hill and he said, "Now you stay in the car and I'll go pick Maggie up." I looked up to the second floor, and here some curtains opened and this young woman looked down, and the next thing I know here comes Bill down the stairs and into the car, and he said, "Well, you and I are gonna go to the show." She wasn't about to go on a date with Bill and his little sister. But that didn't matter to him.

Those are some of my best memories of him. I remember the day he passed his flying test, and Mom let me go with her to watch him solo. He was 17, and I was so excited that I was going to see Bill fly the airplane all by himself. And my mom was convinced that, there's Capitol Hill on one side of Lake Union and Queen Anne Hill on the other side, "Oh, Son is just not gonna make it up over those hills," and of course Bill took off over the lake and flew up over the hills and came back.

When December 7 came, immediately he went down and signed up. He had just barely started college, and he was having to work three jobs to pay for it. He worked managing a playfield, and then he had another job, and at night he worked at Castle Steel in Seattle. And many was the night he'd come home and he'd be so tired, and mom would fix him a bowl of milk and crackers, and he'd eat that, then he'd go stand up against the wall to tell Mom about his day and he'd fall asleep while he was standing up. And after he went into the Air Corps Mom used to worry constantly that he would fall asleep now that he was in the service.

Mrs. John Willet

This letter, titled "A Mother's Plea for Information," was found in Missing Air Crew Report No. 9387 and is reprinted from the 8th Air Force News January 1989 issue. Mrs. Willet was the mother of co-pilot John Willet.

We loved John very much. We were very proud to hear the good report you gave us (9 March letter) on our Son. John always wanted to fly and was very proud when he received his wings at Victoria, Texas.

Some of the other flyers used to tell me what a good fellow John was and how much fun they had together. John was well liked and had lots of friends. Now that John has given his life for his country we would like to ask you if it would be asking too much if you could find out a few things for us as I have been ill and my son never wanted to worry me too much. I have a list of places where John was stationed overseas.

On 1 October John wrote, "Cross your fingers and wish me luck, I am going into combat." We received a letter and a drawing of John sitting in a Martin Marauder with John as pilot. The letter read, "Mom, this is me in my plane. One of the boys drew it. It sure is a good drawing." John also wrote he was flying a Thunderbolt, a very fast plane. In December or January, John sent us an Army picture of a B-17 Flying Fortress and said he had a wreck in bad weather in England or Ireland, I think. He was in the hospital one month, but never told us how he was injured.

John also wrote and said his Squadron went on and he lost out on his promotion to Captain. After John got out of the hospital, he was transferred to the 87th Transport Squadron, from March to

August 1944, and flew to many different parts of the world (Africa, Iceland, Italy and others).

But it seemed he was not satisfied that the time was over a year overseas and he was very disappointed to think he was still a 1st Lt. He went to see his friend, Major Critchfield (700 BS, 445BG; they left Cincinnati for training together in 1941), about getting his captaincy. He was told that if he volunteered for combat he would have a good chance to make the promotion. So he went into combat and was killed and so his wish was never fulfilled. But we know he is more than a captain, he is a great hero. We hope all of our boys haven't died in vain.

I have waited for Christmas to come as John said he would be home by then. We would like to know how many missions and combat hours John had in as he said he had little time to write and was very tired. I really can't believe John will never come back home. It just seems impossible. Please excuse the mistakes and the long letter as I've got to do something to find out more about our son. I thought it would be of great help in our hours of sorrow....

John Ray Lemons

I knew nothing about any of my crew until I got home after the war. I didn't know any of them were killed, and certainly didn't know what happened to the pilot and co-pilot, and certainly didn't know what happened to Byrd. I still thought Byrd was maybe OK. What I did when I got home I finally found out he was killed. So I told myself, I'm going to his home. I'm going to talk to his parents. I had been home on a 30-day leave, and I knew where he lived. Sunset, Texas was a little town close to Wichita Falls. I drove up there and I was kind of apprehensive of what to say. And I walked up and knocked on the door, an old kind of farm house. And the mother and dad came to the door. I said, "I'm John Ray Lemons. I was on the crew with Byrd and I just wanted to come by and tell you what happened on this mission, and I don't really know what happened to him because ..."

They said, "I don't understand. Why are you here and he's not?"

And I just didn't know what to say. I didn't really know what to do. I said, "I'm trying to just explain what little I know about what might have happened."

They said, "We just don't understand why you survived and he didn't."

And I just almost turned around and wanted to leave, but I tried to do a few more words of pacification, but they wouldn't accept it. So I got in the car and left. To this day I never knew what they really went through afterwards, and I don't even know if they ever really knew what happened to him. Because I didn't know that until Hassenpflug told me some of the stuff that he found out.

Erlyn Jensen

In my family, you just bulled your way through things. But my mom never was the same. The only time I saw my mom mellow out was years later, when she was given an anonymous trip to go to St. Avold and see my brother's grave. I was married by that time and had two children, and our friend who was the travel agent called me and said "Erlyn, I want you to come with me. I've got something I need to tell your mom." I got the neighbors to take care of the two kids and I rode down with him, and on the way he told me what he was going to be doing. He said, "You've got to support me, because I promised this person that I would not divulge their identity."

Mom knew Newell and she offered him coffee and we're sitting there, and he said, "Ruth, you've been given a three-week trip to Europe, the first week in France to go up and spend it at St. Avold, and then two weeks on a tour bus all over Europe."

And she said, "Who would do that?"

And he said, "Ruth, I can't tell you. It was anonymous, and the only way that it can be given is if you accept that."

And she broke down and started crying, but she got her trip. And more funny things happened. My sister and I were as excited as she was, because she had dreamed about this. And we had almost forced her to go into Gold Star Mothers. "No, no, I don't want to do that." And she went down and she joined finally a group of women that she really didn't know any of them but they were all Gold Star mothers and she loved it because they had things in common. And when she got this trip, one of the ladies that Mom had never met before Gold Star said, "Mrs. Moore, I'll never get to go to St. Avold. If I give you ten dollars will you get some flowers and take a few to my son's grave?"

And Mom said, "I'd be more than happy to do that" now if you're gonna cry now wait till I tell you, I mean, if you've seen pictures of St. Avold you know that it's thousands and thousands, it's the largest American cemetery in Europe. Mom was taken up there, picked up at the hotel, every step of her trip was planned for her. She was picked up at the hotel in Paris, put on the train, when she got off the train at St. Avold there was someone to meet her there, walk her in, sign in and everything, and then they put her in a little golf cart and she said "Erlyn, it's like I went for miles through these fields of white crosses," and she said finally, this gentleman pulled over and said "Mrs. Moore, there's your son's cross right there," and he gave her a little whistle and said, "When you're ready to leave, you just blow this whistle and I'll be back." And she said she turned around and he just practically disappeared over one of the little hills.

She spent her time at Bill's grave, and then when she blew the whistle he came back. And she said, "Before you take me out," she gave him the number of this other fellow's grave. And he said, "Mrs. Moore, it's right across the walkway." And she was able to come home and tell that mother, "Your son and my son are right across the sidewalk from each other." In those thousands of crosses. So she came home and she was a different woman.

Millie Bean
Millie Bean was the wife of navigator Corman Bean

Why create wounds when there don't have to be any more wounds? Like my maid of honor, that was my godsend during the war when Cormie was gone, her husband was killed in Italy, and he's buried at Fort Snelling. The pilot that was on his plane came and saw us, and he said, "I have to tell you this, Millie. Only his hands were buried." I couldn't go tell my best friend that. Let her think that the whole body is there. And that's why I feel like, why should I go back there? The only thing I would have liked to have seen was Jimmy Stewart. He was at one convention, wasn't he?

Corman Bean

You know, after the war, there were so many of us coming home, many that didn't come home, but I don't recall that the war or war stories or experiences were part of everyday conversations back then. Our best man, who was also a navigator, completed all his missions. I don't recall that he and I ever sat down and compared war stories or whatnot, and we were doing practically the same thing. We were as close as two guys are gonna be. So the attitude was just, "Well, that's a bad chapter in our lives, let's forget about it and move on."

Millie Bean

But it's difficult to deal with emotions. I went to Des Moines, Iowa, to visit Jim Schaen's parents after he was dead. They knew he was dead. And Sarah was pregnant with his first child. And his poor loving mother said to me, "How come your husband came back and my little boy had to die?" Here I am, 21 years old, how do you respond? And when Cormie was missing and a prisoner, people would say to me, "Wouldn't you rather have him dead than a prisoner of war?" I couldn't fathom that. So in my whole life I've been very careful. When they interview on TV, every night there's an interview and somebody says, "How did you feel?" I think, what a dumb question to ask.

Eugene George

I never knew really what happened to Brent. To me, he was MIA, and I thought probably he was killed in the jump or he got caught by civilians who shot him and killed him on the spot. I never knew. He was just straight MIA.

I had an inquiry, it may have been a telephone call, and he said he was from Oregon and he asked if I was Walter E. George who had been a pilot in the Air Force. And I said yes. And he said, "Did you fly with Donald E. Brent?"

I said, "Oh yes, he was my pilot."

And he said, "I'm his great-nephew."

I said, "If you want to know what happened to him, I don't know. I saw him. I think I was the last one to see him alive. He went out of the airplane before I did, but I don't know what happened to him after that."

He said, "He was killed and he was buried in Germany and reburied in an American cemetery." And he said, "I really would like to talk with you. My grandmother would like to talk with you."

And I said, "Well, I'd like to talk with you."

I'd always wanted to see Oregon, so my wife and I went to Eugene, Oregon. It was like going to a funeral. All the relatives, two of them in the military, high up, colonels, who came from the Washington, D.C., area were there. There was another retired Air Force person. There was the family, his former wife, of course, was remarried; his sister, the grandmother of this nephew, and her daughter, and these people really rolled out the carpet, but I told them all I could.

Brent was a good pilot. He was well-coordinated. He thought ahead of the airplane. And he was interested in railroads. He wanted to be a railroad engineer and he'd worked on the railroad for a while. And he was mechanically inclined.

We were in harmony as a team, as pilots. I knew what he was thinking before he said, and he knew what I was thinking, and the way we worked, reacting on the airplane. But he was a good pilot, and I've flown with pilots who are dangerous. In fact, I refused to fly with two pilots because they just weren't with it, and they were trying to be macho.

So we had a good visit. I gave Brent's sister's daughter the Bible that I'd had in my pocket when I bailed out, and she broke into tears. I said, "This rode next to Brent on 17 missions."

So that's about it. I stayed in the Reserves. I flew B-25s. I never flew a B-24 again. When we were evacuated from prison, for a lot of prisoners B-17s came in and picked us up. I was up near the pilot and I said, "Can I fly your airplane?"

He said, "Sure."

So I flew back to an airfield in France at very low altitude in Germany, the low altitude being about 1,500 feet, just looking at the countryside.

Roll of Honor

The Americans

445th Bomb Group

Staff Sergeant William Aaron
Second Lieutenant Daniel A. Abraham
Second Lieutenant Louis P. Ajello
Second Lieutenant Harold P. Allen
Second Lieutenant Daniel H. Appleton
Second Lieutenant Truman Armstrong, Jr.
Second Lieutenant George R. Austin
Second Lieutenant Laurence G. Barben
Second Lieutenant Herbert M. Bateman
Second Lieutenant John J. Becker
Technical Sergeant Roy A. Belouski
Technical Sergeant Glenn A. Bergquist
Second Lieutenant Thomas C. Bibb
Staff Sergeant Ralph H. Bode
Second Lieutenant Roy E. Bolin
Second Lieutenant Newell W. Brainard
First Lieutenant Donald E. Brent
Staff Sergeant James L. Bridgeo
Sergeant Henry Broadway, Jr.
Second Lieutenant Ross B. Brower
Staff Sergeant John E. Buch, Jr.
Staff Sergeant Olen C. Byrd
Captain John H., Chilton
First Lieutenant Virgil Chima
Second Lieutenant Francis W. Costley
Second Lieutenant John W. Cowgill
Sergeant James J. Crowley
Flight Officer Daniel J. Dale
Second Lieutenant John D. Dent

Technical Sergeant John J. Donahue
First Lieutenant Myron H. Donald
Sergeant James M. Douglas
First Lieutenant Oliver B. Elder
Technical Sergeant James T. Fields
Sergeant Ferdinand E. Flach
Staff Sergeant William J. Fleming
Second Lieutenant William E. Flickner
Staff Sergeant Carl W. Forster
Technical Sergeant Andrew Fratta
Staff Sergeant Tage R. Frederiksen
Second Lieutenant James R. Freybler
Second Lieutenant Martin Geiszler, Jr.
Staff Sergeant Joseph H. Gilfoil
Second Lieutenant Edward A. Globis
Second Lieutenant William F. Golden
Technical Sergeant Earl B. Groves
Second Lieutenant Robert N. Hansen
First Lieutenant Edward F. Hautman
Flight Officer Henry J. Henrikson
Technical Sergeant Calvin F. Hess
Staff Sergeant Norman A. Hollis
Staff Sergeant S.E. Howell, Jr.
Staff Sergeant Lee R. Huffman
Staff Sergeant Brian J. Hurt
Staff Sergeant Robert C. Imhoff
First Lieutenant Raymond E. Ische
Staff Sergeant Edward J. Johnson
Staff Sergeant Olin D. Johnson
Technical Sergeant Robert D. Johnson
Second Lieutenant Robert C. Johnston
Technical Sergeant Anthony Kielar
Second Lieutenant William H. Koenig
Sergeant Lars E. Larsen
Staff Sergeant Donald W. Larsen
Sergeant Sylvester V. Lello
Staff Sergeant George B. Linkletter
Sergeant Robert M. Long
Second Lieutenant Michael J. Luongo
Staff Sergeant Milo R. Mann

Major Donald W. McCoy
Staff Sergeant James L. McEntee
Second Lieutenant Kenneth L. Meeks
Second Lieutenant Harold M. Mercier
Sergeant Sigmund C. Mischel
Staff Sergeant Lawrence A. Modlin
Staff Sergeant Stanley H. Morse
First Lieutenant William J. Mowat
Staff Sergeant John B. Neher, Jr.
Staff Sergeant Louis Ochevsky
Sergeant Robert W. Oleson
Staff Sergeant Charles G. Pakestein
Technical Sergeant Charles C. Palmer, Jr.
Staff Sergeant Victor J. Panconi
Staff Sergeant Richard L. Parsons
Staff Sergeant Fred A. Paulus
Staff Sergeant Raymond J. Paulus
Second Lieutenant Porter M. Pile
Second Lieutenant Herbert Potts
Second Lieutenant Hector V. Scala
First Lieutenant James W. Schaen
Second Lieutenant Andrew G. Seeds
Staff Sergeant Glenn H. Shaffer
Staff Sergeant Robert E. Shay
Second Lieutenant Joseph F. Sirl
Second Lieutenant Orville P. Smets
Staff Sergeant Milton C. Smisek
Staff Sergeant Douglas P. Smith
Flight Officer John L. Spingler
Second Lieutenant Arthur E. Stearns
Technical Sergeant William C. Stephens
Sergeant Norman J. Stewart
Second Lieutenant Harold E. Sutherland
Staff Sergeant John A. Tarbert
Technical Sergeant Louis T. Tocket
Technical Sergeant James M. Triplett
Second Lieutenant Charles Vergos
Technical Sergeant Richard W. Vernor
Staff Sergeant Gordon F. Waldron
Staff Sergeant Walter J. Walston

Second Lieutenant Leslie E. Warman
Staff Sergeant Woodard C. Watts
Sergeant Charles E. Weatherly
Sergeant Clare L. Wheeler
First Lieutenant John P. Willet, Jr.
Staff Sergeant Everette L. Williams
Staff Sergeant John F. Wise
Second Lieutenant Dale F. Zornow

361st Fighter Group, 376th Fighter Squadron

Second Lieutenant Leo H. Lamb

The Germans

Jagdeschweder 300

1 Gruppe

Oberfahnrich Heinz Keim
Leutnant Karlheinz Kuhborth
Feldwebel Hans-Joachim Riedel
Oberfeldweber Heinz Weuack

2 Sturmgruppe

Feldwebel Martin Brunotte
Oberleutnant Hermann Kolling
Leutnant Hans Kramer
Feldwebel Hans Kugel
Oberfahnrich Johann Lottes
Oberleutnant Gunter Wasse
Oberfeldweber Johannes Zimdahl

Jagdeschweder 4

2 Sturmgruppe

Leutnant Heinrich Dralle
Unteroffizier Herrmann Hebeisen
Unteroffizier Hans Kalchschmid
Oberleutnant Emil Lubenau
Feldwebel Gerhard Mett
Unteroffizier Werner Penker
Oberleutnant Othmar Zehart

Jagdeschweder 3

4 Sturmgruppe

Unteroffizier Waldemar Hauch

Acknowledgments

After I'd interviewed a number of Kassel Mission veterans, I thought I had all I needed for a book. I was wrong. When I realized I could weave excerpts from my interviews into the wealth of memoirs and letters collected by the Kassel Mission Historical Society, through the efforts of George Collar, Bill Dewey, Frank Bertram and next-generation members Linda Alice Dewey, Jim Bertram, Linda Cadden Gibson, John Elliott (whose father was killed on the mission, and who is still MIA), Bob Toeppe, Doug Collar and Duane Giesler, and J.P. Bertram, Frank Bertram's grandson, who runs the society's web site, kasselmission.org; and the newest KMHS board members, Chris Wahl and Cathy Barton; along with the many photos in the society's archives, and accounts collected by the 8th Air Force Historical Society, it made for a much richer book.

Speaking of memoirs, Mike O'Keefe encouraged his father, Doye O'Keefe, to write his, and it not only provided an important account of the mission and its aftermath, but it is available in its entirety at the KMHS web site. Also, thanks to the University of Illinois (formerly Sangamon State University), which conducted an oral history with O'Keefe). And Rolland Kidder's oral history interview with pilot Ralph Pearson, which is included in Kidder's book "A Hometown Goes to War," about the veterans from Jamestown, New York. Herb Schwartz's entire diary is also at the KMHS web site, along with pilot Palmer Bruland's POW diary which contains many great illustrations of "kriegie" life.

Many years ago I sat down with George Collar and Bill Dewey and we talked about what they would like to see in a book. They envisioned a book like "Black Sunday," a coffee-table type book about the Ploesti mission, with information about each of the planes and their crews. I don't have to look at the honor roll to know that this book comes nowhere close to doing that. Hopefully more stories are yet to be recorded, and more than I could include in this book are available at kasselmission.org, thanks to the efforts of J.P. Bertram, in between a demanding full time job and two young future members of KMHS.

331

Jima Schaen Sparks, the daughter of pilot Jim Schaen, who was killed on the mission; and Erlyn Jensen, kid sister of command pilot Don McCoy, who also died in the battle, supplied me with pictures and stories that were invaluable in showing the effect of war on the families of those who didn't come home.

Mine is not the first book about the Kassel Mission, and it better not be the last (are you listening, Linda Dewey?). Eric Ratcliffe, who runs a gliding club at the 445th's former base in Tibenham, England, has written "The Kassel Raid," published by Pen & Sword Press. But the first and earliest book about the mission was by Luc Dewez of Belgium, who wrote "The Cruel Sky," and brought copies to the Second Air Division reunion at the 8th Air Force Museum in Savannah. Given an opportunity to talk about and promote the book at the reunion's banquet, Luc instead waited in the lobby for an ambulance with veteran pilot Web Uebelhoer, who was having health problems. A recent glance at Amazon shows a listing for "The Cruel Sky" but notes that it is unavailable. Luc's father was in the Belgian resistance.

Also, there is a phenomenal documentary about the Kassel Mission, "Pride of the Nation," filmed over several years at reunions of the 8th Air Force by the Dzenowagis family and containing many interviews.

I and everybody involved with the preservation and documentation of the Kassel Mission owe a tremendous debt of gratitude to Walter Hassenpflug, who overcame a personal tragedy as a child to put aside the bitterness the loss of his family in a bombing raid must have caused to oversee the creation of the Kassel Mission Memorial and to welcome and make survivors of the battle and their families feel at home during their visits. Considering that Walter didn't speak a word of English, thanks also to Guenther Lemke and Carl Lepper for translating for Walter.

I appreciated the suggestions on the editing and cover design from Facebook friends including Frederick Clemens, Matt Garvin, Olan Milligan and Victor Sasson.

Thanks also to Libsyn for hosting the Kassel Mission Chronicles podcast which features interviews by myself and Linda Alice Dewey; as well as my original podcast, War As My Father's Tank Battalion Knew it.

And also to Amazon, for leveling the playing field for independent publishers.

Books by Aaron Elson

Audiobooks

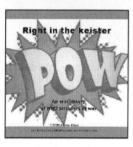

Podcasts

War As My Father's Tank Battalion Knew It

https://myfatherstankbattalion.com

Photo by Walter Hassenpflug

A Spectacular World War II Air Battle and its Amazing Aftermath

The Kassel Mission Chronicles, with hosts Linda Alice Dewey and Aaron Elson, wherever you listen to podcasts.

Documentary

"Pride of the Nation," available at
www.kasselmission.org

Made in the USA
Coppell, TX
31 August 2022

82354955R00186